THE WOMAN WITHIN

ELLEN GLASGOW

The Woman Within

———◆———

AMERICAN CENTURY SERIES

———◆———

HILL AND WANG · NEW YORK
A division of Farrar, Straus and Giroux

Reprinted by arrangement with Harcourt Brace Jovanovich, Inc.
Copyright 1954 by Harcourt Brace Jovanovich, Inc.
All rights reserved
Published in Canada
by McGraw-Hill Ryerson Ltd., Toronto
Printed in the United States of America

FIRST HILL AND WANG EDITION, 1980

Library of Congress Cataloging in Publication Data
Glasgow, Ellen Anderson Gholson, 1873-1945.
The woman within.
Reprint of the ed. published by
Harcourt Brace Jovanovich, New York.
Autobiography.
1. Glasgow, Ellen Anderson Gholson, 1873-1945—Biography.
2. Novelists, American—20th century—Biography. I. Title.
[PS3513.L34Z5   1980]   813'.52 [B]   79-28704
ISBN 0-8090-9783-4
ISBN 0-8090-0147-0 pbk.

Richmond, Virginia, February 8th, 1944

To My Literary Executors

This rough draft is the original and only copy of my auto-biography. It was written in great suffering of mind and body, and the work is as true to actual experience as I have been able to make the written word.

My memoirs may not be worth publishing. I do not know. It may be the part of wisdom to put the manuscript aside, in some safe place, to await the uncertain future. But do not destroy it. I was writing for my own release of mind and heart; and I have tried to make a completely honest portrayal of an interior world, and of that one world alone. It is too late now to revise or to rewrite what I have written. Though I should live for years, I could not find the strength or the courage to go over these rough pages.

So I leave the decision to you, my Literary Executors, and I give you entire freedom to omit or revise pages or passages, or even whole chapters.

If you agree, I should wish you to offer the original copy, with any other papers or letters you may select, to the Library of Congress. Long after I am dead, perhaps in some happier age, an interest may revive in the life of the solitary spirit.

ELLEN GLASGOW

Richmond, Virginia, February 24, 1944,

To my Literary Executors.

This rough draft is the original and only copy of my autobiography. It was written in great suffering of mind and body, and the work is as true to actual experience as I have been able to make the written word.

My memoirs may not be worth publishing. I do not know. It may be the part of wisdom to put the manuscript aside, in some safe place, to await the uncertain future. But do not destroy it. I was writing for my own release of mind and heart; and I have tried to make a completely honest portrayal of an interior world, and of that one world alone. It is too late now to revise or to rewrite the book what I have written. Though I should live for years, I could not find the strength or the courage to go over these rough pages.

So I leave the decision to you, my literary executors, and I give you entire freedom to omit or revise pages or passages or even whole chapters.

If you agree, I should wish you to offer the original copy, with any other papers or letters you may select, to the Library of Congress. Long after I am dead, perhaps in some happier age, an interest may revive in the life of the solitary spirit.

Ellen Glasgow

A NOTE BY THE LITERARY EXECUTORS

Ellen Glasgow died on November 21, 1945. She was then seventy-one or seventy-two years old. Eleven years, or more, before that, when she was about sixty, she had planned this autobiography, and planned for it to be published sometime after her death. At that time she was indeed planning what might be called two companion autobiographies. One was to be her mature comments on the life of the workshop; the other, which in her lifetime she wished to keep completely private, was the life of the woman within.

The actual physical workshop with which a few intimate friends were familiar was, in the years when she was working on this book, the upstairs study at Number One West Main Street, Richmond, Virginia. In that room most of her later, and best known, work was done. In contrast to the rest of the furnishings of the old gray house, there were, within the study, some touches of austerity. The aids to writing were not at all impressive: a rather shallow upright desk with pigeonholes, a rather battered typewriter on a small and none-too-steady table. Long before she used this study, Ellen Glasgow's workshop had been any room which had a closed door behind which she could work, and small, fragile, frail though she was, in the equipment of her study there was, to the end, an assertion that the profession of writing was not dependent on convenient physical aids. The "four dozen sharpened pencils" mentioned in the text were the softest pencils that could be found: Anne Virginia Bennett sharpened them in a pencil sharpener attached to the typewriter table. Pencils, though, were mainly used for making notes. When Ellen wrote with a pen, she used a very broad pen point. But for the bulk of her work she struggled with the typewriter; and it was a struggle. Every three or four years the machine would give up, and there would be a new one. It would be serviced regularly once a month by Mr. Headley, who would also come promptly when, as sometimes happened, there was special trouble. Details of this kind are not negligible. They are part of what the mature Ellen Glasgow had to cope with as she worked on her autobiography, no one with her (but ghosts) behind the closed door of her study.

The professional life of the workshop, Ellen recorded in the series of prefaces to her novels; and, in due course, in 1943, all the prefaces were collected into a volume called *A Certain Measure.* The intensity with which Ellen cared about writing, and her capacity and great achievement, are strikingly exhibited in that life of the workshop. But simultaneously there was tugging at her the life that was even more important, and even more importunate—the life which was the constant companion to the life of the workshop, sometimes friendly, sometimes inimical to it—the really secret life of the woman herself.

The manuscript of *The Woman Within* grew along with the preparation of *A Certain Measure,* and some passages are repetitive. No one, in Ellen Glasgow's lifetime, ever read this manuscript. It was begun in 1934. In 1935 she made a contract to have it published posthumously, subject to the discretion of her literary executors. She treated the manuscript unlike other manuscripts. When it was partially completed, she sealed it in a large brown envelope, identified it on the outside with her own pen as "Important Manuscript," and put it into her silver chest. She seems to have worked on it in 1936, 1937, 1939, 1941, 1942 and 1943, and latterly the successive brown envelopes acquired, as a protective covering, a black leather briefcase, which had a lock and key and two separate luggage tags, each bearing her name and address, and one of them marked, in her own hand, "Private and Personal." This briefcase was then deposited in her safe-deposit vault in the First and Merchants National Bank of Richmond, with instructions that it was never to be entrusted to the mails, but that if anything happened to her the literary executors were to come to Richmond to take personal charge of it. In March, 1944, she invited us both to Richmond to talk about the manuscript, and once more she had it out of the Bank, and on that occasion read aloud to us one short passage, about "the little girl in blue" at Mr. Moody's revival meeting. After that visit she added the instructions which are reproduced here and sealed it in another envelope marked "Original Rough Draft of Autobiography," and added: "Only Copy. Preserve Carefully." Then back it went, into the black briefcase, into the Bank.

We have now read the document many times since the first sad occasion when we went to receive it from the Bank in person, and read it in Ellen's empty workshop; we present it almost exactly in the form in which we found it. The original manuscript is now preserved in the Library of The University of Virginia. That is a deviation from the written instructions reproduced on the page preceding this Note, but it is in accordance with conversations with Ellen that it should reside, with other memorials of her, at "Mr. Jefferson's College."

Ellen called the manuscript an "original rough draft" and said "it will need a lot of editing." However, apart from all other qualities, we have found it to be a document of great psychological interest, and we have preferred to do as little tampering as possible. We have removed a few small repetitions, and at the end have telescoped the rough notes about her later years, which Ellen had been too ill to revise to her own satisfaction. Aside from these small attentions (which, being familiar with her methods of work, with her intentions, and armed explicitly with her permission, we have felt at ease about) we have done nothing to alter a narrative of quite extraordinary human interest.

IRITA VAN DOREN
F. V. MORLEY

CONTENTS

ILLUSTRATIONS

Eight pages of the author and her family:

The young Ellen Glasgow; her birthplace in Cary Street, Richmond; her sister Rebe and brother Frank; her father and mother; her sister Cary; four portraits of Ellen Glasgow; her dogs; the house at One West Main Street, Richmond—garden, interior, and exterior; Ellen Glasgow in 1938.   *between pp.* 68-69

Part One

THE CHILD
AND THE WORLD

ONE

I Feel

Light flickers out of a fog. Nothing but this wavering light is alive in my world.

I see the firelight, but I do not know it is firelight. I hear singing, but I do not recognize my mother's voice, nor any voice, nor any singing. I feel myself moved to and fro, rocked in my mother's arms, only I do not know that I am myself, or that arms are enfolding me, or that I am lulled to sleep with a murmur, with a rhythm, a pause, a caress. All this I learn afterwards. All this is attached, long afterwards, to my earliest remembered sensation. . . .

Moving forward and backward, as contented and as mindless as an amoeba, submerged in that vast fog of existence, I open my eyes and look up at the top windowpanes. Beyond the top windowpanes, in the midst of a red glow, I see a face without a body staring in at me, a vacant face, round, pallid, grotesque, malevolent. Terror—or was it merely sensation?—stabbed me into consciousness. Terror of the sinking sun? Or terror of the formless, the unknown, the mystery, terror of life, of the world, of nothing or everything? Convulsions seized me, a spasm of dumb agony. One minute, I was not; the next minute, I was. I felt. I was separate. I could be hurt. I had discovered myself. And I had discovered, too, the universe apart from myself.

This is my earliest impression: a face without a body hanging there in the sunset, beyond the top windowpanes. All the rest comes in fragments. I scream; I struggle; but my screams and my struggles tell them nothing. I cannot, even now, divide the aftergrowth from the recollection. Only one thing remains, unaltered and vivid as fear: a bodiless apparition, distorted, unreal, yet more real to me than either myself or the world.

My mother and my colored mammy bend over me. I have no words. I cannot tell them. I am too little. My cries choke me. But I remember a cluster of images. I remember passing from arms to arms. I even feel the way something, it may have been my long nightgown, wound about my feet while I fell into spasms. Still, the face never changes. Still the bloated mask of evil stares down through the sunset. Then, suddenly, the light wavers, and goes out, and flickers again into the darkness of memory. . . .

What, I wondered long afterwards, could have caused the illusion? What had I seen or imagined before I could make myself understood? What unknown terror had startled my consciousness, or my senses, awake? Was it merely the pattern of bared branches cast by a dark sunset? Why should that one instant, that one vision, pierce through my covering of unawareness, and pin me to life, as a pin fixes a butterfly? My mother recalled that, as a baby, I had a strange way of shrieking, without cause, apparently, as if I were hurt or frightened. I had come into the world so small and frail that, for three weeks, I was carried on a pillow. I could not be held long in the arms. Again and again, my life appeared to hang by a thread. No one believed I could ever live, first, to walk, then to grow up from a baby into a child, and from a child into a woman. "Born without a skin," my mammy had sighed mournfully.

How old I was when I first saw that face without a body, I have never known. I may have been one or two years old, perhaps less, scarcely more. Fear may have choked back my words. But I do know that I, alone, saw the apparition, and that I saw it hanging there once, and forever. . . .

There has always been a confusion, or simple inaccuracy, concerning the hour and date of my birth. All through my childhood Mother celebrated my birthday on the 22nd of April. I still accept her authority, though I discovered a few years ago, when we consulted the old family Bible, which is now in the possession of my sister, Rebe Tutwiler, that Father had recorded the unhappy event as occurring on April 21st. As I came into the world precisely at four o'clock in the morning, by the testimony of all concerned, I suppose Father had considered it was still night, while Mother, a more sanguine spirit, who welcomed ten children with joy, had dreamed of the more confident morning.

But we made still another discovery in this Bible adventure. It appeared, by the record in faded ink, that I was born, not in 1874, as I had always assumed, but in 1873. Many years ago, in filling in a first slip for *Who's Who,* my sister Cary must have, inadvertently, counted back from January, instead of from April. As long as she lived with me, she looked after all records, business or literary, and so much time had passed when Rebe and I chanced, by accident, upon the mistake that the attempt to track down so slight an inaccuracy appeared trivial. But, after this, I did not give the date of birth, except when I needed it for passports, or for business records, where I gave it as April 22, 1873. For I still believe that Mother was right and that I came in the morning. Not that it matters . . . I have never remembered any birthday, including my own, until my kind friend, Carl Van Vechten, of extraordinary memory, has reminded me by an early morning telegram. . . .

The house where I was born stood on a quiet corner of Cary Street, in Richmond, Virginia. There was a black iron fence enclosing the yard, and once there had been a large old-fashioned garden at the side; but that was before my day. An iron gate opened on a brick pavement, laid in the herringbone pattern, and in April the fine old tulip trees in front were showered with golden cups. The house had three stories, which, from a distance, made it appear tall and narrow. A paved back yard divided the back porch and the area from an oblong brick building, freshly whitewashed every spring, which contained the outside kitchen and laundry, and three servants' rooms up above. The three youngest children (there were ten of us

in all, and I came next to the last, except for a week-old
baby, who died of diphtheria) played in the bricked yard,
where nothing would grow but a single stunted ailanthus
tree at the far end, a blighted creeper or two, and, occasionally, a few geraniums in earthenware pots. The elder
children were all born in the country; but some years
after the war, necessity, and my father's position as one
of the managing directors of the Tredegar Iron Works,
brought our family to the city. It was then that my father
bought the old house with the big garden, in a neighborhood which was pleasant and attractive, though it was
rapidly becoming unfashionable. Four of us were born in
that house, and we were still living there in the early years
of my childhood.

I remember the nursery as a big, square front room on
the second floor. When I was very small, much of my time
was spent at the windows, where I could watch, a little
wistfully, other and more robust children at play in the
street. At dusk, I watched, too, for the old lamplighter,
going by on his evening round. I could not have been
more than two or three when I first noticed him, or perhaps my mammy pointed him out to me; but, even now,
after a lifetime, the recollection is ringed with a fading
brightness. The season must have been early spring, for
there was a pale green twilight under the great tulip trees,
when the old man raised his stick, and a pointed flame
suddenly flared up in the tall lamp on the corner. One
after another, the lights would bloom out, shining, across
all the years, like a row of pale daffodils. And while I
watched them, I was seized with a new feeling of joy.

I clapped my hands, and laughed with Mammy, while my eyes followed the gleaming track of the lamplighter. Once again, I had discovered my world. I was separate; I had learned to know delight; I had learned to recognize beauty and wonder. . . .

But I was to learn, too, a little later, that pain could cut deeper than pleasure, that the edge of it was rougher, and more twisted. From that tide of darkness we call unconscious memory, two recollections are flung up on a wave, and embedded in the very structure of life. They are fixed there, alone, in that vast area of unapprehended sensation. Yet they influenced, and it may be altered, the whole pattern and texture of my personality. Fear entered into them, but it was a wider fear, shot through with an agonized pity. Before these incidents occurred—many months, possibly a year, apart—I had felt the thrill of sensation, but I was, as yet, unaware of any stronger emotion. Though the outlines are blurred as I try to recall them, the accompanying shock and recoil of sympathy, of that strange transference of identity, the power to suffer for something outside oneself, remain among my most enduring impressions. I am trying to write simply and honestly, avoiding alike the patter of science and of superstition, and describing merely the images that sank deeply into the glimmering consciousness of a little child. I am speaking truth, as I know it, because the truth alone, without vanity or evasion, can justify an intimate memoir. . . .

There is blue and gold everywhere, fluttering leaves in the sunshine. My perambulator stands in front of a house with a low doorway, which is not ours, and I am playing happily about the roots of a big tree, sweeping into piles the small green pods that have dropped from the low maple boughs, and littered the pavement. Mammy sits on a doorstep, talking to another nurse, who has just trundled up a second baby carriage, for we never said either "pram" or "perambulator." I was too old to be trundled far; but after many illnesses, my carriage, with its quaint phaeton top, was sometimes used for a rest or a nap out-of-doors. I remember this scene, not for itself, but because it was arrested and held fast by a blow, by a thrust of emotion. Grave, attentive, absorbed, I played on, alone, heaping the small green buds into mounds and borders for a doll's garden. Then, in the midst of my earnest play, I hear a scream of pain, a sound of stones flung and falling, the heavy tread of feet running. Down the middle of the street, coming toward me through the sun and dust, a large black dog flees in terror. The dog passes me; he hesitates. He turns his head and looks at me, and he flees on. The men and boys shout. I run out into the street. My mammy and the strange nurse rush after me. Mammy reaches me first. She swoops down and gathers me up into her arms. But I have seen what it means to be hunted. I run on with the black dog. I am chased into an area over the street. I am beaten with clubs, and caught in a net. I am seized and dragged away to something unseen and frightful. "Hush, baby," Mammy pleads with me. "Hush, my baby." But I cannot hush. I have felt cruelty, and I shall never forget. Something deep down in me has, for the first time, awakened, something with a passionate, tormented hatred of merciless strength, with a heartbreaking pity for the abused and inarticulate, for all the helpless victims of life, everywhere. . . .

Again darkness closes in, and again the darkness is cut in two by an anguish which is sharper than joy. Why, I ask myself, long afterwards, does pain flash up so often from the lower depths of the memory?

It must have been in this instant of horror that I began to think, or to feel, that cruelty is the only sin. I cannot remember when the thought first formed in my mind, but I do recall that, all through my childhood, I felt, as strongly as I feel now, in after years, that cruelty is that unforgivable sin against the Holy Ghost. . . .

In the other memory, there is a crowd, or it may be only a few persons, gathered out on the pavement. I am standing, with my hand in my mammy's, watching the struggles of an old Negro, Uncle Henry, as he is brought out from his cellar and put into the wagon from the almshouse. Afterwards, I am told that the wagon belongs to the almshouse. At the time, I saw only the white mule that pulled it. I am told, too, that they are taking him away, because he is penniless and half-witted and old, and he would starve if he were left in his cellar. Now, I see only that he is very old, that he totters, that he shakes, that he mumbles, that the tears roll down his blue wrinkled cheeks and into his toothless mouth. But he does not want to go to the poorhouse. He is still young enough to dread that. He struggles; he fights off the men who hold him; he cries out in a loud mournful voice, "Don't put me in! Don't put me in!" A group of little boys begins to jump up and down, and I jump up and down with them, though I do not know what the noise means or what it is all about. "Don't put me in! Don't put me in!" we shout over and over, until my mammy jerks me by the arm and tells me to be quiet. And then, suddenly, I stop and burst into tears. A flood of misery pours over me. I am lost and hopeless. Nothing that I can do will stop them from taking the old man away. Nothing that I can do will keep the old man from crying out in his grieving voice that he does not want to be taken. Nothing that I can do will make the world different.

Then the recollection vanishes as swiftly as the glimmer of phosphorescence on waves of darkness.

TWO

————◆————

I Observe

Inside the black iron gate there were two oleanders in immense green tubs. White and red, they flowered so high above me that I thought of them as trees, and, in early summer, I watched for them whenever I came home from a walk. Every morning, when I was very young, my mammy would take me down to the Capitol Square or to Gamble's Hill, or sometimes to the gathering of nurses and children in front of St. Paul's Church. Almost the only thing I remember from these years is the happiness of walking or playing. Yet I was ill again and again. I was thought to be dying of diphtheria, and, in the same year, of scarlet fever. But these afflictions I have forgotten, while I can still see vividly the golden buttercups that I picked on Gamble's Hill, and the white and the red oleanders at the foot of our front steps. I remember, too, a little pink coat and bonnet (my mother kept them for years) of which I was very proud. My growth was not rapid, and this coat, with its delicate embroidery, was altered for me until it became too small, and was cut down for my little sister. So much has been forgotten; yet I have a clear memory of hearing a strange man, who turned out to be a cousin, exclaim, "Why, she looks like an angel!" as he dropped on his knees and gathered me and the pink coat into his arms. For the word "angel" sounded beautiful to me, and my mother was already teaching me to sing in a fluting, tuneless treble,

> I want to be an Angel and with the angels stand,
> A crown upon my forehead, a harp within my hand.

But was I really, without louder hymn-singing, an angel?

My mother was the center of my childhood's world, the sun in my universe. She made everything luminous— the sky, the street, the trees, the house, the nursery. Her spirit was the loveliest I have ever known, and her life was the saddest. I have two images of her, one a creature of light and the other a figure of tragedy. One minute I remember her smiling, happy, joyous, making gaiety where there was no gaiety. The next minute I see her ill, worn, despairing, yet still with her rare flashes of brilliance. I am as old now as she was when she died; yet my heart breaks again whenever I remember her life. A tragic shape dims her light. Then it passes as the drift of cloud over a star, and she shines there, in solitary radiance, unalterably fixed in my memory.

As life goes on her face becomes clearer and more youthful. I look beyond the misery of her later years, and see her smiling at me from between the blossoming oleanders, on the steps of the porch. Her face was oval, with so fair and fine a skin that she was called "the lily" in her girlhood, old ladies have told me. Her hair was as soft as spun silk, of a light chestnut shade, and very lustrous where it was parted over her wide beautiful brow and delicately arched eyebrows, over eyes that were blue when she smiled and gray when she was sad. She loved life until it bore down upon her, and she suffered the long anguish of a nervous illness. When I was a baby she lost her eldest son, my brother Joseph Reid, and though she was never really happy again, she recovered her gaiety and her laughing spirit. I can never read "My Last Duchess" without seeing my mother, as I first remember her, through a rainbow mist of tears.

> . . . She had
> A heart—how shall I say?—too soon made glad,
> Too easily impressed; she liked whate'er
> She looked on, and her looks went everywhere.

Her whole nature was interwoven with sympathy. She would divide her last crust with a suffering stranger. I can still see the streams of old servants and the descendants of old servants, who came to the house for baskets at Christmas. Though she had very little herself (having lost all her modest fortune from the war) no one who had the slightest claim upon her ever went away empty handed. Her feeling for animals, in an age when no laws and little humanity protected the speechless, was a constant torture. My father had little compassion for the inarticulate, and as his Calvinistic faith taught him, the soulless; and because of this and for many other reasons, including this iron vein of Presbyterianism, he was one of the last men on earth that she should have married. Though he admired her, he never in his life, not for so much as a single minute, understood her. Even her beauty, since he was without a sense of beauty, eluded him.

When I look back now, after time has softened my long perspective, I can see plainly and do proper justice to my father's character. His virtues were more than Calvinistic; they were Roman. With complete integrity, and an abiding sense of responsibility, he gave his wife and children everything but the one thing they needed most, and that was love. Yet he was entirely unselfish, and in his long life (he lived to be eighty-six, surviving my mother by a quarter of a century) he never committed a pleasure. For pleasures were not only unnecessary to the scheme of salvation, they were also extravagant, and he held fast to property, not for his own sake, but for the sake of his family. He spent nothing on himself, and except in the matter of education, for he had all the Scottish respect for learning, and kept his Latin until the end of his life, he could not bring himself to be a cheerful giver. It is true that, by the time I was born, he had little left. Eight children had come before me. Four years of war, and of the Reconstruction Acts, which were harder than war, had swept away his possessions. I understand, now, that he must have suffered, beneath his stern fortitude, at the thought of leaving his wife and children in poverty.

A man of fine presence, with an upright carriage, I have heard old ladies say that they used to wait, at the window, to see him pass in the street. At his death, many of the men who had worked under him at the Tredegar Iron Works came to express their feeling of grief and loss. Over and over, they repeated: "He was always just. We knew we could get justice when we went to him." Though he had never had an intimate friend, he possessed a vital sense of responsibility, and he became attached to one or two of the younger men at "the Works." After his retirement, in his middle eighties, he spent much of his time looking after their interests. He was, moreover, one of the first Southerners to become interested in prison reform, and he served for a number of years as one of the directors on the board of the Virginia Penitentiary.

But we were made of different clay, and I inherited nothing from him, except the color of my eyes and a share in a trust fund, which he had accumulated with infinite self-sacrifice. Everything in me, mental or physical, I owe to my mother; and it is possible that from that union of opposites, I derived a perpetual conflict of types. Even in childhood, my soul was a battleground for hostile forces of character, for obscure mental and emotional antagonisms. Stalwart, unbending, rock-ribbed with Calvinism, yet richly endowed with the irrepressible Scottish sense of humor, my father regarded every earthly affliction, from an invading army to the curdling of a pan of milk, as divinely appointed by a God, who must have been the first dangerous Experimentalist. . .

When my brother Joseph died, I was a baby. I do not remember him, but the sorrow for him, the consciousness of my mother's loss, ran like a nerve of grief through all my earliest childhood.

Later, there came a day (I was three years and nine

months old) when my colored mammy took me down to
a toy shop, presided over by Mrs. Does, of pleasant memory; and I was allowed to play there a whole morning,
among wax dolls with real hair, and dolls' houses, and
little red wagons, and painted Noah's Arks with variegated
animals. This was the day my younger sister Rebe, the
last of Mother's ten children, was born; but I can remember nothing of it except the rows of wax dolls, and the
gaily colored animals marching into the ark. Even these
impressions are probably mingled with later ones. When
I was older, my mammy told me how bitterly I had wept
when I was shown a new baby in my mother's arms. Even
Mrs. Does may be imagined, as I knew her afterwards—an
enormous and benevolent German woman, in a gray calico
dress and a small white cap—always smiling and friendly,
and generous with gumdrops. Until I was quite a large
child I envied and loved her. Did she not live in a perpetual playhouse, an unending fairyland of delight?

My little sister does not come into my life until she can
run about and go out with us in my black baby carriage,
with the phaeton top. My brother Frank, several years
my elder, and the only one of my mother's children who
never failed her (as he never failed my father, or anyone
else in his strangely tragic life), was my idol, after my
mother and my mammy; but for a long time I still felt
myself to be the smallest and the most favored. At this
time, my most vivid recollection is of traveling on a train
that stopped for a long while, when my mammy and I
got out, and wandered off in the woods to pick flowers.
This was on the slow old Virginia Central Railway. I was

three years old, my mother said; and before the train could go on the conductor and all the passengers alighted and began searching for us. We were found at last, hunting for pipsissewas under the leaves in the woods. I can see quite clearly the precious milk-white waxen blossoms; I can feel the new sensation, the love of beauty, rushing over me; I can see the indignant passengers bursting out of the pine woods. . . .

When I look back now, through that fast-vanishing perspective, it seems to me, though I had suffered every illness known to the childhood of that day, that my happiest years were those between the ages of three and seven, when I lived, with my Mammy Lizzie, a life of wandering adventures. For we sought adventures, not only in the tales we spun at night, while I undressed before the fire, but even in the daytime, when we roamed, hand-in-hand, in search of the fresh and the strange, through the streets and back alleys, and up and down the hills of old Richmond.

My beloved mammy, Lizzie Jones, was an extraordinary character, endowed with an unusual intelligence, a high temper, and a sprightly sense of humor. If fate had yielded her even the slightest advantages of education and opportunity, she might have made a place for herself in the world. But she could neither read nor write, and since she had not attracted her own race in her youth, her emotional life was confined to the love she lavished upon the children she nursed. But no, there was still another romantic memory. In her youth she had cooked General Lee's supper on the night before the Surrender!

Mammy Rhoda, who had taken my mother as a baby a week old, and had brought her up and nursed all her elder children, died just after my brother Frank was born, and a new nurse was sought and found in Lizzie Jones, who had belonged to the family of Blantons in Cumberland County. She came to us the month after I arrived (screaming, and with long brown hair that rubbed off and left a bronze fuzz) into a hostile world. For the next seven years, we were never apart, except at night—for I was frail and nervous and dreamed dreams and saw visions, and my mother kept me in a crib by her bed, where she could put her hand on me when I cried out in my sleep.

Waking early, Mammy and I would be dressed before the family had risen; and we were ready to start out on our roving as soon as breakfast was over. There is a photograph of me looking very shy and proud, in the embroidered pink French flannel coat and close lace cap with a pink lining, which an elderly cousin had given to me on my second or third birthday.

It could not have been always spring in our wanderings. Yet, in my recollection of that far-off time, the sky is of changeless blue, the trees are in green leafy foliage, the grassy hills are starred with daisies or buttercups, the birds are singing high in the boughs, the golden air is as soft as the scent of a flower on my cheek.

As soon as we left the house there would be brief calls on the neighbors, or long chats with the neighbors' cooks going to market, basket on arm, and with the neighbor's maid sweeping the brick pavement. Sometimes we would meet "old Mr. Warner," the rag-picker, an ancient colored derelict, bent double, and hobbling under his bags of trash, who had told me that I must call him "Mister Warner" if I did not want to be poked into his bag and taken away. Occasionally, to my unfailing delight, we were given a blue and white china pitcher and allowed to fetch milk or cream from Mrs. Staples, who owned, not only a soft-eyed Jersey cow, but a giant microphylla rose-bush over her lattice gate, and a red and green parrot, Pharaoh, who was so highly educated that he could talk, they said, in two tongues. His big green cage fascinated me, and when I gave him the lump of sugar I had brought to tempt him, it seemed to me his harsh tones would soften.

My little legs must have grown very tired on our rambles. But, like my mammy, I was spurred on by an inborn love of adventure, a vital curiosity to know what was hidden round the next corner. When I dragged too heavily on her hand, Mammy would pick me up in her arms, or we would sit for hours on one of the green benches, at the edge of the terrace on Gamble's Hill, or linger in the group of babies and nurses in Capitol Square, in Monroe Park, or on the pavement in front of St. Paul's Church. All the nurses were sociable, and all the new babies were swathed in veils of sky-blue silk grenadine, which were pinned to the nurses' right shoulders and allowed to float down over the sleeping infants.

On the corner of Main Street, there was what we still called, in classic English, "Mr. Childs' apothecary shop," and one of my brightest memories is of the morning I cried for a big green bullfrog made of soap in his window, until hearing my voice Mr. Childs came out and put it into my eager hands. Generous Mr. Jesse Childs was, after Mrs. Does and Mrs. Moesta, the most beloved of my friends. And beloved, too, was the kind policeman on the block, who once took me home with him, and gave me a mealy yellow sweet potato from his dinner; and the friendly very light colored letter-carrier, named Forrester, who, as a Republican, was once threatened with the loss of his place, until the children of the neighborhood rose in resentment, and circulated a petition. I remember rushing in and out of houses, and begging people, especially fathers, to sign —but this must have been long afterwards.

We made friends, in those years, all over the city, from the Governor's house in Capitol Square to the City Almshouse, beyond Shockoe Cemetery, on Shockoe Hill. We must have appeared strange companions, except that everyone knew us, a dark, lean, eager colored woman, with an animated expression, and a small, pale, eager little girl, with defiant brown eyes, and thin legs that ended in ribbed white socks and black slippers strapped over the ankles. I must have had other clothes, but I recall only the pink coat, and I recall, too, that at parties, or on Sunday, I wore pink kid slippers instead of black.

There was only one visit, I think, to the almshouse. All I remember is that I was petted by old women in drab clothes, and that I was allowed to play with several children under big spreading trees, while my mammy gossiped with these old women on the steps of the porch. When my mother heard of it, she forbade Mammy to take me there again. I had already had as many maladies as I could bear, she insisted, and she wanted me to avoid catching anything else. But cemeteries were then, and have remained ever since, among my favorite haunts. Even at that early age, I found them strangely romantic. There was Hollywood, where I played over the graves while Mother and Mammy planted flowers, and almost deserted Oakwood, and once at least I was taken far out to Shockoe or even to the old colored cemetery, which was fast falling to ruins.

Returning home to an early dinner, I would have a nap, and then we would start out again for Gamble's Hill, probably, which had grassy terraces made, I imagined, for children to roll on. My life could not have been always like this when I was so very young. Yet this is all that lingers, now, in my memory, against that green and gold perspective of time. I can still see the pale flower-like shadows falling through the old tulip trees, as we came up Cary Street in the late afternoon. Overhead, the tulip-tree blossoms and the clusters of bright leaves would ripple and wave in the spring breeze, casting gauzy shadows over the herringbone pattern of the brick pavement. If Cary Street lacked a future, or even a present, it still jealously preserved a distinguished past. There were several old houses, with dwindling gardens, which sheltered lilacs and snowballs and calycanthus, and the delicious hundred-leaved roses. On the opposite corner stood a very old red brick house, with a square George the Second porch in front, and, at the back, a fascinating garden, where I used to gather bunches of these old-world flowers.

But my brightest recollection is of our own open gate,

and of my mother's face watching for me from the door-way, beyond the tall red and white oleanders.

Indoors, I was kept upon a rigid diet, and relentlessly doctored with a preparation called Scott's Emulsion of Cod-liver Oil. But no sooner were Mammy and I free to roam than we hastened, with all our pennies, to Mrs. Moesta's confectionery a few blocks away. There, we would buy delicious sticky buns, stuffed full of currants; and I can still see Mrs. Moesta's large, smooth, very plump hands, as they sorted out the biggest and stickiest buns, and wedged them into a brown paper bag, which was always so small that it left the top bun poking out. I can see, too, the green bench under the trees, where we would sit, munching happily, while we planned our morning's adventure. Once, some meddling busybody caught us with the buns in our hands, and immediately betrayed us to Father. When we reached home, just before lunch, we met a stormy reception.

"Currant buns!" cried Mother and Father, upbraid-ingly. "To let our delicate baby touch currant buns!"

But we had been happy. We had enjoyed life. I wonder, indeed, whether I was ever again so carefree as in those early rambles with Mammy.

Although my actual adventures were over at dusk, I knew that more thrilling occasions were still ahead of me. After a supper of bread and milk, as I was undressed in front of the fire, or by candlelight, Mammy and I would take up and spin out, until I fell asleep, the story we had left off the evening before. Out of the dim mists of infancy a hero named Little Willie had wandered into the strange country of my mind, or, it may be, at the start, into Mammy's. I cannot recall either his earliest background or his first appearance. But, after Little Willie had entered our lives, he stayed there, as the closest and dearest of companions, until at last I outgrew him. With him, I was lost in trackless forests; I was pursued by bears; I joined an imaginary circus; I discovered buried treasure on desert islands; and, for weeks at a time, we lived with the Swiss Family Robinson, and shared in all the delights of "Mrs. Swiss Family Robinson's" inexhaustible bag.

When or where or how I learned to read, I could never remember. When I look back, it seems to me that one day the alphabet was merely a row of black or red marks on paper, and the next day I was earnestly picking out the letters in *Old Mortality*. I must have taught myself, for the doctors had warned my mother not to begin teaching me, and had prophesied that it was unlikely I should ever live to grow up. There were few things one would need less in Heaven than a command of the alphabet. "Don't push her, whatever you do. Let her take her own time about learning." But the trouble was that my own time was quick time. After hearing dear old Aunt Rebecca, my father's elder sister, and the perfect story-teller, relate the plots of *The Waverley Novels,* I resolved, apparently, that as soon as possible, I would read them for myself in my own way, which meant spelling out the words, letter by letter, as I went on. All that I now remember clearly is that *Old Mortality* and a little blue book called *Reading Without Tears* were the beginning of my serious education, and that, so far as I am aware, nobody ever taught me to read. "As soon as I learn my letters, Mammy, I'm going to teach you yours," I promised. But I never taught her, and to this day, I regret that I did not.

At this age, the monosyllable Why? Why? Why? was on my lips so often that my father, worn out after a day at the Tredegar, would pay me a new penny to stop asking questions, just as years later, anticipating the principle of the New Deal, he offered to pay me not to read Lecky's *European Morals* and *Rationalism in Europe*. I must have been a tiresome and exhausting child; yet never again in my life, perhaps, have I had so wide a circle of friends and admiring acquaintances. At least two offers of adoption were made by childless couples whom my parents had never seen. Since I lacked not only class consciousness, but the normal anthropomorphic delusion of grandeur, I was quickly responsive to the mortal touch in both the human and the animal species. That morbid shyness combined with almost constant headaches, had not yet overcome my natural exuberance, and set me apart from the well and happy in childhood. Not until I was eight or nine years old was I driven to unchildlike brooding over my sense of exile in a hostile world, and back again to that half-forgotten presence of the evil face without a body. . . .

THREE

Early Joy

When I was very small, my father bought a farm, and, a little later, he sold the old house on Cary Street, and moved his family into a still older and larger house on the corner of Foushee and Main Streets. This is the square gray house where I have lived for the rest of my life, and where I have written all my books, with the exception of *Life and Gabriella*. The many tragedies of my life, and a fair measure at least of the happiness, have come to me in this house. The fibers of my personality are interwoven, I feel, with some indestructible element of the place; and this element is superior to time and chance, as well as to the material substance of brick and mortar.

But, before I came to this house, I loved, as a child, the farm of Jerdone Castle, in the way one loves not only a place but a person. In the first summers Mammy was with me, and we ranged over the wide fields, some plowed and planted in corn or tobacco, but the greater part of them left to run wild in broomsedge, and scrub pine, and life-everlasting. Farther away, there was a frame of virgin woods, where small wild violets and heartsease and a strange waxen blossom pushed up from under the dead leaves of last winter. Every vista in the woods beckoned me; every field held its own secret; every tree near our house had a name of its own and a special identity. This was the beginning of my love for natural things, for earth and sky, for roads and fields and woods, for trees and grass and flowers; a love which has been second only to my sense of an enduring kinship with birds and animals, and all inarticulate creatures. Mammy and I gave every tree on the big blue-grass lawn a baptism. We knew each one by name, from Godwin, the giant elm, to Charles, the oak, and Alfred, the shivering aspen. I remember running out at night, when I was only half dressed, to clasp my arms, as far as they would go, round a beech, because somebody had cut into the bark, and I was sure it was hurt.

I was five that first summer; and it was not until a year or so later that my mother gave Rebe and me each a tiny garden to work; and we planted a Safrano rose-bush, mother's favorite, and slips of heliotrope, sweet alyssum, and lemon verbena. Until Father sold the farm, and left us broken-hearted, we raised our flowers every spring in our own little gardens, just inside the big garden where the flowering shrubs had been uprooted by the overseer, to make way for the plow.

For the first few summers we had no dogs; but when I was older my "bosom friend," Lizzie Patterson, gave me a beautiful pointer puppy, and I learned what the companionship of a dog can mean to a child. After Mother and Mammy, Pat came nearest to me; and I never forgave Father, who did not like dogs, because, when he sold the farm, he would not let me bring Pat to town, and gave him to an indifferent overseer whom I disliked. For years I agonized over Pat's fate; and that incident was one of the things, but not the only thing, that encouraged a childish affliction of nervous sensibility.

My elder sisters hated the farm as much as I loved it. There were no amusements for them, and only one family of neighbors. These were the Colemans, from whom my father bought the family plantation, which had been, originally, a grant of three thousand acres, made by George the First to Francis Jerdone. Immediately, our two families became one united family, in lasting affection. The day when little Carrie Coleman was first brought over to play with us was the beginning of our most intimate friendship. I have forgotten the details of that visit, but Carrie, who is a year and nine months younger, remembers them vividly. She even recalls that my mother brought out beaten biscuits with ham between them, and that, as I opened my biscuit and stripped the fat from the ham, I remarked, solemnly, "I never could abide fat."

Though I adored my mammy, I lived in perpetual terror of Aunt Jane, the cook, a tall, straight, handsome Negress, who wore large loops of gold in her shiny black ears. She was a born autocrat, with the regal bearing of an empress. The whole family suffered under her dictatorship, but it was impossible to discharge her because she was the granddaughter of Mammy Rhoda, and had belonged to my mother before the war. The long low brick house in the back yard at Richmond, which contained the kitchen and laundry and two upstairs rooms, was her special province. She defended her rights with cold authority, and my little sister and I dared not venture so far as the kitchen doorstep. Her permission was always asked before we invited a playmate to dinner or supper, and this stern rule was enforced even upon my grown-up sisters and their numerous admirers. Again and again, I have seen the family cluster round my father, behind closed doors, and beg him to break the news to Aunt Jane that we wished to have company on Sunday, or perhaps a guest for a few days. Father was the only member of our household who was not afraid of her. Several times I had heard him advise Mother to dismiss her, with the assurance that Aunt Jane wouldn't starve because she had managed to save up (Heaven only knows by what denials in those lean years) a tidy little property. But Mother would invariably protest, "We couldn't, Mr. Glasgow. She is Mammy's granddaughter."

Yet even Aunt Jane was not without her touch of nature. Once, when we were peeping into the kitchen window, she suddenly charged out on us, and in our panic, little Rebe stumbled and skinned her knee on the bricks. Hearing her cries, Aunt Jane picked her up, and after administering first aid to the injured knee, gave her a bright new penny.

When I was a half-grown girl, she decided, of her own accord, and to the unspeakable relief of our family, to move into a home of her own.

Just after my seventh birthday, Mammy left me to go to Reveille, where the Pattersons lived, a few miles away in the country.

When the carriage came for her, I stood by the fence in the front yard, and watched her driving away. This was the first real sorrow of my life. It was the beginning of that sense of loss, of exile in solitude, which I was to bear with me to the end. Choking back my tears, I watched the carriage roll down the street, while it tore my world apart, and left a great jagged scar on the horizon. It was as if I could look ahead and see that the happiest time of my life was now over. The long rambles were over. The circle of my friends, in every shade of white, black, or yellow, had melted away. The stories in the evenings were over. Little Willie had vanished. It may be he was dead. Whatever had happened, he never came back after they let Mammy leave.

I had on a pink and white cambric dress and the front of it was wet with tears, while I hid away in the long side yard, on the periwinkle under a drooping mimosa. Mother called me. Frank, my brother, called me. My little sister called me. Cindy called me. And then they called together, startled and alarmed. But I did not answer. I wanted only my mammy, and they had taken her away from me forever. Forever. What was forever? Did it never end? Was there anything that did not end some day—somewhere? But I knew, at seven, as well as I know now, at sixty, that the happiest time of my life was already over, that I had crossed the bridge between childhood and the grown-up years when you have to have trouble, I told myself, and more trouble as long as you live.

The dust rose, scattered, settled again after the carriage. There was only a speck of black now in the distance;

there was only that jagged scar in my heart, and on the horizon. It was spring, and the tulip trees were flowering under the lonely blue of the sky. I knew suddenly that I was alone. I had always been alone. Nobody could come near enough to shut out the loneliness. Not even my mother. Not even Mammy. Not even my big sisters, of whom I was terribly afraid, not even my brother Frank who was three years older than I, or my sister Rebe, who was more than three years younger. I stood between them, but they might have been miles away.

The carriage was gone now. I was staring at an empty world, while I felt only a slow ache where there was nothing, while I heard only the strangled sobs I tried to choke back in my throat.

But, though Mammy had gone, happiness followed her. Three days after Mammy left me, she came again, in the big carriage with a pair of proud-stepping horses, and she brought her new charges, little Lizzie and Pernet Patterson. As soon as Lizzie and I saw each other, the second strongest and deepest friendship of my life began. She was a year older than I, and Pernet, her little brother, was younger. I was just reaching the age when my brother Frank was my idol, and I trotted after him whenever he would permit it as earnestly as my sister Rebe trotted after me. But, except for Carrie Coleman, who was one of the family, we were without what we called "bosom friends" of our own age. When I was well enough we were allowed to play in the street with the neighbors' children; but I was often ill, and games like "Fox in the Warner" and

"King William was King George's Son" and my favorite "Here Come Three Dukes a-Riding" were considered too exciting. After Mammy went, the most vivid recollection I have of the city for the next few years is the memory of standing by the window and watching stronger children playing "Fox in the Warner" under the tulip poplars. I longed with all my heart to be with them; but my mother was always anxious about me, and the doctor had warned her that too vigorous exercise might bring on those nervous headaches no little child ought to have.

Not long after this I went to spend the night at Reveille, in the big attic nursery, which covered the entire top of the house. All the children slept there, and in one corner there was Mammy's bed under her spotless calico quilt of the Star of Bethlehem pattern. In the evening we played roaming games over the slippery floor, as smooth and wide as a ballroom, or "pulled" spun candy, which we made in a big copper pan over the log fire.

On winter evenings, when the sun was sinking in a red ball over the snowy country, old Doctor Patterson would stop by for me in his cozy buggy with the big bay horse. Then Mother would carefully bundle me up in a thick coat, and woolen stockings and mittens, and tie a knitted red cap under my chin. I would snuggle in, under the great bearskin robe, close against the fur-lined greatcoat of the old doctor, who looked exactly like Santa Claus, with his ruddy face framed in a thick gray beard. He would flick the reins, and the bay horse would start off, cloppity, cloppity, clop, up Franklin Street and far out into the rugged fields, which are now Monument Avenue.

The lamplighters would have gone by, and one after another, the gas lamps in the street would fade out in the
blue dusk. Ahead of us, while I cuddled happily, too blissful for words, for I was a painfully shy child, I could see
the heavenly twilight of the country, with the red sun
sinking—sinking—sinking, and the first stars pricking the
greenish blue of the sky. But my thoughts would be on
the big, flickering nursery under the dormer roof, with the
bright fire, and the big brass kettle of molasses candy on
the trivet. The room would fill slowly with happiness, with
all the fairies and ghosts and talking animals that Mammy
would evoke from her secret magic, when the time came
to tell stories.

But there were other evenings, frozen in bitterness even
now, when I watched from the nursery window because
I was not well enough to go out into the cold night air,
which was regarded with suspicion by my parents, as well
as by the medical profession of that period. Then, through
my tears, I would see the old doctor shake his head regret-
fully, before he jerked the reins over his horse, and drove
away, with an empty place beside him under the bearskin
robe. . . .

In the later years of my childhood many of our happiest
hours and days were spent at romantic old Reveille.
Mammy was with us then, and we were all happy together.
She had an inventive mind, and we were never at a loss
for new games or stirring adventures. Sometimes, when
other interests failed, she would make one of the colored
"hands" harness a horse to an old wagon, and tie another

horse to the back, or perhaps leave a young colt trotting beside the mare. Then she would dress us as gipsies, darken our faces with a burnt cork, and wrap our pigtails in strips of red flannel. The five of us, Mammy, Lizzie, Rebe, Pernet, and I, would start on a long journey, telling fortunes wherever we came upon a farm house or a Negro cabin. The only thing I remember now of those masquerades is that I was always the one who could think up the most exciting or plausible fortunes. But such recollections are only sunny interludes. . . .

A few weeks after Mammy left me, I think—though I cannot be sure of the exact date, and, while I vividly remember the incident, the details are obscure—I was overwhelmed by a religious conversion.

Mr. Moody, the celebrated evangelist, was holding a "revival" in what I recall as "the old armory" (or was it "the tabernacle"?), and my Aunt Rebecca, who was visiting us at the time, invited me to go to the meetings. She was a beautiful old lady, with the face of an elderly madonna framed in a bonnet of black taffeta, and in any crowd she invariably aroused admiration. As long as the "revival" lasted, we listened, entranced, to two fiery sermons a day, and we never failed to secure seats on the front bench, immediately under the soothing or warning voice of the preacher.

So faithful was our attendance that, on the last afternoon, to my burning humiliation, I was singled out for praise by the evangelist.

"The little girl in blue on the front bench has been an example to us all," he said. "She has never missed a

meeting, and she has followed every word of the message.
Now, she will start, for us, the Gospel hymn, and we will
all sing together."

While I tried to hide from his relentless gaze behind
the narrow figure of Aunt Rebecca, I found myself un-
willingly hypnotized into obedience. "Now, little girl in
blue," prompted the awful voice. "Now . . ." And, the
next instant, with shame and horror, I heard two reedy
tones, Aunt Rebecca's and mine, thinly piping:

> "Rescue the per-ish-ing, Care for the dy-ing,
> Snatch them in pit-y from sin and the grave.
> Weep o'er the err-ing one, Lift up the fall-en,
> Tell them of Je-sus, the migh-ty to save.
> Je-sus is mer-ci-ful, Je-sus will save."

That was the end. The evangelist passed on to wider
fields and to riper harvests, while I relapsed, permanently,
into "original corruption," and was "bound over to the
wrath of God." . . .

FOUR

I Become a Writer

In my seventh summer I became a writer. As far back as I remember, long before I could write, I had played at making stories, and, in collaboration with Mammy, I had created Little Willie and his many adventures. But not until I was seven or more, did I begin to pray every night "O God, let me write books! Please, God, let me write books!"

One summer day, lying on the blue grass at Jerdone Castle, beneath sweeping boughs of the "old elm," which was so large that it took five of us to measure its bole, I found myself singing aloud in time with the wind in the leaves. Beyond the clustering leaves, I could see the sky as blue as the larkspur in the field below the garden fence, and over the blue a fleet of small white clouds was sailing.

"I would that I with the clouds could drift," I began to sing under my breath. "Quietly, happily onward—" And then suddenly, with a start of surprise, I exclaimed aloud, "But that's po'try! That's po'try! And I made it!" Joy flooded through me. Running into the house, I seized

a paper and pencil from my sister's desk, and came back
to the elm, while the rhythm ran on and on and on in
my thoughts, making a new hymn—a hymn of my very
own.

> Drift from this land of mist and snow,
> Drift to the land where I long to go,
> Leaving behind me the world's sad choices,
> Hearing alone the angels' voices,
> At the foot of my Father's throne.

"That's po'try," my heart sang over and over, "and I
wrote it!"

For days my new happiness lasted, as if I had entered
some hidden forest of wonder and delight. I wandered
"lonely as a cloud" in that strange exile to which all
writers who are born and not made are condemned. Then
the end came with a shock that plunged me from joy into
despair. One morning, seeking more paper and a sharpened pencil in my sister's room, I heard her voice reading
my precious verses aloud to her guests, and I overheard,
too, the burst of kindly ridicule and amusement. Noise-
lessly, without the flutter of a curtain, I fled back through
the window, and down the columns of the porch to the
shelter of the big box-bush beneath. My skin felt naked
and scorched, as if a flame had blown over it.

Was that the beginning of my secrecy, I have sometimes
wondered. Was the sensitiveness I have always felt about
my work rooted in the sharp mortification of that awakening?

After this bitter humiliation, I wrote only in secret;

and I began to live two lives twisted together. One was my external life, delicate but intense, devoted to my few friends, Mother, Mammy, my brother Frank, my sister Rebe, Carrie Coleman, and Lizzie Patterson. Without, in the objective world, there was, also, dear Miss Virginia Rawlings, a large, happy, genial spinster, with a Roman profile, like Caesar's, and the first short curly bob I had ever seen on a woman. Many years before my birth she had come to my mother, as a companion and a governess for the three eldest children. They had shared the war terrors and anxiety, and the worse horrors of Reconstruction, and when these were past, and only the stricken country and the general poverty remained, Miss Virginia had stayed on permanently, as one of the family. She had garnered, through fifty years, a ripened store of recollections, gay and solemn, comic and tragic. Frequently, she would while away a rainy afternoon by telling us stories of the war. Unlike my Aunt Bec—that born story-teller, who could make the Bible and *The Waverley Novels* rise from the grave and put on incorruptibility—Miss Virginia knew only the drama that was reality.

There was the adventure of my great-aunt Cassie, an old lady of over eighty years, the wife of my father's uncle, Colonel John Thomas Anderson, whose house, "Mount Joy," one of the loveliest places in the Valley, was burned by General Hunter in his ruthless invasion. Great-aunt Cassie was given only one hour in which to save her favorite possessions, and with the help of the house servants, she chose to preserve a few family portraits. The nearest refuge was my father's farm, "Far Enough," three miles

away, and the old lady was carried in the arms of her
servants, by woodland paths, fearfully avoiding the troops
on the turnpikes, to Far Enough, where my mother, with
a baby of three months in her arms, heard her older babies
crying of hunger.

One day the Federals would swoop down, and the next
day, there would be a rush from the Confederates. The
regular troops were a blessing compared to the hordes
of stragglers from both armies. The soldiers, after snatch-
ing the scant store of bread from the larder, would, occasionally, break off a crust of the crude war loaf and share
it with one of the hungry babies. But the stragglers took
everything and gave nothing but insults.

And there was another story I liked even better. After
a day of terror, my mother sent a note to General Hunter,
asking him to place a guard on her porch for the night;
but the General's answer was to tear the note across and
reply to her colored servant: "Tell her to make her
damned Rebel husband come home and protect her."
Shivering with dread, as night approached, Mother and
Miss Virginia hushed the crying children, and had just
drawn the bolts and closed the shutters, when a knock
fell on the door. Mother, the frailest but the bravest, went
herself to unbar the door, and saw, to her astonishment,
a Federal officer on the porch. "Madam," he began, "I am
Colonel . . ." (though Mother never forgot his name, in
my long life since her death, this has escaped my mind)
"of the . . . Massachusetts Regiment. I was present when
General Hunter received your request for a guard. I heard
his reply, and I have come to tell you that I shall spend

the night on your porch." Though I can recall neither his name nor the name of the regiment, I can still see Mother's face when she told me the story. I can remember, too, that his name began with "M," and that he had come from Massachusetts.

A small thing to happen, the merest incident in the midst of great battles; but my mother remembered that officer long after she had ceased to feel either the thrill or the pain of defeat. She often wondered, in the desperate struggle of rebuilding a world, whether he was still alive; and for many months, with the old, tender, futile piety of her age, she included the name I have forgotten in her morning and evening prayers. The stragglers came and swept by. For three nights, as long as General Hunter remained in the neighborhood, this unknown New England soldier guarded my mother's house.

She talked less of the war than Miss Virginia did. Yet one remark impressed me so vividly that I seem still to hear the sound of her voice, a thrilling and lovely voice, as she spoke. "Even in the midst of the horrors," she said, "a wave of thankfulness rushed over me when I heard that the slaves were freed." The few servants we inherited were happy. But there were others. There was the auction block; there was the slave trader; there were the parted families; there were the returned fugitives; there were the rice plantations in the Deep South.

My interior world was thickly woven of recollections, but these recollections had no part in the remote, hidden country of the mind. In that far republic of the spirit I ranged, free and wild, and a rebel. From the moment when I heard my first verses read aloud, not with ridicule, but with the kindly merriment that holds a withdrawn sting, I wrote always in secret, but I wrote ceaselessly in dim corners, under beds, or, in the blessed summer days, under the deep shrubbery and beneath low-hanging boughs. Until my first book was finished no one, except my mother, who suspected but did not speak of it, was aware that, below the animated surface, I was already immersed in some dark stream of identity, stronger and deeper and more relentless than the external movement of living. It was not that I had so early found my vocation. At the age of seven my vocation had found me. The one permanent interest, the single core of unity at the center of my nature, was beginning to shape itself, and to harden. I was born a novelist, though I formed myself into an artist. Looking back on my life I can see that a solitary pattern has run through it, from earliest childhood. Always I have had to learn for myself, from within. Always I have persevered in the face of an immense disadvantage—in the face of illness, of partial deafness, which came later, of the necessity to blaze my own trail through the wilderness that was ignorance. To teach one's self is to be forced to learn twice. Yet, no doubt it is true, as my friends assure me, that when one hews out from rock a philosophy or an understanding, it stays fast in the mind. Only a hunger and thirst for knowledge can bring perseverance.

I must have been seven or eight years old when I was sent to school for my first term, which lasted less than a day. Although I was innocent of arithmetic and geography, I was well acquainted with English literature and with English history. It was my father's habit to read aloud to us every evening, and since we had a good old library, and no money to spend on current books, my taste was already formed. Or perhaps, as I have felt, I was born with an appreciation of the best, and an equal aversion from the second best. I was, even at that age, a social rebel. I cannot recall the time when the pattern of society, as well as the scheme of things in general, had not seemed to me false and even malignant. Later on, I read widely in Adam Smith, Malthus, John Stuart Mill, Henry George. I was a radical when everyone else I knew was conservative, and now I am conservative when most other people appear to be radical. This, of course, is merely the inevitable recoil from youth to age. If I were still one and twenty, I suppose I should continue to believe in both romantic love and the theory of collectivism. So it was, a little later, with votes for women. At eighteen, after discovering John Stuart Mill, I was an ardent suffragist, and the only one, except my sister Cary, in our circle of acquaintances. Years afterwards, when the cause had triumphed and attained respectability, I lost interest, and regarded it merely as one more reform that had ceased too soon to be exciting. The whole design of my life ran like that, in a rhythm and pause, forward and backward. By the time an idea has won its way in the world, I have rushed ahead to another.

But, at seven or eight, beginning my first day at school, I was an inarticulate rebel. I can see myself, carefully dressed by my mother in a pink and white cambric frock, with my schoolbooks under my arm, and a little white straw basket neatly packed with buttered beaten biscuits and sponge cake, all folded in white napkins with a turkey red border. Two big girls, friends of my elder sisters, came by for me, and I started out, with eager curiosity, into the unknown—into the strange universe which was an enemy to the sensitive and the fearful. It was a mild morning in early October, and I walked delicately over sunbeams.

I remember the long room crowded with pupils, the sweet face and tender voice of the gentlewoman who taught the infant class. I remember thinking that in some ways (pleasant), the ways of literature and history, I knew more than my teacher did, and in other ways, in the dreadful ways of arithmetic and geography, that I knew less than the least of these infants.

Sitting primly on the hard bench, with my feet dangling above the floor, I felt the familiar palpitations of fear. Fear that crept, that quivered, that rushed upward. Fear that began in an icy chill and ended in the blackness of a sick headache. "Why, your hands are cold!" exclaimed Mrs. Garnett, the pleasant teacher, who had promised my mother to take care of me. "Did you eat a good breakfast?" I shook my head. The very thought of school, of the unknown, had choked me. "Well, you must have your lunch now. Nellie will take you out before recess, and you may play for half an hour in the yard. Nellie is good at play."

Nellie, a plump, red-cheeked child of my own age, slipped promptly from the bench and picked up my lunch

basket. She looked pleased, and merry, and utterly un-
afraid. Dashing ahead of me into the yard, which was
paved with bricks and bare of grass and flowers, she caught
me by the hand, and ran to a dilapidated swing between
the two twisted ailanthus trees in one corner.

"Is this your first day?"

I nodded. The lump in my throat was as hard as a
marble.

"Do you like it?"

I shook my head. Were all strange little girls enemies?

"I've been comin' a long time, goin' on two years," she
was reciting proudly. "Why did you wait till you were
so old?"

I swallowed the marble with a gulp. "It was the doctor,
the doctor wouldn't let me."

"I hate doctors. Don't you?"

This pricked me to resentment. I adored Dr. Coleman.
"Not my doctor. He knew me when I was born. He is
finer than anybody."

Though I may have forgotten her exact words, I can
still recall the shock of my revolt from her rudeness. In
that place and time, boys might be rude, but little girls
were supposed to remember their manners.

"Well, I hate them anyway. I'm glad I'm not delicate
too." Then she picked up my lunch basket. "Do you know
what's in it?"

"Beaten biscuits and sponge cake and breast of chicken."

"Aren't you going to open it? Mrs. Garnett said you
were to eat your lunch."

I shook my head. Not to save myself from school forever could I have swallowed a morsel.

"Will you let me look?"

She had opened the top of the basket and was peeping beneath the red and white napkin. "I might eat it for you," she said. "She would never know unless you're a tell-tale."

I wasn't a tell-tale; that act required greater moral courage than I possessed; but I knew my Dickens, of whom the rude little girl seemed never to have heard, and I recalled the friendly waiter at the inn, where David changed stages.

A black chill was creeping up my spine and into my thoughts, a chill I learned afterwards to associate with my few school days and my bleak endeavor to acquire a systematic education. I was not over eight, and school lasted until you were old—until you were eighteen. I would rather be dead. Passionately, I decided that I would rather be dead, even with the awful God of my father in Judgment.

Sick from nervous despair, I watched Nellie unfold the napkin, and inspect the dainty lunch with which my mother had lovingly tempted my frail appetite. I watched her take out the two buttered beaten biscuits, the slice of chicken, the sponge muffin, and the red apple. I watched her as she began, at first slowly and then more rapidly, to nibble a beaten biscuit. The teacher had sent me out to play in the yard, and I sat in sullen misery, with icy hands and an aching head, watching a rude little girl devour my lunch. When she had eaten the last crumb, she tucked in the napkin, closed the top of the basket, and returned it to my lap.

"I have my own lunch too," she said, "but that doesn't come till later."

How many important things have I forgotten, and how vividly do I recall that moment of disillusionment! She began swinging violently, until I grew sick from emptiness and fear and frantic detestation of what grown-up people called education. Now children enjoy school, I am told, and do pretty much what their teachers do not wish them to do; but in that benighted period, in the middle of the aesthetic 'eighties, from nine till three, one acquired learning. And learning comprised the dates of old battles, the names of dead kings, the number of rivers in Asia, and the way figures multiplied in a table. I know I should have gladly exchanged every dead king and every date in history or river in Asia for the blameless and irresponsible joy of illiteracy.

"Let's eat our lunch together every day," Nellie was saying affectionately. "I want a bosom friend. Let's you and me be bosom friends."

Then, before I could grasp at the rag of an excuse, a bell rang, and a little girl from my class tripped out to tell us that our recess was over.

"This isn't the real recess," Nellie explained, as we returned to the schoolroom. "When that comes, I'll give you a bite of my apple."

So I went back, sick and empty and shaking, to the torture chamber, where gentle Mrs. Garnett, with her lovely face and voice, tried to fit me into the proper class and the exact right spot. No, I didn't know the multiplication table, but I knew the names of all the heroes and heroines of *The Waverley Novels,* and I had read (or had read to me) the tragedies, but not the comedies, of Shakespeare. I was totally ignorant of American history, except of course the part that told of General Lee and General Jackson, and of the victories, without defeats, of the Army of Northern Virginia. For poetry, too, my memory was endless. I could recite, whenever I found courage, a varied collection of what I called my "favorite poetry," from "Sigh no more, ladies, sigh no more" or "Call the robin redbreast and the wren" or "An Elegy in a Country Churchyard" to "Ivry" or "On Linden when the sun was low" or even "When we two parted." But, as I grew older, the poem I loved best for years was *The Rime of the Ancient Mariner.*

Because of my low standing in arithmetic, I was put at the foot of my class. I remember this, and I have not forgotten that while I sat there I felt a chill crawling up my spine, like a beetle. Sickness, black and chill, attacked the pit of my stomach, and all the stamping feet and treble voices coming closer were stabbing down into my ears, into my throbbing head. It was the beginning of one of my nervous headaches, and a cold sweat broke out while I struggled not to disgrace myself by throwing up before my natural enemies, strange children, on my first day at school. If the children had been cannibals, and I a missionary prepared for the feast, my doom could not have seemed more dreadful to me, or more inevitable. Presently

I should be sick on the bench; I should be jeered out of school; I should be in eternal disgrace.

Then, suddenly, without the shadow of an approach, destiny overtook me. A door opened; there was a thunder of feet, a rumble of voices, a crowd of figures surged toward me, hemming me in, shutting me out, with my headache, my sickness. The older girls of the history class, like released colts, brave, strong, fearless, with clear heads and quiet stomachs, were thronging through to the schoolroom beyond.

Terror seized me, blind panic terror. A wave of darkness rushed over me and I bit my lips till they hurt, in the frantic effort not to disgrace myself. My ears rang; my elbows quivered; my ice-cold hands even were afflicted by this agony of physical shyness.

One of the older girls turned her head, as they tramped through the room, laughed maliciously, and whispered, "Look at the white rabbit!" Mirth convulsed them. For the first time in my brief unhappy life I was an object of mirth, a figure for ridicule. Though I knew this was not wit, that it was not even sport, I felt the heart of a rabbit tremble and leap beneath the tucked pink and white cambric.

Flight remained. Flight could save me. Jumping down from the bench, I dashed out of the door, into the paved yard, through the gate, and down the empty street to my sure refuge with Mother. Mother alone knew. Mother alone understood. Mother alone could protect me from this despair of being different, of being outside the world. I heard calls. The class was on my track. Without turning my head, I could see with the inner eye the whole school pursuing. Or, may be, not the whole school. Maybe it was only Nellie's voice on the wind and the patter of Nellie's feet on the pavement.

At the head of the steps my mother waited with open arms to receive me. I flung myself upon her bosom, while the throbbing in my temples filled the world, filled the universe.

"A headache, my darling child! There! There! Is it another headache?" She folded me in her tenderness, in her sympathy. I was undressed. I was tucked into bed. I was comforted. "No, you needn't go back. Only stop sobbing so. You didn't eat any breakfast. Lie still while I make you some cocoa. Then we'll send for Dr. Coleman. You'll like to see· Dr. Coleman. No, you won't ever have to go back."

The room was darkened. My head was rubbed gently with Eau de Cologne. Cocoa, which I could not touch, was made for me, and brought on a little tray to my bedside. Gradually the retching, which was the worst part of those headaches, grew quieter. By the time dear old Dr. Coleman, who had brought me through diphtheria and scarlet fever and measles, and the general misery of an exile in a malignant world, had arrived and felt my pulse and gravely looked at my tongue, I was beginning to doze from sheer weariness. If I had listened, I should probably have heard him whisper, "She must not go back. Not to a large school, with long hours. These headaches must stop. Above all, don't force her, or she may slip through our hands. She is a frail little thing, and she suffers too keenly."

Then he went, after leaving a prescription, and again the room darkened and grew as quiet as night. The room, but not the street outside, under the big tulip trees, where other children, children without headaches, without nerves, without fears, children who neither dreamed dreams nor saw visions, were playing my favorite "Fox in the Warner." Their gay cries and happy laughter floated in to me while I lay with Mother stroking my head, and the long shuddering throbs growing fainter and fainter, and farther and farther—and farther— "At least I didn't throw up in school," I remember thinking, with a kind of sick comfort. For, at that age, proper behavior, not to disgrace one's self before other people, seemed to me the most important thing in the world. And the moral, as the Duchess might have observed, is that something may be said in favor of the Spartan method with delicate infants. Death from exposure would have been a simple way of escape for a child who knelt down every night and prayed that she might die before the time came for her to go back to school. But this was in the middle 'eighties, and schools today, I am told, are scarcely more than pleasure gardens for pupils.

Impressions and Illusions

But even in an unhappy childhood life has its moments. My escape from hostile circumstances—from school and fear and God all together—came in the summer. On the farm, I was free, I was alive within, I even knew happiness. My headaches disappeared, when I roamed all day out of doors, and I have wondered whether my early frailty was imposed by conditions, or at least increased by the perpetual conflict between my nature and my surroundings.

At Jerdone Castle, I knew and loved every meadow, every stream, especially every tree—for I was born a tree worshiper. I bled within when my father cut down any tree on the road or the lawn. During the week he was in Richmond; but, from late Saturday afternoon until early Monday morning, when he came up on what was known as an "accommodation train," I grew nervous and apprehensive for the dogs and the trees. My mother loved Pat, my beautiful pointer, and Toy, my small "mixie," as much as I did. All the week they lived in the house, but on Saturdays they would glance up, uneasily, at the whip in the hall, knowing why it was hung there, and they would begin to grow anxious. Yet my father was good in his fashion, and unselfish to a fault in his own way.

I still followed Frank everywhere, and, because my little sister Rebe followed me so closely, I named her "Shadow." I adored them both, and it is pain even now, after fifty years, to look back on that comradeship. Often we would wander to the far red gate where the farm began, and, farther still, into the strange leafy ways, where the narrow roads were strangled in mud. Sometimes we would stop at one of the Negro cabins, especially the cabin of Uncle Will, a grand old gentleman whom we loved best. He gave his life to a crippled grandchild named Betsy, who was abused by her family. These Negroes had never left the land on which they were born. At the end of the war, their former master, the grandfather of our close friends and only neighbors, the Colemans, had divided the greater part of his estate among his three hundred servants. They were fine Negroes, intelligent, thrifty, hard-working, and greatly superior to the "poor whites" whom they regarded with merited contempt. But, then, the Negroes on such a plantation possessed security, and the "poor whites" possessed nothing but the freedom of malnutrition. As for us, we would play eagerly with little colored children, but we were ashamed of association with the "poor whites."

Even my writing was done out of doors—and, when I was not playing, there was always a book in my hand. I had been born with a genuine passion for words—for rhythms, and by this time I had read more English poetry than I could well assimilate. Why I chose to write prose, instead of verse, I have never known. In those days, poetry possessed me. My first stories were all allegories, done in a kind of childish prose-poetry. "Only a Daisy in a Garden of Roses" might as well, at the age of seven, have been written in rhyme. But perhaps the shadow of Little Willie still hovered over me. Or it may have been that the grim realities of my mother's illness and death were already impending.

As a child I loved a storm. I loved to fly out, with my hair streaming, and embrace the rush of the wind. When the thunder muttered far off, and the tongue of forked lightning bit into the horizon, some caged bird in my bosom would break free. All the terrors of living were stripped away, like leaves from the trees. My eldest sister, Emily, would shiver with fear, and bury her face in the midst of a featherbed; but I ran out through the gate, which would creak as it swung back, and down the long road to the ice pond. The things I feared were not in the sky, but in the nature and in the touch of humanity. The cruelty of children, the harshness of health and happiness to the weak, the blindness of the unpitiful—these were my terrors. But not the crash of the thunder overhead, not the bolts of fire from the clouds.

As I raced on, I would chant majestic verse to the wind. The tremendous rhythms of Dryden I loved even at that age, and I would sing aloud, with ecstasy, lines that are pure music:

> Fallen, fallen, fallen, fallen,
> Fallen from his high estate . . .

or perhaps:

> None but the brave,
> None but the brave,
> None but the brave deserves the fair. . . .

Then I was happy. I was happy with that strange, secret, hidden happiness that belonged to myself alone. A happiness so shy that it would start and flee before a shadow, yet so fearless that it would rush, singing, into the very heart of the storm. But all this was a part of the summer. When winter came I crept back into the cold darkness, where there were set tasks I could not do, where nightmares came in my sleep, and sinister apprehensions stayed by me in daylight.

Perhaps—perhaps— But I believe my predispositions were formed, and the deepest impressions made on my mind, in the earliest years of my childhood—certainly before I was eight years old.

It has become the habit of our Freudian era to represent the infant mind as oppressed by a heavy burden of sex. It may be that the curiosity of modern children is more advanced on such subjects. For myself, I cannot recall that I speculated about sex, or singled out this instinct as a special province of wonder. Only once was the alien topic thrust into our little world, and then it was introduced as a curious mystery by a visiting child—a small precocious girl whom we avoided, afterwards, as not entirely "nice" in her conversation. Over the universe in general, I burned with curiosity. Why were things what they were? Why did God let people and animals suffer when he could prevent it by a word or a gesture? Though I longed passionately for a God I could love, I could not, either from profit or piety, love the God of my fathers. I prayed to Him constantly—to help Mother when she was ill, to keep people from hurting animals, to let me die before school opened again; but these supplications might have been addressed to any heathen god, instead of to that Awful Power in the Old Testament. "A Fountain Filled with Blood" was an agonized obsession of my childhood. I wept for hours after the story of the Crucifixion was read to me. It was enough to wake and find misty images standing beside my bed. Those hallucinations—or dreams—I could convert into the shape of my guardian angel. But the agony of the Cross, the despair of Judas, who, my infant sense of justice protested, was appointed to Hell, and the avenging torments of the damned—all these eternal terrors of the Shorter Catechism were beyond the outspread wings of any hovering angel.

To the average child of seven, "moiling," as some solemn psychiatrist has remarked, "over the mystery of sex," these minor interests of an avenging God and eternal damnation might appear unimportant—or at least unexciting. Yet I was not ever a normal child. Far and wide as the common denominator might expand, it had never benignly included me. My mental responses, like my physical reflexes, were purely private affairs.

But an emotion is not dependent upon the investigation of sex. An intellectual sublimation may become as possessive as, and certainly more profound than, a natural instinct. Almost from the beginning, I was to discover that, if physical instincts did not bother me, the illusion of romantic love was an ancient antagonist.

What I had wished to do, when I looked into the future, was to leave the permanent record of an adventure into the far unknown. I had planned, in these memoirs, to deal only with my intellectual changes and pursuits, with the continuous search for a creed, for the reality of spirit, which would explain, if it could not justify, the truth of facts (things). In looking back, I see, now, that my emotional and my intellectual lives formed a single strand, and could not be divided. So closely were they intertwined that I could not tell where one began in pure feeling, and the other ended in pure speculation. I have lived to the fullest of my nature in thought and in emotion, and I have lived my own personal life as it seemed good to me —or, if not good, at least compelling.

At this very time, scarcely more than a block away from me, a grave little boy was beginning his perpetual conflict with dynamic illusions. His name was James Branch Cabell, but I saw him only when I called on his grandmother, an old lady of invincible spirit. Then he and his brothers would stare at me, indifferently, until they were able to slip silently out of the room. I was always pleased when they went. The grandmother amused me, but I did not like strange little boys. They seemed to me exciting, but insufficiently civilized. They were rude; they were indecent; they were boisterous; they were impolite to animals; they even (an offense against Nature or the Holy Ghost!) found some godless pleasure in robbing a bird's nest. To all these enormities, my brother Frank, whom I adored and imitated, was a shining exception. For the rest, I felt only a sensitive aversion, as if they or I had dropped from some inhabited star. I had never forgotten that boys had laughed and mocked at me when, at the age of six, I had robbed a squirrel of his hoard of chestnuts, and then, seized by remorse in the night, had got up on a frosty morning at sunrise to carry the nuts back to the woods in a vain effort to replace them in the empty hole. But there were so many big trees in the woods, and they all looked alike at a distance. Even Mr. Goodman, our favorite hired man, who excelled at everything, from carpenter's work to minding children, could not remember where the squirrel had had his house, or whether he had lived under the boughs of an oak or a chestnut. He laughed with the boys; but on cold nights, or when the snow was on the ground, I would think of that plundered squirrel and wonder if he and his family were hungry.

I can still say, with a pang of longing and regret, that Cary, my elder sister, had the most brilliant mind I have ever known. Her intellectual integrity must have prepared for her a tragic fate, in a period when truth walked alone, and the second best was exalted. She had a singularly winning charm, an iridescent personality. Even when she turned away to the strange gods of heterodoxy, her older friends were still ardently faithful, and remained devoted until the end of her life. Wherever she went, she invariably drew the best and brightest about her. But a girl who read Darwin and Henry George in the last decades of the nineteenth century was known as "the eccentric Miss Glasgow" to the orthodox youth who walked home from church with her sisters. When I was eighteen, she was married to a man with the face of a poet, and the mind of a scholar. His fidelity to truth in an age of pompous pretense left with me, after his early death, an indestructible standard. But I am running away from my time. Now I am still a little child, and I am beginning to feel, with Dryden, that "pity melts the heart to love."

Among the bland admirers who crowded our drawing-room and cast sheep's eyes at "Sister Emily," as I then called her, or listened, in amorous abstraction, to "Sister Annie" when she sang "Strangers Yet" or "Douglas, Douglas, tender and true" in a sweet small voice, with a yearning expression, there was a silent, sallow young man, who walked with a limp, and bore the marks of a hard childhood. Though I never spoke to him, I lavished on him a vague and completely ethereal sentiment. His poverty and his incredible pathos awakened an emotion I had not known until then, though it was associated, in some way I could not understand, with the rage that flared in me at the sight of cruelty and injustice. On wet evenings he would bring a cotton umbrella, slightly greenish from wear, and place it in the umbrella stand in the hall. To think that he had fallen so low, for he possessed the uncertain quality we still called "blue blood," was all that I needed for my budding romance.

I was too frightened of my grown sisters to enter the

room, unless I was sent with a message from Mother, or especially invited to hear Sister Annie sing a hymn on Sunday evening, or trill a love song on a night that was not sacred. At that time, all my family, with the exception of my mother, who had been brought up in the Episcopal Church and had a long line of high-church Episcopalian clergy and scholarly free-thinkers in her ancestry, were devoutly Presbyterian. Afterwards, only a single member, my eldest sister, preserved that stern creed through years of mingled happiness and adversity; but in my childhood I was, in our household, the only dissenter from orthodox Christianity, and the only rebel against the Calvinist conscience.

And so, while the music or the laughter floated out to me, I would sit in the cold hall, with my gaze on that sad umbrella, and wish I could be kind to the lame young man, who seemed to fear life as I did, and to suffer, as I did, too, in a proud silence, a rebellious and angry silence. Yet I never once spoke to him, and he did not suspect that the thin, pale little girl, with grave eyes below a straight bang, who looked far younger than her age because of her delicate frame, was weaving bloodless illusions around him. Ever since I watched the black dog pursued by cruel men, and old Uncle Henry taken, screaming, to the almshouse, life, in my imagination, was divided between the stronger and the weaker, the fortunate and the unfortunate. Either by fate or by choice, I had found myself on the side of the weaker. But, for the first time, I had discovered that, in my own small circle, there was a grown-up person, a man even, who could by no twist of pretense be placed among the victors of life. For my sisters scorned him, and I felt that he knew it.

Then, abruptly, he stopped coming. Perhaps my sisters discouraged his visits. Perhaps he felt that his rivals were too strong for him. I never knew why he left us. I never had the courage to ask whether he had been hurt or had simply dropped away without resentment, without reason. In a week my interest in him disappeared as quickly as it had come. After all, there was no lack of unfortunates. Destiny, without my connivance, had arranged that in advance. By the time I was grown my sense of humor, tinctured with irony, enabled me to laugh at myself and my own follies of temperament. Once at least in my experience, when I believed myself to be approaching death, with my world, within and without, overwhelmed by catastrophe, I found that I could laugh at the spectacle. But at the age of eleven, my senses, including the sense of humor, were still developed imperfectly. In that earliest romantic episode, I failed utterly to see the point of the jest.

———◄•►———

SIX

Early Sorrow

I could not have been more than ten years old when I was overtaken by a tragic occurrence which plunged my childhood into grief and anxiety, and profoundly affected, not only my mind and character, but my whole future life. In a single night, or so it seemed to us, my mother was changed from a source of radiant happiness into a chronic invalid, whose nervous equilibrium was permanently damaged. A severe shock, in a critical period, altered her so completely that I should scarcely have known her if I had come upon her after a brief absence. She, who had been a fountain of joy, became an increasing anxiety, a perpetual ache in the heart. Although she recovered her health, in a measure, her buoyant emotion toward life was utterly lost. Even now, when she has been dead so long, I cannot write of these things without a stab of that old inarticulate agony. . . .

At Jerdone Castle, when my father was away, Rebe and I slept in small twin beds in Mother's big airy room; but at the week end, when Father returned, we moved into the adjoining room, with the door between left open. Night after night, we would lie awake, listening to Mother's voice, as she walked the floor in anguish, to and fro, back and forth, driven by a thought or a vision, from which she tried in vain to escape. After I was in bed, before I could fall asleep, I would draw the sheet over my head, holding it fast to the pillow, in a fruitless effort to shut out the sound of her voice, and to ease the throbbing pain in my throat, that unavailing passion of sympathy. In those years, the most impressionable of our lives, Rebe and I knew scarcely a night that was not broken by a sudden start of apprehension, or by a torment of pity and terror which was as physical as the turn of a screw in our flesh. All through her nervous illness Mother refused steadfastly to take even a mild sleeping potion. Her horror of drugs was inborn, and there was no one in our world who understood either the cause or the inevitable course of her malady. Her mind remained clear, brilliant, and reasonable, and she kept to the end an extraordinary sense of humor. No visitor, hearing her merry laugh, or listening to her gay stories, would have suspected the constant pain hidden under her sparkling vivacity.

I have wondered since why she was allowed to suffer without the slightest alleviation. The physicians she consulted were as helpless as the rest of us. One after another, they solemnly advised her to divert her mind by cheerful thoughts, or to try a change of scene. It was the ancient superstition that unhappiness resides in the country without, not within, and that one may cure a broken heart by a simple change of address. For many years I bore a

passionate resentment against her family, against her physicians, against the universe, against God. Why? Why?
Why? I asked myself, as I lay, half smothered, under the
sheet, Why did this have to be? But I could find no answer, not in any universe, not even by a bald denial of
the reality. Nor have I ever understood why my mother,
who had never known a selfish thought in her life, whose
nature was composed of pure goodness, could have kept
her two youngest children beside her, day and night, in
her period of melancholy.

Rebe and I, and through the day, Frank, who was the
finest of us all, lived and breathed and moved, for months
at a time, in the atmosphere of despair. The very bread
we ate tasted of hopelessness. Not always, not without
brief interludes of brightness and joy, and a renewal of
vital expectancy. For weeks, perhaps, my mother would
again become her radiant self. She would recover her
cheerfulness, her look of effervescent delight, and sometimes she would join with us in our games, or dance with
us in the immense hall at Jerdone Castle. Then, by magic
it would seem, our whole world would be suffused with
light. As she changed, so we changed with her. Even school
would appear less threatening when the intolerable burden of anguish was lifted. If only the change could have
lasted! But it was barely more than a semblance of brightness. Inevitably, the glow would fade from life, and the
air of melancholy wash over us. This was our actual life,
beneath the smooth conventional surface. A fate such as
my mother's has been called, by one of the wisest of all
philosophers, unbearable even as a subject of drama:—the

spectacle of an innocent soul suffering an undeserved
tragedy. . . .

My mother was married at twenty-one, and she bore ten
children, not including one that came prematurely, and
died stillborn. Two of her children were born immediately
before the Civil War, two came into the devastated Valley
of Virginia, in the midst of the conflict, when there was
not bread enough for the other babies, and the rest followed a sudden descent from affluence to comparative
poverty, and the bitter struggle to build a home, and to
bring up a family, among ruins. My mother, who in her
youth, as the Negroes were fond of saying, "had never
stooped to pick up a handkerchief," braced her strength
for the long struggle, and worked harder, during her child-
bearing period, than any servant had been allowed to
work for her in the past. Her courage never failed, but
her delicate physical constitution, and her heightened sen-
sibilities, reached the breaking-point, before her nervous
system was injured by an emotional shock.

How much this affected her children's future, I have
never known. The eldest escaped. My brother Arthur,
who left home at sixteen, when the youngest children
were still very small, has remained untouched by the past.
Yet he was born at the end of an invasion, and he paid
for a brilliant success in his profession with impaired
health and failing eyesight. But only the two eldest sisters
grew up with the normal responses to life.

These details are of little interest, I am aware, to the
casual reader; but, I am aware also, that the merely casual

reader will have given up long before he reaches the beginning, or the end, of the page. Only the student of
heredity and environment may find a stubborn problem
to solve. . . .

Although the images of my earliest childhood are quite
clear in my recollection, the years between ten and fifteen
swim in a haze, whenever I look back. My mother's unhappiness obscured everything. I could not see far beyond
it. Even in play, and I loved play, we were never free
from the pressure of anxiety, from the sense of foreboding,
and of something else, strange and terrible, hanging over
us. The children I played with, the friends of my own
age, began to feel that I was too old for them. Frank, Rebe
and I were inseparable. When Frank was sent away to
school, my childhood, I think, was over forever. We were
at Jerdone Castle when he left, and I remember stealing
off, in my grief, until no one could see me, and then crying, silently, over the heads of Pat, my pointer, and little
Toy. We were beside the old ice pond, where Frank and
I had once released a small alligator, and I can see, in
memory, the green and brown sedges, and the colored
leaves floating on the still water. Clouds of dying blue
and yellow butterflies lingered, through September, over
the rushes, and they were drifting there on that last sad
afternoon. The next day, we would leave, for the summer
was ended.

Frank was a shy and delicate boy, with immense dark
eyes, and handsome, reserved features. Father had selected
the Virginia Military Institute, in the vain hope that the

training might "harden" him; but Frank was the last boy
on earth who should have been sent to a military academy.
He endured it to the end, without a word of protest or
complaint. I can only imagine what he must have suffered;
for his reserve was the strongest I have ever known, and
he wore it, throughout his life, as an armor. He never
spoke, except perhaps to Mother, whom he adored, of his
four years at the Institute. Yet he made several devoted
friends there, and he was scrupulously loyal to his class
and to the school. But he was not "hardened" by the training. He was never strong, and his years away from home
increased his unconquerable remoteness. No human being
could have been more self-contained, more inarticulate
under suffering, or more unselfish in his association with
the only two persons he really loved, first Mother, and
then, in a lesser degree, Father. Because I have regretted
so deeply I did not say this to Frank himself, while it was
still possible, I repeat that he was the only one of Mother's
children who never failed her in word, or in act, or in
sympathetic understanding.

From that moment when he went away to school, Frank
was lost to me. A door shut between us. His reserve turned
to stone; and from that autumn afternoon until the April
morning, long afterwards, when he found life too intolerable to be borne, he lived a stranger among us. If Mother
had still lived, his fortitude would not have broken. But
Mother was dead; his health had failed; the doctors had
told him they could do nothing to help him; and, in his
complete loneliness, he had come to dread, quite without
reason, a mental breakdown. To the end, he showed that

delicate consideration for others which had always been
a second nature. Alone, except for Mother in his early life,
he had lived among us, but not with us. In a last effort
to spare us as far as it was possible, he went, alone, from
the house, and, alone, into a future where we could not
follow him. . . .

But this was years afterwards. If only I could have
looked ahead, I have said to myself, over and over, I might
have made everything different. . . . Weeping beside the
old ice pond, in a mood which indelibly impressed the
scene on my mind—green and bronze rushes, silken gray
water, bullfrogs plunging and leaping from the leaves of
the water lilies—weeping there in the vast loneliness of
childhood, I grieved for my lost playmate, and perhaps,
with one of those uncanny premonitions of the very young
or the very old, I suspected he would never come back
to me.

When Frank returned for the holidays, at long intervals,
we spoke reservedly to each other, from a widening distance, as if we were friendly strangers, on guard lest we
betray ourselves. We were alike in this. When we recoiled
from experience, we went deeper and deeper into ourselves. Around us, we spun the protective cocoon of in-
difference. I was still a child when I learned that an artificial brightness is the safest defense against life.

Rebe was left to me as a playmate, and we had wonderful times with Carrie Coleman and Lizzie Patterson from
Reveille. Every child, if it survives, must discover or invent its own special joys. When we were smaller, we had

delighted in boisterous romping, and in the old out-of-door games. . . .

From the mist and sunshine of those years a few stark shapes emerge. We had moved, now, into the big gray house on the corner of Main Street, and after my mother's nervous breakdown, we left Jerdone Castle forever. Mother had conceived a horror of the place I loved, and she could not stay on there without greater anguish of mind.

For Rebe, and for me, leaving the farm was like tearing up the very roots of our nature. This was the only place where I found health, where I had known a simple and natural life. It was the place where I had begun to write, and had discovered an object, if not a meaning, in the complicated pattern of my inner world. It was the place, too, where I had felt hours and even days of pure happiness, where I had rushed down the road to meet the advancing storm, while I felt in my heart the fine, pointed flame that is ecstasy.

All this was distressing, but far worse even than this was the enforced desertion of Pat, my beautiful pointer. For years, the memory of Pat, left with an overseer who might not be kind to him, would thrust up, like a dagger, into my dreams. What would they do with Pat when they moved? What would happen to him when he grew old? Why was it people made you do things that would break your heart always? Even now, I sometimes awake with a regret, that is half for Pat himself, and half a burning remorse for some act I have committed but cannot remember.

Ellen Glasgow in her twenties

The house at First and Cary Streets, Richmond, where Ellen Glasgow was born (Ellen and Rebe on the porch)

Francis Thomas Glasgow, Jr., aged six

Rebe Gordon Glasgow, aged four

Anne Jane (Gholson) Glasgow,
the author's mother

Francis Thomas Glasgow,
the author's father

Cary Glasgow McCormack,
aged twenty-eight

Ellen Glasgow at the turn of the century

At age seven

A portrait made in the 1920's

In her early thirties,
with "chrysanthemum" bob

The garden of Ellen Glasgow's house at One West Main Street, with the grave of Jeremy, her dog, at right

Billy and Pat, the author's dogs, in 1935

One West Main Street, Richmond

Ellen Glasgow's study at One West Main Street

Ellen Glasgow in 1938

Only a delicate child, rendered morbid by circumstances, could have suffered as I suffered from that change
to the city in summer. Though I went to school for a few
months each year, until my health grew frail again and
my nervous headaches returned, I would wonder all the
way home whether I should find my mother cheerful or
sad. Usually, she sent us off brightly; but the brightness
would fade as soon as we turned the corner, and the deep
despondency would creep over her. Once in those years
she went away on her only visit to her brother, whom she
had adored since she was a baby. He lived in Holly Springs,
Mississippi, and the doctors advised the long trip as a
diversion. Rebe went with her, and they were away several months. It was my first long separation from them,
and I missed them both with an ache that was like physical pain. Most of my time was spent alone, for in our
large family the three elder sisters lived in a different, and
a larger, world, where they had their own interests and
their own pleasures. No doubt they had their own troubles
also, but they seemed, to us, creatures of a more fortunate
sphere.

I still had little Toy, but, in Mother's absence, he was
set apart, though I did not suspect this, as another victim.
One afternoon, I could not find him when I was urged
by my father to go to walk with Lizzie Patterson, and that
night, after I had looked for him in vain, one of the servants told me that Father had had him put into a bag, and
had given him to two men who worked at the Tredegar.
They told me fearfully, wondering what "Miss Annie"
(my mother) "would say when she came back"; but, with-

out a word, I turned away and went straight to Father.

Rage convulsed me, the red rage that must have swept up from the jungles and the untamed mind of primitive man. And this rage—I have not ever forgotten it—contained every anger, every revolt I had ever felt in my life —the way I felt when I saw the black dog hunted, the way I felt when I watched old Uncle Henry taken away to the almshouse, the way I felt whenever I had seen people or animals hurt for the pleasure or profit of others. All these different rages were here; all had dissolved and intermingled with the fury of youth that is helpless. If I spoke words, I cannot recall them. I remember only that I picked up a fragile china vase on the mantelpiece and hurled it across the room. It shattered against the wall, and I can still hear the crash it made as it fell into fragments. Then I rushed into my room, and locked the door on my frightened sisters and the more frightened servants. I should never see Toy again, I knew. I had never seen Pat again. My father would not change his mind. Not once in my knowledge of him had he ever changed his mind or admitted that he was wrong—or even mistaken.

I poured out my heart in a letter to Mother. And she did not reply. Day after day, week after week, I waited, but when her letters came, they made no mention of her affection for my dog, or of the injustice from which I suffered so desperately. Not until long afterwards, when Mother was at home and ill again, did I discover the reason for her apparent neglect. Then, one afternoon, while I was studying my lessons in a corner of the library, I overheard my sister Emily, the eldest of the family, relate

an amusing version of Toy's betrayal. It was a good opportunity to get rid of him, she explained, while Mother was
away. He was sick and old and troublesome, and none
of them liked him but Mother and Rebe and me. So they
had meant to keep it a secret from Mother, and when
they found that I had written, Emily had gone to the postmaster and asked him to return a letter which would give
Mother a shock if she received it. And the postmaster had
obligingly returned the letter from the post. An incredible
incident to anyone who has not lived in a small Southern
community.

The remembrance of children is a long remembrance,
and the incidents often make milestones in a personal history. In those months of Mother's absence, I know that I
broke forever with my childhood. For the first time I was
standing alone, without the shelter and the comfort of her
love and her sympathy. Her silence, inexplicable and utterly unlike her, seemed to thrust me still farther and
farther into loneliness, until at last—for months may have
the significance of years when one is very young—I began
to love, not to fear, loneliness. During this time, and indeed through all my future life, I shrank from my father's
presence; and only one of my elder sisters ever won my
reluctant confidence. At the time, angry, defiant, utterly
unsubdued by pleadings and rebukes, I told myself, obstinately, that if they cared nothing for my feelings, I
would care nothing for theirs. For weeks I hated them all.
I hated the things they believed in, the things they so
innocently and charmingly pretended. I hated the sanc-
timonious piety that let people hurt helpless creatures.

I hated the prayers and the hymns, and the red images that colored their drab music, the fountains filled with blood, the sacrifice of the lamb.

And, then, much to Father's distress, and to my sisters' consternation, I refused to attend divine service—and there was nothing left that they could do about it. My will, which was as strong as Father's, plunged its claws into the earth. Nothing, not lectures, not deprivations, not all the pressure they could bring, could ever make me again go with them to church.

If I had won nothing else, I had won liberty. Never again should I feel that I ought to believe, that older people were wiser and better than I was. Never again should I feel that I ought to pretend things were different. Dumbly, obstinately, I would stare back at them when they talked to me. I could not answer them. I could not refute my father when he opened the Bible, and read aloud, in his impressive voice, the sternest psalms in the Old Testament. All I could do was to shake my ignorant head, and reply that, even if all that was true, it made no difference to me. I was finished with that way of life before I had begun it.

And, then, in the midst of it all, while my mother was still away, I was seized, I was overwhelmed by a consuming desire to find out things for myself, to know the true from the false, the real from the make-believe. The longing was so intense that I flung myself on knowledge as a thirsty man might fling himself into a desert spring. I read everything in our library. History, poetry, fiction, archaic or merely picturesque, works on science, and even *The Westminster Confession of Faith*. Lizzie Patterson and Carrie Coleman came frequently in the afternoon; but even with them, my two closest friends, I felt that I had changed beyond understanding and recognition. They lived happy lives on the outside of things, accepting what they were taught, while I was devoured by this hunger to know, to discover some meaning, some underlying reason for the mystery and the pain of the world.

For I had ceased to be a child. My mind and the very pit of my stomach felt empty. I needed the kind of reality that was solid and hard and would stay by one.

When, at last, Mother and Rebe returned, I felt shy with them and vaguely uncomfortable. It seemed to me, for the first few days at least, that they had changed, that they had seen things I had not seen, that they treasured recollections I could not share. Or perhaps I was the one who had changed. Something had gone out of me for good, and, in exchange, I had found something that, to me, was more precious. I had found the greatest consolation of my life; but I had found also an unconquerable loneliness. I had entered the long solitude that stretches on beyond the vanishing-point in the distance.

Part Two

YOUTH
AND THE WORLD

———◄·►———

SEVEN

The Search for Truth

With a firm, wide-reaching power to retain the words and rhythms of poetry, as well as all visual impressions, scenes, colors, and scents which may evoke, or be translated into, images of the mind, my memory has always been, and is now, incapable of permanently recording a date or a number. Pictures are indelible, but figures are immediately washed from the slate of my recollection. When, therefore, I have not been able to verify certain or uncertain dates in my life, I have been obliged, however reluctantly, to make a reasonable guess at the probability.

This is especially true of the years between my sixteenth and my twentieth birthday. The four years glide into one another as if they were a single year. Yet they began pleasantly, even happily, at sixteen, with my first ball, a Saint Cecilia ball, in Charleston, where I was spending part of the winter. I remember that I was eager for gaiety. I was light and graceful on my feet, a natural dancer. I wore a frock of white organdie, with innumerable flounces, which whirled around me in the waltz. There was a red rose in my elaborately curled hair. Because I was a visitor, as well as the youngest girl present, I was made, according to the gracious courtesy of old Charleston, one of the belles of that brilliant and unforgettable evening.

In the following June I went to Commencement at the University of Virginia, and I was almost startled to find how easy it was, as soon as I had forgotten my shyness, to mingle with strangers, and to become popular among them. After my sad childhood, it was like breaking out of a cage. Several light romances budded and bloomed and dropped, as I passed on; but I was, at seventeen, incredible as it sounds to modern ears, still ignorant of what we call, euphemistically, "the facts of life." It was during this visit that an older woman, deploring my "dangerous ignorance," delicately but painfully enlightened me; and, from this enlightenment my earliest idea for *The Descendant* was born—from this, and from my awakening interest in social history and in theories of economics.

But neither my ignorance of life nor my serious tastes interfered with my pleasures. For a few weeks, at least, I won all the admiration, and felt all the glorified sensations, of a Southern belle in the Victorian age. Two years before, I had found myself neglected by the Virginia Military Institute, in Lexington; but, now, at Mr. Jefferson's University, I was not ever a wallflower, I was, indeed, a brilliant success. No girl was allowed, of course, in the classroom; but my old friend, Dr. George Frederick Holmes, professor of political economy, gave me, in the seclusion of his study, a private examination on economics. Though he used the examination papers he gave to his students, I passed with distinction. It happened that

I knew my John Stuart Mill by heart, and I possessed, too, a fair acquaintance with Walker's less interesting work. My mind had been turned in that direction by the man my sister Cary married a year or two later. This was George Walter McCormack, of Charleston. He was a sound and brilliant thinker, and, in his too brief life, he exercised a vital influence over my intellectual outlook.

At that time, I was looking forward to the normal life of a Southern girl in my circle. Yet my vital interests were not objective, and I put aside, indifferently, the offer of the usual "coming-out party" and the "formal presentation to Richmond society." For I was writing, or had already written, a long novel, of some four hundred pages, entitled *Sharp Realities,* a name borrowed from Beaumont and Fletcher; and in the year between the burning of this manuscript and the beginning of *The Descendant,* it had dawned upon me that I was gradually attaining a culture before I had acquired what we have agreed to call an education.

Guided by chance or inspired by my instructor, Walter McCormack, I had found, on the dusty shelf of a second-hand book shop, a copy of *Progress and Poverty.* After buying it for thirty cents, I had brought home my discovery, and I had plunged, eagerly, into the absorbing first chapters, with their able analysis of social conditions. As I read, I was impressed by Henry George's review of the world's poverty, and by his logical and unrelenting inferences from the facts. He may or may not have influenced my theme when I began my crude first book, *The Descendant.* I was striving more for art than for inspiration, which, as a beginning author, I needed far less; but, at least, he encouraged the revolutionary slant in my point of view. Why did not people rebel when they had nothing to lose? I wanted to know why. I wanted to discover what it was that kept the poor in their place. Was it merely the pressure from without? Or was it that still more demoralizing pressure from within? I had none of the early Christian belief that poverty was eternally blest. Only when it was chosen as a symbol of compassion had it ever blest anybody. The shaved head and the yellow bowl were the outward signs, not of material destitution, but of spiritual abundance.

Nevertheless, I might learn the effect of poverty on the will to live while I investigated the actual lives of the poor. I had never forgotten Uncle Henry and the wagon from the almshouse. That childish rage against social cruelty and injustice had not burned out; it had melted into a more general conflict with the world's inhumanity. After all, social savagery was only a part of the whole barbaric nature of life. In those years I was ripe for revolution; but I wanted a revolution against inhumanity, and every social revolution in the past had been merely against one special aspect of inhumanity. Some familiar Devil's advocate invariably found the safe shelter of the barricade. I could not be in favor of any particular series of cruelties, and against another series. I abhorred them all, and I knew that freedom had its own favorite witch-finders. No, I liked human beings, but I did not love human nature.

A little later, at seventeen, I gave my first party, and, in the same winter, I joined the City Mission, and became

the youngest "visitor" in its membership. Though my
health was frail, my mental energy was inexhaustible, and
I was eager to test life on every side and in every situation.
The squalor I saw horrified me, and, in the majority of
cases, I felt that I was dealing with inanimate matter.
Certainly, there was not any blessedness in the spiritless
whining with which these particular paupers gave up the
struggle, and leaned back upon God. Society was to blame,
I innocently told myself. Society was responsible. No doubt
that was true. But the trouble with society is now, and
has always been, that it has no entity apart from the individual human beings of which it is composed.

All that winter I worked with the City Mission, but I
learned so little that I decided the independent poor, the
poor who were "too proud to beg," must be different. The
next year I went once or twice a week to The Sheltering
Arms, a private charity which well merited its romantic
name. That was a small hospital, down on Governor
Street, with no winding of red tape, but a pitifully small
income. Still, one could reach these people, and I came
very close to their personal lives. It was, however, a foolish
effort to learn something of life from the outside, and
ever since that first failure, I have been suspicious of all
such endeavors.

For a few months, scarcely longer, I was a convert to
Socialism. I called myself a "Fabian Socialist," until it
seemed to me the Fabian Society had become flabby with
compromise. But I was feeling deeply the wrongs and the
general unfairness of what we call modern civilization,

and I used to dream foolish dreams of running off to join some vague revolutionary movement. But where, at the end of the nineteenth century, could one find the Revolution? In what mean streets and dark alleys of the South was it then lying in ambush? Though I suffered with the world's suffering, though I told myself the few had no right to seek happiness at the expense of the many, or to remain satisfied with a mortal lot that meant only pain to the great majority of human beings, and to all animals —though I might feel, and even believe this, still I could see, in the sky, no promise of better things, not the faintest glimmering signs of an approaching millennium. If history proved anything, surely it proved, beyond a doubt, that the blood of revolutions had never washed a people's soul clean of cruelty and greed and intolerance. What most rebels wanted was, not a new and fairer order for all, but a conqueror's share in the state they inhabited. In the mass of recorded conflicts, whether foreign or civil, booty for one, not blessedness for many, had been the inspiring motive. . . .

As I grew older, the sensitiveness of my childhood was beginning to wear away, and I was losing my shyness with strangers, if not entirely with my elder sisters. My fear of them had now disappeared. I had stopped calling them "Sister Emily" and "Sister Annie," and Cary, the most brilliant member of our family, had begun to notice me, and even to become interested. Though I did not confide in her, she was the only person, except my mother, who encouraged me to write, and to have faith in my future. But that was long afterwards. When I was sixteen or seven-

teen, she was doing her best to discourage me. She remembered that she herself had tried and had failed as a girl;
and she dreaded, for me, a renewal of that old disappointment.

Nevertheless, I had not yet found myself. I was still in
search, less of abstract truth, than of a very private and
personal destiny. Youth is without finality, and, like all
young and ardent creatures, I craved change, adventure,
delight. I felt a thrilling sense that mystery surrounded
me, that life stretched ahead, like a forest of luminous
vistas. . . .

Then, just as I was turning from the knowledge in books,
and eagerly grasping at the careless youth I had never
known, life struck again, and the blow left me writhing
in anguish. My mother became ill with typhoid fever, and
died after a week's suffering. She had begun to feel a new
interest in living, and, in September, she had gone, with
Cary, to a summer resort in the Virginia mountains. At
first, she had appeared to improve, but a little while after
she came home, typhoid developed. To her three younger
children, it was as if the world rocked suddenly, and fell
to pieces. Well or ill, she had been the supreme figure
in our universe.

It is more than forty years now since she died, yet a
part of me seems still to live on, in that hour, in that
moment. A part of me, buried but alive, was held there,
imprisoned and immovable, while the rest of my being
flowed on as time flows, relentlessly. Strangely enough, the
external incidents have survived, the wild tumult, and

even the memory of grief, and of the more agonizing remorse for all the things I might have done for her, and
had not done. The sorrow that seemed eternal is now dead.
I cannot recover a vital emotion, or bring back a throb
of that old agony. Yet some other self stands in the center
of that desolate room, looks through the blurred windowpanes, and still watches, without knowing what it watches,
two sparrows quarreling in the slow rain on a roof. And
while I stand there, a mountain of things I had left undone is torn up from the earth, and crashes down on my
life.

Of her ten children, Frank, as I have said before, was
the only one who repaid her unselfish devotion. He had
never failed her, though all the rest of us, in our blind
egoism, had failed her when she needed us most. A profound, an unbreakable, sympathy united them, mother
and son. She was the only human being who ever saw
Frank as he really was, incurably faithful in his affections,
and yet completely disillusioned with life, wanting nothing from experience, because all experience seemed to
him to be inadequate. After his first wild torrent of grief,
he retreated into his invulnerable reserve. Never once,
in the years afterwards, did I hear him mention her name.
To the end, he tried to do whatever was in his power to
make Father's life easier, and he never lost patience with
a nature so utterly unlike his own. Horseback riding was
his solitary pleasure; the hours at the office were long, and
Sunday was the only day he could use for exercise or
diversion. His health had always been frail, and he suffered agonies from insomnia. The doctor had told him

riding would help him more than anything else he could
do. Yet when Father objected to his riding on the Sab-
bath, he gave up his only recreation, without a word of
protest, and spent the long Sunday afternoons either sitting indoors or going with Father to church for the second
service. Why he did not rebel, I have never known. It
may be that he felt sorry for Father. It may be that he
felt nothing, not life itself, was worth making a fuss about.
Until the end he was Father's right hand, going with him
to work, and helping him as he grew older and less active
in mind. Then, when the burden became too heavy to be
borne, and suffering was incessant, without hope of relief,
he died as bravely and as quietly as he had lived. . . .

That was many years later, but, in the weeks that followed Mother's death, Frank was kinder than anyone else
to Father. He would sit patiently, with an inscrutable face,
while Father gathered us about him, and read aloud his
favorite belligerent passages from the Old Testament.
What comfort he could have found in the slaughter of
Moabites or Amalekites, or even of Philistines, it is hard
to imagine. Certainly, he could have had no special griev-
ance against any one of these tribes. But, I think, he
needed comfort as little as he needed pleasure; and a God
of terror, savoring the strong smoke of blood sacrifice, was
the only deity awful enough to command his respect. He
never read of love or of mercy, for, I imagine, he regarded
these virtues as belonging by right to a weaker gender,
amid an unassorted collection of feminine graces.

Whatever softening I might have felt toward Father in
our grief was swept away by the discovery that, within a

few weeks of Mother's death, he had sold her pet mare,
Winnie, to be used for light hauling at the Tredegar Iron
Works. Mother had loved Winnie. She was the only person who had driven her to the phaeton, and Winnie had
known her voice and her touch on the reins. The mare
was taken away before we discovered her empty stall, and
then I pleaded with Father to give her back to us. But,
as usual, he would not reverse a decision. Winnie was
growing old, he explained. Didn't I know that she had
fallen with a kind of fit in the street? When I begged
him to have her shot, instead of selling her down into
servitude, he replied that he would hate to have to do
that. I turned away blinded with tears, and with the memory of Mother. There was nothing else I could say or do.
I did not own, at the time, so much as a penny to spend
as I pleased. . . .

Yet it was amazing how gentle Father could become in
a sickroom. In the presence of pain, physical, not mental,
rooted in flesh and bone, not in spirit or in nerves, he
would sit quietly and stroke a fevered head, forgetful alike
of the massacre of the innocents or of the death of the
firstborn. I used to be perplexed, too, by the easy tears
he would shed over sentimental fiction. Though he had
never made the slightest effort to win the affection of his
children, assuming, no doubt, that filial devotion was a
product of unaided nature, his voice would quiver and
break, and tears would overflow his eyes, whenever he
encountered in print the return of a prodigal daughter.
Oddly enough, the prodigal son left him untouched, at
least to all outward signs. He was cold equally to the husks

and to the fatted calf. But I recall an evening in his library, when he was absorbed in one of his favorite stories —I think it was *Beside the Bonnie Briar Bush,* if that is the name—and we were suddenly startled to hear a loud sob burst from his lips. For an instant, nobody spoke. Then Cary remarked, with a faintly ironic smile: "The lamp has been set in the window to welcome the prodigal daughter." He always wept over that scene, yet I cannot remember, though I may be mistaken, that he ever shed a tear over a death in his family. Though he was cold, he was not naturally cruel. There was no tinge of sadism in his mind, and he never hurt anything simply for the satisfaction of hurting.

Through the varied illnesses of my early childhood, he bore his part, Mother said, in the nursing. She told me once that, when they thought I was dying of diphtheria, he was the only person I would let touch me, after Mammy, who, for three days, never left my bedside, except for a few minutes at a time. I was only two, and I insisted that "the thing in my throat" would leap up and choke me if Mammy took her hands away. Then Mother, who was in bed with a week-old baby in the adjoining room, would beg me to let Father hold me while Mammy ate a mouthful of soup. And he would sit there at my side until Mammy returned. But, even then, I must have felt, instinctively, that his attention was more patriarchal than paternal, and that I was not myself to him, but merely one of his ten children.

All over town other children were dying, at that time, for there was a fearful scourge of diphtheria. Frank and

I fought the illness under tented sheets, with the ante-
diluvian remedy of slaked lime in tubs by our beds. All
I remember of that desperate time is that I was lying
under something white, with steam or fog floating round
me. But this might well be a later act of the imagination.
. . . How Frank came through, I have never known;
but old Dr. Coleman declared my life was saved by
Mammy's nursing; and after her unselfish devotion, he
became her physician, without charge, till the end of his
days. Nobody appears to have thought of the week-old
baby, Samuel Creed, who caught the disease and died all
in a single night. I am able to place my age as two, because exactly one year and nine months after that baby's
death, Rebe, the youngest of Mother's children, was
born. . . .

Living through diphtheria was nothing compared to living
through the months immediately after Mother's death.
We were alone now, Frank and Rebe and I, with Father
and Emily, who was not married until a few years later.
Cary was married to George Walter McCormack, and they
were living in Charleston. Until I met Walter I had never
known a man with an intellect of the highest order, and
my brief association with him, for he died at the age of
twenty-six, overthrew the last of my inherited prejudices,
and exerted a far-reaching influence over my future. He
sent me books, and it was owing to him that I carried on
my study of economics. I know that he was responsible
for my discovery of the great scientists of the Victorian
age. By his advice, I studied *The Origin of Species,* until
I could have passed successfully an examination on every

page. My health had again failed, and for the winter months I was confined to my room. If only I had been encouraged, or even permitted, to take exercise, I might have built up my frail constitution. Years later, after I decided that I would rather risk dying than live to be an invalid, I won a fair measure of health by cold baths, summer and winter, and long walks in all weather. Nothing ever benefited me so much, or gave me such zestful enjoyment, as golf when I played it; but this came long afterwards, and entirely from my own determination to get well or to die. In that winter, after my mother's death, I was suffering from my old headaches, and all the doctors could advise was a permanent rest cure.

For two years I had been working on *The Descendant;* but, after Mother's death, I burned the uncompleted manuscript, and a year or more passed before I found courage to return to my writing. All my impulse and ambition seemed to be buried with Mother, and I looked, instead, for some hidden clue to experience, for some truth, or at least for some philosophy, which would help me to adjust my identity to a world I had found hostile and even malign. How could one live on without a meaning in life? Fortitude alone was not enough to support life.

There was no public library in Richmond, and I borrowed the few scientific works, mostly old editions, or obsolete, from the State library. History, especially philosophical histories, contributed what I craved in that time of emotional bleakness; the hard truths irradiated with genius. For I craved truth that was concrete and indestructible.

In the year of Mother's death, I did not leave the old

gray house in Richmond. If I went out at all it was only into the small garden at the back, or as far as the spreading shadows of the big tulip poplars on the front pavement. Rebe and I were very near to each other at that time. For Frank, in spite of his iron reserve, we both felt a shy and yearning tenderness. We could feel his suffering, but we dared not speak of it.

Early that spring, Cary and Walter sent me a subscription to the Mercantile Library in New York, and then the doors of a new world were flung back. When I pause to think, now, of the way I waste money on books I can never read—that I give away, merely to have them out of the house—I am touched by the recollection of what that library and those weekly or fortnightly parcels of books meant in my life. I had no money to buy books; but I had all the time in the world to read them, and I begrudged the hours I spent asleep or talking to my acquaintances, who regarded books as not only unnecessary in well-bred circles, but as an unwarranted extravagance. Besides, did not everybody know what happened to bluestockings? Was not New England full of them? And did not they invariably end as abolitionists—or, since abolition was itself ended, did not they become either temperance workers or women's rights advocates? "You are too attractive to be strong-minded," they would remark, reassuringly.

When the first parcel came, I opened it eagerly. After this, I would read all day, stopping only for a cup of tea or a plate of soup, which Emily would send me in the hope of "tempting my appetite." I was supposed to go to bed early; but after Rebe had fallen asleep, I would slip from the adjoining bed, and steal down the dark stairs, feeling my way to the library, or—but this was after I had published a book and had been given a place to write in —I groped through the hall to the tiny study, which is now a bathroom, between the two rooms at the front. Here I would light the "students'" lamp, for this was before we had electricity in the house, and I would read, breathlessly, searching always for something I never found, until two o'clock in the morning. The only sounds that reached me were the rumble of occasional wheels in the street, or, if the windows were open, the slow, even tramp of a policeman's walk on the pavement.

From the Mercantile, I borrowed the works of all German scientists I had heard mentioned, or had seen quoted in books. Not until long afterwards did it occur to me that the German philosophers, especially Schopenhauer, would have been better reading, and that they possessed more of the hard truth I required—more, too, of that intellectual fortitude I was seeking. A few years later I read Kant and (though I could never read Hegel) the whole wide group of idealists, which included Fichte and Schelling. Of the German philosophy, only *The World as Will and Idea* stayed with me, until, by pure accident, I discovered the great prose-poem, *Thus Spake Zarathustra*. But we are in the early 'nineties, and I am running entirely too far ahead. . . .

In that dark winter of my mother's death, I was made the victim of a minor religious persecution. Father was keenly distressed by my unbridled pursuit of knowledge. He had heard Gibbon denounced from the pulpit, and, on both general and particular grounds, he disapproved of Gibbon's superlative history. However, at least one Presbyterian divine had declared the work to be scholarly, and had suggested that the danger of reading it might be diminished if one were careful to omit, in reading, the famous fifteenth chapter. Two of my elder sisters had even boasted of dipping, recklessly, into that forbidden chapter, and of emerging with their faith unimpaired.

But, if Gibbon appeared as a menace, the very name of Darwin was anathema among the few Southerners who had ever heard it pronounced. "Pish! Tush! Doesn't the man say we are descended from monkeys!" When Father actually surprised me with the sinister work, lent to me by Walter McCormack, there was at first rebuke, then moral suasion, and, after that, since milder methods had proved futile, righteous rage stormed about me. The humorous or ironic point of the jest was that, at the time, I was too young to comprehend a word of the Darwinian hypothesis, and it was not until years later that I came to understand and to value the book. Even then, I was influenced, less by the special scientific theory of natural selection than I was by the older all-embracing philosophy of organic evolution. But, throughout that hideous winter, I read what Father and my eldest sister feared and hated rather than what I, myself, enjoyed. Right or wrong, I could not be moved. Long ago, when it might have been easy to win a child's confidence, Father had estranged me, without thinking a child could be estranged; and now all the tumult of unreason provoked only a clash of two wills equally strong. Over and over, I repeated my variation of the modern creed: Not "my life is my own!" as youth cries today, but "my mind is my own!"

Emily supported him, that eldest sister, more than eighteen years my senior, who had once hidden a copy of Ouida's *Moths* beneath her shirtwaists, in a bureau drawer, to keep me from finding it. Frank stood apart, smiling, indifferent. Only Rebe, the youngest, was bold or heretical enough to stand by me. Cary would have fought for me, but she was living in Charleston.

In the end, after a stormy discussion, a truce was agreed upon. Father and Emily went to Sunday service, twice a day, and to another service on Wednesday evening, while I rushed, with renewed enthusiasm, to puzzle over books which, at twenty, I read in a dazed wonder of admiration and awe and misunderstanding. Nothing more was said, until Emily stole in one evening, when Rebe was away, and offered me a shining gold-piece if I would let her exchange Lecky's *History of Rationalism in Europe* for some "nicer book like *The Lives of the Poets.*"

And all the time, if only they had suspected it, I needed God more than they needed Him, and, in my own rebellious way, I was trying to find Him. At that age, had I known the God of Plotinus, or the God of St. Francis, I should have sought Him as a refuge. But, all my life, Father had offered me, not Christ, but Jehovah. . . . "Oh, Thou who dost take the shapes imagined by Thy worshipers!"

EIGHT

The Search for Art

Except for the first six chapters, which I had overlooked, the entire manuscript of *The Descendant* was lost; but the theme and every incident, with detail complete, were stored away in some recess of my memory. Gradually, after a year or more of unavailing sorrow, my creative impulse awakened, and the whole book returned to me. A vast discouragement overwhelmed me, and, while it endured, I tried to forget that I was born a writer, that, as far back as I could remember, I had wanted to be a novelist. It was not for nothing that I was born, too, with an innate sense of what is good, and of what is merely second best in any intellectual pursuit. I knew that my work, so far, was not right; but I did not know the exact way I could follow to make it better. Every step of that way I had to plan and to hew out, unaided. One help alone I possessed (I repeat this because it has meant so much in my career) and that help was the native instinct that warned me, unfailingly, "This is not right! That word will not do!" My earliest books were crude and blundering, because though I heard the warning voice, I did not know how to obey it. As I went on, slowly evolving my own theories, and working out my own peculiar technique, this voice seemed to grow clearer, and no longer to speak a strange language.

Two winters before we lost Mother, I had gone to New York with a group of girls, whose parents had decided that music, and especially the opera, was a necessary part of their daughters' education. We stayed all together, four of us, in one room on the top floor of a boarding house, which was kept by a handsome, and very strict, Southern lady, in depressed spirits and reduced circumstances. Whenever we went to the opera, she was our chaperone. Occasionally, however, we were allowed to go, unattended, for a walk on Fifth Avenue, and for a glance into the shops. It was on one of these strolls that I separated myself from the others, and achieved the genuine purpose of my trip to New York.

Somewhere in the advertising pages of a magazine, Cary or I had seen the advertisement of a "distinguished" literary critic, endorsed by many members of the Authors' Club, who could be induced, for the sum of fifty dollars, to give advice to young authors, and to assist them in selecting the right publisher. At the time, I did not have fifty dollars of my own, and, at eighteen, I saw no possibility of ever having that much to spend as I pleased. But we cut out the notice; and, oddly enough, we had alluded to it just before we heard of the Southern lady who would receive, for a moderate sum, any number of girls of good families provided they stayed all in one room. When Mother or Cary asked Father to let me go, he con-

sented, rather to our surprise. But I had some slight
trouble with my ears. Nothing serious, the doctors in Richmond assured me; but my terror of anything like deafness
made Cary suggest that I should consult one of the leading
aurists in New York. Incidentally, I did consult one, and
he told me that there was no danger of my becoming deaf,
and that I had better go home and forget all about it.

But when I was leaving home Cary had sent me fifty
dollars, which she had subtracted from a present Father
had given her when she married. This I had sent with
the manuscript of *Sharp Realities* to the unknown literary
adviser, and, after reaching New York, I had made an
appointment to call on him. I called to the minute of the
appointed hour, and was received by an elderly gray-
haired man, in a velvet coat, who finally, after prolonged
fumbling, disinterred my unwrapped manuscript from beneath a mountain of papers. Though he cut the string,
he scarcely glanced at the title. He was not interested in
the manuscripts of young women. All he cared for, I discovered to my dismay, was their physical charm. After a
vague and disconcerting prelude, he began to ask questions more personal than literary. Where was I staying?
When would I come again? Would I come late in the
afternoon, when he was usually alone in the building?
All of this I was too startled or too stupid to understand.
But I did understand when he said in his blunt Northern
manner, "You are too pretty to be a novelist. Is your figure
as lovely in the altogether as it is in your clothes?" One
must have been stupid indeed not to have taken that in.

Another minute, and his hands were upon me, who, even as a child, had hated to be pawed over—especially to be pawed over by elderly uncles. This was my first encounter with such inclinations in age. Heretofore, I had attracted only inclination in youth. "If you kiss me I will let you go," he said presently; but at last I struggled free without kissing. His mouth, beneath his gray mustache, was red and juicy, and it gave me forever afterwards a loathing for red and juicy lips.

At last I was out of the office; I was out of the building; I was in the sheltering publicity of the streets. He had let me go only after I had promised to come again, and he had kept not only my manuscript but the fifty dollars belonging to Cary. I was bruised, I was disgusted, I was trembling with anger.

The next morning I sent a messenger for my manuscript, and when I returned home, where there was an open fire, I burned *Sharp Realities*, without unwrapping the parcel. "I will never write again," I resolved; but before the year was half over I had begun *The Descendant*. My revolt from the philosophy of evasive idealism was seeking an outlet. I hated—I had always hated—the inherent falseness in much Southern tradition, and *Sharp Realities* was an indignant departure from the whole sentimental fallacy, not only in the South, but all over America. Those superficial critics who classify me as "beginning in the local color school" can have read none of my earliest novels. On the contrary, my native impulse, as well as my later theories of the novel as a mirror of life, sprang directly from my dislike for what I called "little vessels

of experience." Never, at any time, have little ways and
means of thinking made a particular appeal to me. If I
prefer fine workmanship and delicate embroideries of
style, I demand that both material and pattern shall be
ample in form and richly varied in texture.

When I burned *Sharp Realities,* I had told myself that
I should find relief from the pressure within. Yet the
ashes were barely cold before the figure of Michael Akersham walked out of nowhere into my mind, just as Little
Willie had walked into my infant imagination. Immediately I was possessed and dominated by this figure of
revolt. All I suffered from convention was embodied in
his strange image. I would write, I resolved, as no South-
erner had ever written, of the universal human chords
beneath the superficial variations of scene and character.
I would write of all the harsher realities beneath manners,
beneath social customs, beneath the poetry of the past,
and the romantic nostalgia of the present. I would write
of an outcast, of an illegitimate "poor white," of a thinker,
and of a radical socialist. I would take as my theme those
ugly aspects of life the sentimentalists passed over. The
impulse flamed into a vision. If only I had learned to
write before writing, my first book might have been not
entirely unworthy of my idea.

Ignorant as I was of New York, I had determined to
use that city for my background. I needed a big city, and
New York was the only one in which I had stayed as long
as two weeks—or even two days. To be sure, I did not
need landladies in reduced circumstances—I had seen too
many of those in Richmond—but I did need my only

glimpse of what was called in the eighteen-nineties, "bo-hemian New York." A man I had met in my boarding-house—I have forgotten his name—had heard me inno-cently enquiring if New York had "a Latin quarter," and he had taken me for dinner to a little restaurant named "The Black Cat." Today it would seem but a tame affair even to a girl of eighteen fresh from Virginia. But, at the time, I was thrilled and enchanted; and immediately I saw the second part of *The Descendant,* and the meet-ing of Michael Akersham and Rachel Gavin in the shabby little restaurant. Once again, in spite of my reluctance, I was enslaved by an idea.

In the early summer, after Mother's death, Cary and Walter came up from Charleston for a brief visit. They adored each other, and were as happy as any other young couple without enough money to live on could be. With my first glance at Walter's face a chill of foreboding—one of those dark childish fears of some approaching doom—rushed over me. He looked ill, and his face—a poet's face, if poets ever looked their poetry—was drawn and pallid. He was suffering from a severe spinal malady, which gave him attacks of acute pain. Like so many Southern men of his generation, which was still feeling the deprivations of a conquered and wasted country, he had never been robust in health, and at twenty-six, after his struggle for an education and a start in life, he was unequal to heavier responsibilities, and to the simple drudgery of securing the bare necessities of living. The afternoon before he went on to New York, ostensibly upon a legal matter, we walked up the street together, and we had a talk that I have always remembered. Grief had benumbed me—grief and illness. "If I knew the open door was just before me," I confessed, "I should keep straight on, and I doubt if I should even slacken my pace." And he replied, "But I don't want to stop now. I want to go on until I see what folly the world will commit next. Sheer curiosity, if nothing else, would keep me clinging to life."

The next morning he left us, and we never saw him again.

Days passed, and we heard nothing. Other days dragged by, in slow torture. When at last we found him in New York, he was dead.

There are some tragedies too terrible to write of—to speak of—to think of. The air of tragedy had been my native element since I was two years old, and Joseph, Mother's darling, and the most promising of her children, died at sixteen. But this was different from all the others. This was different even from Mother's long illness and death. Walter was so young, so brilliant, and his end was so sudden, so unexpected, and so lonely. Even today, after forty years, as I write of it I burn with moral indignation, because so much brilliance, so much pure intellectual fire and radiance, was wasted, in an age and a place that valued only tepid sentimentality. I burn with indignation when I think that a little money—not much, but enough to supply a simple living, while he struggled to regain the health he had lost—that this very little might have saved him.

No one who has not lived with a broken heart, hour by hour, day by day, week by week, month by month, year

by year, can know what the next two or three years meant
in this house. It was like living in a tomb, for Cary spent
her days in Hollywood Cemetery, and her nights brooding in anguish. She clung to me, and I knew that I was
the frailest of comforts. It was agony to watch her, to
listen to her, year after year; but I was immersed again
in the old sense of doom, of fatality, which rested upon
all of us, from the eldest to the youngest. Poor little Rebe
was engulfed also, but I was the only one of us whom
Cary wanted. Walter had been fond of me; we had understood each other; and I was the only person who could
feel and know why he had chosen the one way of escape.

Our salvation, and this came at the end of the first
terrible year of sorrow, was an intellectual awakening.
Cary had always read and studied with Walter, and at
last, with a pathos that tore the heart, she persuaded herself that the more widely she read, the more companion-
able she might be with Walter, when they met in eternity.
For, strangely enough, she had not, at this time, lost her
faith in personal immortality. She had been deeply religious through all her early life, and long after she had
relinquished her faith in creeds and dogmas, she still re-
tained a beneficent hope that the principles of Christianity
might contain some spiritual truth.

With this pathetic hope in her mind, Cary turned back,
with me, to the study of economics, and of the more
recent theories of biology and ethnology. Darwin became
her prophet; but we read far and wide, and I cannot
recall all the names of the works that came down from
the Mercantile Library. When I look back now, I cannot
see the slightest benefit I derived from these studies, which

we pursued whenever she was not watching by Walter's grave. I am glad to have had a thorough grounding in both philosophic and scientific theories; I am glad to have had a profound acquaintance with *The Origin of Species,* and even with Spencer's *Synthetic Philosophy.* But I cannot see today that this knowledge gave me more than a wider intellectual horizon and a longer perspective. But I saw that intellectual excitement was slowly easing the pangs of Cary's tortured imagination. She had found a fleeting appeasement, though her torment would return as soon as her mind wandered back into the familiar channels of grief. And how beautiful she was in these first years of her widowhood! She was young enough to be enhanced, not wasted, by suffering, and her skin had the luminous texture of some transparent lamp with the flame burning within. I have never seen anyone in the least like her, though the portrait of *The Parson's Daughter,* by Romney, might have been painted from her in her exquisite girlhood. Her small, expressive face was very changeable. At times she would look quite plain, and at other times her features would flash into beauty. But her charm was her own, and singularly elusive. What startled me was that grief intensified both her beauty and her brilliance.

As Cary grew better, or at least able to divert her mind from her sorrow, I began to feel that my own capacity to endure had reached the breaking-point. I could not go on as I was, and I had never found, I could never find, I knew, but one vocation. If I were to survive in the struggle, I must go back to my work, to that inner world of creation. It was then that I wrote over again, in secret, and in the night hours, *The Descendant,* and, after it was completed, I read it aloud to Cary and Rebe. They were both at last convinced that I had not been mistaken, and Cary, in her generous way (she was the most generous creature I have ever known) threw her whole mental interest into helping me with my work. Though she knew as little as I did about the craft and mere technique of fiction, she possessed a peculiarly vital mind and a rare instinct, not only for characteristics (which is not uncommon) but for the elemental sources of character. She is the only human being who was of the slightest help to me in my work, and without her sympathy and inspiration, I doubt if I should ever have had the spirit to take up again the old discouraging struggle. "If only I can have one book published," I had said in the beginning, "I think I should die of happiness. . . ."

Something was wrong, I felt, in the mental state of the eighteen-nineties. I felt it, I knew it, though I could not say what it was. Ideas, like American fiction, had gone soft. In a world and a period that were simply waiting to be examined, to be interpreted, in terms of reality (by which I do not mean literary "realism"), the literary mind had gone delirious over novels that dropped from the presses already mellowing before they were ripe. Critics and public alike rushed to devour incredible romances placed in impossible countries. The American literary scene had become a kindergarten. Romances whirled madly. Everybody was happy. Nobody wished to be different. "But life isn't like this," I would reflect. "Life never was and never will be like this."

I suppose we had sprung up too quickly. We were grown before we had had time to grow up. Then, as now, immaturity was our dangerous age. Then, as now, we were a nation of glorified amateurs; we were possessed by the delusion that the easiest way is merely the democratic name for the royal road. Then, as now, we continued to mistake facility for genius. Emotionally, too, we were more effervescent than stable. Our innocence may have been as real as our gentility; but our sentimentality was so close to the skin that it would drip if it were touched. Years later, when an interviewer asked me what I thought the South needed most, I replied instantly, "Blood and irony."

Yet, if I could criticize, it was not because I had escaped from the elegiac tone that surrounded me. All America had dropped back into adolescence in fiction; but in the South there was not only adolescence to outgrow, there was an insidious sentimental tradition to live down. I had been brought up in the midst of it; I was a part of it, or it was a part of me; I had been born with an intimate feeling for the spirit of the past, and the lingering poetry of time and place. Underneath my revolt there was, I believe, an uprising of that old hatred of inhumanity. I revolted from sentimentality, less because it was false than because it was cruel. An evasive idealism made people insensitive; it made people blind to what happened.

———◄•►———

NINE

My First Book

The Descendant was finished four years after I had written that first sentence: "The child sat by the roadside." It is not a good novel; but "something told me" that, if life ceased hostilities, I should live to write a good novel. At the time, I had done my best—but where was the publisher? To us, publishers were a strange race, suffused with a mild glamour, because of the mysterious powers they possessed to give life or to destroy it. We knew that there were such tribes, as we knew of agnostics, and conjurors, and magicians, and dipsomaniacs, and people who believed in free love; but we had never encountered, except in books, a member of any one of these romantic fraternities. Southerners did not publish, did not write, did not read. Their appetite for information was Gargantuan but personal; it was either satisfied by oratory, or it was sated by gossip.

For several months we pondered this question. Then Cary and I decided that I must go on to New York and invade the territory of publishers. An impression had reached us (by what road, I cannot recall) that a manuscript received a warmer welcome when the author accompanied it on its travels. At this point, Cary had one of her frequent flashes of inspiration. She remembered that old Dr. Holmes, of the University of Virginia (who had given me my examination in political economy) had once spoken to her of a friend who was the president of a New York firm that published schoolbooks. Perhaps he could help me. We laughed over this, while we continued to plan ways and means, and Cary's sparkling wit was able to extract amusement from the relentless malice of fate.

The letter came from Dr. Holmes, and at the same time a new friend, Louise Collier Willcox, gave me a note of introduction to her brother, Price Collier, who was acting as the final critic for Macmillan's publishing house. Then the precious manuscript was sent off to that firm, and I followed a fortnight later, with a trembling heart but a defiant chin. It amuses me now to think that I should ever have stood in such awe of any human beings, especially of publishers, who, I have reason to know, are more than ordinarily human. But I was young, I was ignorant beyond belief, and I was consumed with the longing to write and the will to be heard.

The brownstone boarding-house in the upper Forties had not changed. The hall and the Southern parlor were still as gloomy as I had remembered them; the soup was still as thin; the boarders were still as depressed-looking. This time I occupied a hall bedroom on the third or fourth floor, so cramped by a bed like a cot, a bureau, a wash-stand, and a single chair that there was not room inside for my small trunk. There was a tiny gas-stove, which pretended to give heat, in one corner, and from

the narrow window I could look out on rows of fire-
escapes, where the week's washing of the next street fluttered on clotheslines.

No sooner had I settled myself than I addressed my letter
of introduction to Mr. Collier. After I had stolen down
three flights of stairs to the post-box on the corner, I crept
up again to my hall bedroom, where I waited, in anxious
expectancy, for the next turn of the wheel, which so frequently, in my small affairs, revolved backward.

But, forward or backward, the wheel turned with
promptness. By the next post, I received a note from Mr.
Collier, who asked me to lunch with him at Delmonico's.
The lunch, I recall, was delectable, and the wine all that
artless ignorance, nourished on Father's temperance views
and the rare mint juleps of neighbors, could imagine.
Price Collier was pleasant, friendly, attractive, and patron-
izing, without offense, to a Southern girl who believed
that she could break into American letters. I felt that in
his heart, he esteemed American letters, barring Henry
James, his close friend, as lightly as I did; but, in any
case, he wanted no more writing from women, especially
from women young enough to have babies. "You don't
look more than sixteen," he said, and when I told him
I was twenty-two, and still growing, he pretended to be
astonished. It was true that I looked too young. If I had
not known that already, every publisher I met would have
made me aware of it—but, as I hastened to assure them
all, that aspect was in the shape of my face, not in the
shape of my mind.

In the end, as in the beginning, Mr. Collier gave me

no encouragement. He appeared to think that providing food of the best quality was sufficient; and he told me frankly that there was no hope for me with Macmillan. No, it would not do the slightest good if he read my manuscript; he could tell, without reading it, that there was not a chance of Macmillan's accepting the book.

"The best advice I can give you," he said, with charming candor, "is to stop writing, and go back to the South and have some babies." And I think, though I may have heard this ripe wisdom from other men, probably from many, that he added: "The greatest woman is not the woman who has written the finest book, but the woman who has had the finest babies." That might be true. I did not stay to dispute it. However, it was true also that I wanted to write books, and not ever had I felt the faintest wish to have babies. Other women might have all they wanted, and I shouldn't object. But I was not made that way, and I did not see why I should pretend to be what I wasn't, or to feel what I couldn't. At that age I suspected, and later I discovered, that the maternal instinct, sacred or profane, was left out of me by nature when I was designed. I sometimes think that a hollow where it might have been was filled by the sense of compassion; but even of this, I am not entirely sure. All I know is that, at any time in my life, it would have seemed to me an irretrievable wrong to bring another being into a world where I had suffered so many indignities of the spirit. After my deafness, this became a moral conviction.

Mr. Collier and I parted amicably, and years afterwards Mr. Brett, the president of Macmillan, told me that the rejection of *The Descendant* was one of the two gravest mistakes he had ever made as a publisher. He was kind enough to add that if he himself had read the manuscript, instead of leaving the decision to others, he should not have declined it.

But it was a month or six weeks before the manuscript was returned to me. In the 'nineties publishers were slower, and certainly less active, than they are nowadays. Breaking into print was much more difficult for a young writer, and a first book was not snatched at so eagerly. The autocrats of American literature composed a self-centered group of benevolent old gentlemen in the Authors' Club, who are now turning in their graves, I imagine, before the modern apotheosis of the amateur. But the rage for "rough stuff" and raw material would have seemed incredible to a literary generation who wrote only what "the ubiquitous young girl" could pick up with safety from the drawing-room table. Yet, even though I couldn't read their pale, consumptive novels, I longed, in my hall bedroom, to know these old gentlemen, who, however uninteresting in print, were at least "literary." And to be "literary" appeared to my deluded innocence as an unending romance. If only I could meet a few "people who wrote," and listen, humbly, while they discoursed, I might learn something I ought to know, something that would make the practice of writing less difficult. Only one thing could destroy those fond illusions, and that was a gathering of the bearded meteors in our literary firmament. I was invited to the Authors' Club. I went. I saw. I listened. I waited for enlightenment. "If these writers are no better than their books," I reflected, "then when and where can I reach the literary mind in America?" What I learned on that festive occasion was merely that the enjoyment of the second best was not confined to the South. And I learned, too, that a literary reputation, if it were skillfully arranged, might remain as thin in substance as current refined realism. All one needed to make a reputation as a novelist was to belong to the oldest and the most respectable of the fraternities. There wasn't even the bother of donning a cap and gown. One might patch up one's old garments as long as one agreed to relinquish one's identity.

But I did not like to be patronized, and I had not come so far from home in search of benevolent old gentlemen. That was a product in which the South was never found wanting. What I needed was to find higher intelligence than any I had ever known, a way of reason better than any I could invent for myself. And, more than anything else, I wanted the right to be heard.

In those six weeks I had become friendly with the other boarders, and several girls and I had frequently gone to the opera. In my later years, when I have come to look upon opera as a hybrid art, and I prefer music, when I prefer it at all, without useless accessories, it is amusing to recall the many nights when, standing in the aisle for hours, I listened enraptured to the silliest of Italian operas.

At last—at last the manuscript came back to me, and I tucked it under my arm and went down to see Mr.

Lawrence, of the University Publishing Company. As a contemporary of Dr. Holmes, I had expected him to be eighty or more, and he was, indeed, a kindly, charming, and distinguished old gentleman. No one could have been more sympathetic, but he told me he published only textbooks, and he did not know, personally, any of the younger publishers in New York. "The best thing I can do for you," he said, "is to turn you over to one of the younger men in the firm. I'll ask Mr. Patton what he can do for you." He touched the bell, said: "Tell Mr. Patton I'd like to speak to him," and in less than a minute, a man of middle age came into the room, and all my helpless waiting on publishers was ended forever. The fate of my first book was whisked, as if by magic, into Mr. Patton's kind and competent hands. At first, he did not appear overeager, but after Mr. Lawrence had talked to him, he consented to read the manuscript, and to do what he could. Publishers were not interested in first books, he said; they liked writers who were already established, and too many Southerners, he thought, were trying to write the same thing. "I suppose it's Page all over again," he remarked, dubiously, and it is odd how well I recall every word of that interview. "Well, anyhow, I'll do the best I can for you."

He went out with my manuscript, and, in a few minutes, I parted from pleasant Mr. Lawrence, and returned to my boarding-house. All the afternoon and night I was seeing a sharp, wise face bending down over my book. I was too excited to sleep. I could only lie awake and wonder what passages he would like best as he went on.

The next evening after dinner, Mr. Patton came to see me, and fortunately, for a little while, the drawing room was empty of boarders. For an instant he looked at me without speaking, while my heart, as they say, seemed to miss a beat. Then he said slowly and gravely, for he was a silent man, "I read the manuscript last night without putting it down until I finished it at dawn. Don't worry, my child. That book shall be published if I have to build a publishing house in order to publish it." Then while I was groping for words, he saw tears in my eyes, and he added impulsively, "I haven't been so moved since I was a boy and read Victor Hugo."

Victor Hugo! Well, well— But I had won my first convert, and I knew that everything would be easier, now, because somebody, besides my two sisters and one friend, believed in me.

Again that night I could not sleep. For hours, until a glimmer of day extinguished the white glare in the street, and splashed like water over the bulging clothes on the fire escapes, I lay awake and tried to imagine what the world would be like when one had published a first book, and had found recognition. I had known few of what we call the natural pleasures of childhood and girlhood. Fear and illness and heartbreak had pursued me as far back as I could remember. I thought of the face without a body that had marked me as a victim, before I learned to put my fear into words. I thought of the days and weeks of pain when I had watched other children play in the street, or had gazed after old Dr. Patterson's buggy until it was lost in the twilight. I thought, too, of my mother's slow martyrdom, which had drained the joy from my veins. Life had defrauded me of something infinitely precious that I could never recover. Yet I was not disposed, by temperament, to self-pity. I had had to struggle for everything I had ever had, from health or knowledge to the very elements of my own identity. But I was willing to struggle. I had never asked of life anything more than the fair rewards of endeavor. Years afterwards, a friend remarked to me in a casual tone, "Your whole life has been simply the overcoming of one obstacle after another." She was thinking, chiefly, of my deafness; but, on that night in New York, watching for the dawn of a brighter day, my deafness, which was only beginning to afflict me, had not become "a wound in the soul" from which there is no escape until death. That morbid sensitiveness, the hidden horror of an infirmity to proud and independent natures, had not split my personality in half from center to surface. "If only I can have my work and adequate recognition," I told myself that night, "I shall be satisfied to give up everything else."

It was as well, perhaps, that I could not look ahead into the troubled future. Ironic as it might have appeared, it is probable that I should not have been wholly amused. I was too young, even though I had had no youth, to relish the full savor of laughing at one's own misfortunes. Later, I was to cultivate this subtle aptitude at its finest —but when I attained that point in my culture, I was no longer a simple two-and-twenty.

Part Three

ON NOT TAKING ADVICE

———◄•►———

TEN

Alone in London

Yes, publishers must have been less active in those days. It was now early spring, and I had heard nothing from Mr. Patton. My second book was more than half finished, and I expected to go to England in June. My brother Arthur, who had made a brilliant reputation as an engineer, was in London, living in chambers in Victoria Street, and he had invited me to spend the summer with him. A man of great personality and charm of manner, he had, too, a kind of royal generosity with money. He had arranged passage with some friends who would look after me. I was to be his guest from the time I left Richmond, and it was characteristic of him that he should have provided me with the right sort of clothes.

It was Cary who persuaded me to go. She had felt deeply my blighted childhood, and Rebe's; and it seemed to her an opportunity for me to discover the nature of pleasure. But the trip was a mistake. It came at the wrong time, either too late or too soon. I was on the brink of a nervous breakdown; the old headaches were returning more frequently; and my state of mind was deeply despondent.

Suddenly, after a sharp attack of influenza, I had discovered that my deafness was increasing, and morbid sensitiveness was tracking me down, like a wolf waiting to
spring. Still, Cary, Rebe, Frank, and even Father, were
all assured that a change, and especially a change to England, would be good for me.

Just as I decided, against my intuition, to make the
trip, a letter came from Mr. Patton, telling me that he
had submitted my manuscript to the Century Company.
They were enthusiastic, he said, and would publish the
book if I would consent to make a few changes in the
first chapters. These were the six chapters I had written
at eighteen, and then rewritten, after Mother's death, as
I remembered them. I felt that they were not in character
with the rest of the book, and I knew exactly what ought
to be done to them. I sat down immediately and rewrote
this part, but after sending it off, I heard nothing more
from my manuscript before I sailed in June.

Not ever before in my life had I felt so suffocated by
melancholy as I felt when I sailed, alone, among strangers,
to England. I knew that I was in a cloud of nervous de-
pression; but it was impossible for me to break through
the restraint, or to be natural. It was the first time since
Mother's death that I had left off mourning, or at least
a severe black dress, high at the throat and long in the
sleeves; and the blue suit I had chosen made me feel
conspicuous and uncomfortable. I had never looked worse
in my life, and I knew that whatever charm I possessed
was dimmed by the terror of not hearing strange voices,
and of not understanding the words that were said to me.

That was the time in my life when the sound of the word
"deafness," or even the sight of it in a newspaper, would
send chills of horror, like crawling beetles, along my
nerves. Years afterwards, when a miracle had occurred,
several persons who met me on this voyage told me they
would never have recognized me, and even refused to
believe that I was the same person.

What the trip abroad gave me was the ancient concrete
body of London. The day after I landed, I went out alone
with the feeling that I had come home, and I walked
slowly down the Strand and Fleet Street to St. Paul's.
I was alone every day until my brother came up from
his office, and in my freedom, I roamed for many miles,
or rode on top of an omnibus, seated next to the driver,
who would talk to me all the way. Customs have changed,
they tell me, and one is no longer permitted to occupy
that favored seat, and to enjoy that spicy conversation,
which was made easier by the tumultuous vibrations. For
the matter of that, I suppose, all London has changed
too; but in the summer of 1896, I found the London that
was like home to me. Not ever again, in any other summer, have I seen it so thoroughly, or loved it so deeply.
I rode on every omnibus I could reach. I walked miles
each day into streets that had been made familiar by
books. I lingered in every gallery and in every church;
and for days, I made my home in the British Museum.
One morning, after wandering far away, through unknown roads and streets, I found myself in what seemed
to be strange surroundings. "Will you please tell me
where I am?" I asked the kindly bobby at the corner,

and he answered placidly, "You're in Billingsgate Fish Market, Miss."

I was alone most of the time, but someone—I cannot recall who it was—took me to tea with Mrs. W. K. Clifford, and we became fast friends for years. It was in her house, either then or later, that I met an attractive elderly man, who said to me, "I suppose, like all other Americans, you have been to Westminster Abbey, to lay a rose on Chaucer's tomb?" When I replied, innocently, that I had taken a rose to Westminster Abbey, but it was for the grave of Charles Darwin, he appeared interested, and before leaving, he came back to talk to me once again. After he had gone, I asked my hostess who he was, and she answered: "Why, that's the eldest son of Charles Darwin." How I should have enjoyed confessing my ignorance of his identity!

That summer I made my first visit to Scotland. One of my brother's friends took me through the Highlands, and though, in the good old times, we should have been looked upon as despised lowlanders, I felt that I had come to my home in the past, because of my childish adoration of Sir Walter. I spent the month of August, with the family of this friend, on the Kyles of Bute, four weeks of unforgettable beauty. If I had not been nervously ill, and hunted, even in my dreams, by this secret wolf of deafness, which, in my mistaken pride, I was trying desperately to pretend away, I might have known my first happy summer since early childhood. . . .

In September I went over to Paris, with some friends of my brother; but I saw nothing more interesting or improving than dressmaking establishments. Once, it is true, I escaped into the Louvre, and I have a vague recollection that I was shown the tomb of Napoleon. But I have one unfading memory. While I was there a cabled message, from home, told me that Harper had eagerly accepted *The Descendant,* and were enthusiastic about it. Afterwards, I learned that Mr. Patton had taken the manuscript to Harper instead of back to the Century Company. My name was not on the title page, and none of the firm had suspected that it was the work of a girl who had spent only two weeks in New York. One of their critics had insisted that it was an anonymous work by Harold Frederic. So much for the perspicacity of publishers and of critics!

With the blue slip still in my hand, I went out, alone, to walk in the streets, because I was too excited to look at clothes that afternoon. It was the first time I had been to walk by myself, and I did not know when or where I was going. I had, at the moment, no external vision, for my world was within, and the little Hotel Louis le Grand might have been hemmed in by desert spaces. It was one of few moments in my life when I knew the sensation of joy. Winged, fugitive, gone like a ray of sunshine, but still pure joy while it lasted. For the rest, Paris, with its gray September skies, its damp roving winds, its yellowing leaves underfoot in the parks, with all its gaiety and sadness—Paris meant nothing to me. All I felt (and for so frail a cause) was that at last I knew happiness.

But the recoil came almost immediately. The years of my youth had been too much for me. When I landed in

New York, at the end of September, I was in constant pain, I was despondent, and I was in the clutch of that wolfish terror. Never in the future, not even when, years afterwards, I triumphed, in a measure at least, over my infirmity, did the terror of deafness ever release its grasp on my mind. But in the beginning, while I helplessly watched its approach, knowing that, sooner or later, it would spring on me and fasten its unendurable burden, I lived in a state of nervous apprehension that was more wasting than pain. I, who longed to stand alone, was forced to depend, intolerably, upon others. Some day, I used to tell myself, I will go alone round the world. Now, I was finding it too difficult to receive callers in my own drawing room unless Cary or Rebe was with me. All this crept upon me gradually, but it was creeping nearer, and I knew, as the animal in the trap knows, that there is no way of escape. . . .

I remember that I was alone when I made the return voyage; and one of my brother's English friends had arranged for the captain to look after me. I remember, too, that I was placed at the captain's table, and that when no one met me, one of the officers of the boat saw me safely behind the bleak door of my boarding-house. After all these years, I am still grateful, in memory, to that kind English captain, though I have forgotten the name of his ship.

I spent only one day in New York; but early on that morning I went down to the old house of Harper in Franklin Square, and met one of the members of the firm —I think this was Colonel James Thorne Harper. I am not sure of his name, though I am perfectly sure that he appeared to me to be the most delightful of men. For he, also, was astonished to find that I was, not Harold Frederic, but a Southern girl. He was enthusiastic; he was kind; he was charming; and, best of all, he was helpful. On that morning, the firm of Harper seemed to me to be a haven for wandering souls, and for lost aspirations. I left with a dancing heart, and I even forgave the absence of critical judgment which could confuse my crude innocence with the depressing theological flavor of *The Damnation of Theron Ware*. . . .

Well, I had had one book published, and I was not happy, I was not even appeased. *The Descendant* was somewhat of a success, and more of a little sensation. Published anonymously, it had excited curiosity among reviewers, who hesitated either to praise or to blame, because, after all, it might turn out to have been written by somebody.

But one novel, as I had long since observed, does not make a novelist. Wasn't the American literary scene dotted with such tombstones to promising authors, who had died when they were born? For myself, I wanted more than a memorial of what might have been. I wanted not an inspiration (wasn't my mind bubbling with inspiration?); I wanted an art. I wanted a firm foundation; I wanted a steady control over my ideas and my material. What I understood more and more was that I needed a philosophy of fiction, I needed a technique of working. Above all, I felt the supreme necessity of a prose style so pure and flexible that it could bend without breaking.

Where could I find this by seeking? Who could direct me? Others were imitating, or at least serving a successful apprenticeship, under Henry James. As James Branch Cabell observed a few years later, "Mrs. Gerould's story is so much like Mr. Henry James that it might have been written by Mrs. Wharton." No, I did not wish to be like anyone, not even like Henry James, whom I admired with fervor. I wanted only to be myself, and to be myself perfectly. Still, I read Henry James from beginning to end, and then, tracing Henry James to his source, I immersed myself in Flaubert and Maupassant. I tried to take *Madame Bovary* to pieces, and to put it together again. The most flawless novel, I thought then, that I had ever read, and yet something was wanting. The hand of the master was too evident; his fingerprints were too visible on every paragraph. Realism this might be, I decided, but it is not reality. Life is a stream, it is even a torrent; but it is not modeled in clay; it is not even dough, to be twisted and pinched into an artificial perfection. The twisting may be there in the novel, but it must not be visible; it must remain always below the surface of art.

From Maupassant, I gained a great deal, and to this day I am grateful. My second book was unfortunately brought out when the publishers were on the brink of failure and reorganization. It was written when I was still under the influence of Maupassant as a supreme craftsman, if not a supreme novelist. I read every line of his novels and short stories, and I yearned to write a novel as perfect in every sentence as *Une Vie*. Just as *Madame Bovary* had seemed to me the most flawless, so *Une Vie* seemed to me to be the most beautiful novel in all literature. Yet, even here, after the first wild enthusiasm had worn off, I felt that something was missing. As I studied Maupassant's short stories, phrase after phrase, I was conscious of an inner recoil from the world as art made it. Surely the novel should be a form of art—but art was not enough. It must contain not only the perfection of art, but the imperfection of nature.

The inevitable reversal of the situation at first excited, then amused, and finally bored me. When the reversal is inevitable, it ceases to be surprising. And in O. Henry, who borrowed Maupassant's famous trick ending, the artifice becomes infinitely tedious and even grotesque. Yes, something was missing. Very positively and impatiently, I repeated, "Life isn't like this. Things don't happen this way." After all, in this fine method of doing things, the essential thing was not done. Was it possible that literary "realism" was not an approach to reality, but a pattern of thought, with no close relation to the substance of life?

Then, suddenly, in the midst of my confusion, I happened, quite by accident, to read *War and Peace,* and I knew what was missing, I knew what I wanted. Life must use art; art must use life. My first reading of Tolstoy affected me as a revelation from heaven, as the trumpet of the Judgment. What he made me feel was not the desire to imitate, but the conviction that imitation was futile. One might select realities, but one could not impose on Reality. Not if one were honest in one's interpretation, not if one possessed artistic integrity. For truth to art became in the end simple fidelity to one's own inner vision.

It has been said again and again that *War and Peace* proves the assertion that a great novel can stand on its merits as fiction without style. But I have never believed this, and I believe it less than ever when I look back on my first reading of Tolstoy. The critic who invented this theory must have had an ignorant or superficial idea of the meaning of style in prose. For, even in translation, *War and Peace* is saturated with the effervescent flow of a great style, which, at its best and truest, is not a petrified form, but a life-giving fluid. Even in a translation, one feels the tumultuous rhythms and pauses of a style that has the power of genius brooding over creation.

And a few years later, when I came to Chekhov, I found the quality I had found "missing" in Maupassant. Here was art used by life for its own purpose, and because it had been so used, art itself had become living. Here was all the difference between the small and the great, between the shadow and the substance, between the reflection in art and the reality in nature.

I had learned from Maupassant the value of the precise word, of the swift phrase, of cool and scrupulous observation. After my study of Maupassant's complete work, I felt that I must form a style that was balanced yet supple, a style that was touched with beauty and yet tinctured with irony. An interest in Science had already impaired a way of expression that was naturally precise and epigrammatic. That any style should have survived the whole of the *Synthetic Philosophy,* to say nothing of an invincible battalion of German scientists, provides, I suppose, an occasion for wonder or congratulation. And here, Mau-

passant was my liberator. He impregnated my mind, I like
to think, with artistic integrity. My old childish pleasure
in singing words came back to me, and I passed on from
Flaubert's theory of the one, the only, the exact word for
every object, to a wider range and an increasing delight
in the rhythms and the minor cadences of English prose.
But it was not until I came to write *Barren Ground* and
my later books that I felt an easy grasp of technique, a
practiced authority over style and material. I had worked
too hard for this to be modest about it. I had found that
French sentences had a way of going to one's head too
quickly, and I had turned from Flaubert and Maupassant
to the sobering English tradition. Always, I have felt by
intuition when I needed an author. I may not have thought
of him for years, but, suddenly, his name will spring into
my mind, and I will say to myself, "I must read Bacon
now," or "I must read Swift or Sterne, for a change."
Fielding I had loved ever since I had first discovered
Amelia and a little later *Tom Jones,* and I turned to the
robustness of Fielding much as one might flee back to
roast beef and ale after an indulgence in French sauces
and Sauterne. Yet I brought my preference for the precise
word back to American fiction. In the final writing, or
revision, of a novel, I would find myself bound and enslaved by *words,* just as Gulliver, in one of the illustrations
from our old nursery copy of *Gulliver's Travels,* awoke
to find himself bound and enslaved by the Lilliputians.

   From Tolstoy, I learned immeasurably more, though
not in awareness of technique. What he gave me was my
own immature vision of life in a transcendant maturity.

I had always wished to escape from the particular into the general, from the provincial into the universal. Never from my earliest blind gropings after truth in art and truth in life had I felt an impulse to write of a single locality or of regional characteristics. From the beginning I had resolved to write of the South, not, in elegy, as a conquered province, but, vitally, as a part of the larger world. Tolstoy made me see clearly what I had realized dimly, that the ordinary is simply the universal observed from the surface, that the direct approach to reality is not without, but within. Touch life anywhere, I felt after reading *War and Peace,* and you will touch universality wherever you touch the earth. Before I discovered those two greatest of all novels, *Anna Karenina* and *War and Peace,* I had tried to make use of the sudden light, the deepened illumination which, as I found later, Tolstoy has magnified to perfection in such living scenes as Anna Karenina's drive through the streets on the day of her death, in Prince Andrey's return to the little Princess after she is dead, and in his later visions when he himself is dying.

This, I felt, with that piercing certainty of an almost miraculous revelation, is both life and art at their highest, their truest.

———◄◆►———

ELEVEN

James Branch Cabell

By the time *The Descendant* was in print, I had finished
my second novel, *Phases of an Inferior Planet,* and I was
planning to write a series of books which would deal with
the Virginian background, from the Civil War down to
the present year. Much of this design I worked out in the
next twenty years. In *The Battle-Ground,* I dealt with the
war. In *The Deliverance* and in *The Voice of the People,*
I treated the Reconstruction period. In *Virginia,* the best
of my early books, I analyzed the whole tradition of the
Southern lady. And in *The Miller of Old Church,* I de-
picted the small farmers, neglected by Southern writers,
who had confined themselves to the portrayal of the
planters and the romantic legend of the great plantations.

Yet I was faithful to my resolve that I would write of
the universal, not of the provincial, in human nature, that
I would write of characters, not of characteristics. I knew
my part of the South, and I had looked deep enough
within and far enough without to learn something of
human beings and their substance. We write better, I had
discovered by my experimental failures, when we write

of places we know, and of a background with which we
are familiar. A guidebook is a poor scene for a novel, and
already I was regretting that I had made the mistake of
placing my first scenes in New York. In these later books
I would keep at least a basis of exact knowledge for the
imagination to work over. Though I had missed the mental discipline that makes a scholar, I had been born with
a literary conscience, and with the scholar's instinct for
exactness.

It was May, and I was in Williamsburg, studying the
scene for *The Voice of the People,* when I met James
Branch Cabell for the first time since he had been a little
boy at his grandmother's. Between this meeting and our
next meeting, when we became intimate and devoted
friends, there stretched a period of sixteen or seventeen
years. All those years passed, dark years for both of us in
many ways, before I saw him again; yet I think we had
always been friends without knowing that we knew one
another. What I am writing now of that spring in Williamsburg, when he was graduated from the College of
William and Mary, may never be published. But, then,
as I go on, trying to write the simple truth of things, without vanity or evasion, I begin to wonder whether I should
wish any of this autobiography to be given to strangers—
or even to friends who are still strangers. So I am recording these episodes chiefly in the endeavor to attain a clearer
understanding of my own dubious identity and of the
confused external world in which I have lived.

Cary and I spent the month of May at the Colonial Inn,
beside the old Courthouse and the Courthouse green,

which was golden with buttercups. Staying with us at the Inn were several famous gossips of the "best families," and every evening the news of the day would be imparted to us in the shelter of the Inn's "private parlor." For, strangely, I, who so seldom happen anywhere, from the world to a literary party, at the exact right moment, had arrived when the ancient sleepy village of Williamsburg was involved in what it would have called a turmoil, and the distinguished College of William and Mary was split in two by the first scandal in its history. Moreover, to make matters worse, the scandal was of that peculiar nature which, in the nineteenth century, before Oscar Wilde and our recent postwar fiction had made it a household word, relied entirely upon innuendo and parenthesis for distribution.

What had happened, as I gathered, however inaccurately, from the cheerful gossips, was simply this. The leading middle-aged intellectual of the village, or so I was told, had exercised a pernicious influence over some of the students, and the faculty of the College, uniting with certain people of importance, had banished him forever from Williamsburg. But, instead of stopping here, they had attempted to root out and exterminate every trace of the scandal, and condemned, without proper investigation, every student who had even a literary association with the supreme offender. A number of students, and a number may include any figure, would be dismissed from the College because they had been seen in unfavorable company. Among them—I am relating merely what I was told—was the most brilliant youth in the student body. His name was James Branch Cabell, and he was to receive

his diploma in the spring. Hearing this, his mother had
come from Richmond with an attorney, and in the end
the College had been obliged to withdraw its charges. Mrs.
Cabell, who had been a beauty in her youth, was now
staying at the Inn, and the attorney, after a triumphant
dismissal of the case, had left town a few hours before I
arrived. But there was not a shred of evidence to connect
James in any way with the scandal, or with the Author
of Evil. There was, indeed, not anything more compro-
mising than a shared preference for *belles-lettres*.

It was the first time I had encountered the mob spirit,
except in histories of the French Revolution, and in one
or two imperfectly suppressed stories of the South, by
persons who were known among us as "those Yankees."
But, here and now, in this lovely village under its whispering leaves, the mob spirit, carefully veiled, had awakened in the minds of the best people, in the midst of the
first families. I could not fail to see that the charming old
ladies were eager to relate more than they knew and all
they suspected. "There's no use denying it," a playful husband remarked to me, "they're having the time of their
lives, every last one of them. They're crammed so full of
scandal that the first thing they know, there'll be an explosion." He found it amusing, I gathered, but to me a
refined mob with a character on a pinpoint was scarcely
less appalling than a vulgar mob with a head on a pike.

But sheep are not the only creatures that run together.
More from shyness than from intellectual exclusiveness,
James was drawn into a small circle; yet he had not been
intimate enough with this circle to have it tighten in his

defense. For weeks before the Commencement, he lived
utterly alone in his College center, and the acquaintances
he passed in the street had fallen into an abstracted habit
of sky-gazing. In those weeks my sister and I longed to
approach him, but we were doubtful whether he would
wish to be spoken to by persons he did not remember.
Every afternoon he would sit, alone, on the porch of a
tavern across the street, while Cary and I were reading
on the porch of the Inn. Then, at last, one afternoon we
did walk across the green to the tavern porch, and I recall
still how grave, inscrutable and disdainful he appeared,
while groups of students and citizens of the town passed
by in the street. He had, even then, that air of legendary
remoteness, as if he lived in a perpetual escape from actuality. I was young enough to feel that he was a romantic
figure, innocent but persecuted, and I admired his aristocratic detachment, the fine, thin modeling of his features,
and the enigmatic quality of his expression. There was,
too, even a flash of envy in my heart as I watched him.
What was an unjust passing scandal compared to the permanent burden of deafness? Silly people might avoid him,
but at least he did not have to wear out his nerves pretending that he heard all they were saying.

When we called to him, he rose and came down to the
street, and we stood talking about trivial matters. The
words in our minds were never spoken; but that was the
moment, I think, when our lifelong friendship began. . . .

Surely one of the peculiar habits of circumstances is the
way they follow, in their eternal recurrence, a single
course. If an event happens once in a life, it may be de-

pended upon to repeat later its general design. A mis-
adventure in love will be constantly renewed, not in subtle
variations, but in a similar pattern. A heart once broken
appears to be forever looking for trouble of the same
nature. And so, though James was leading a blameless life,
absorbed in work, he was selected to become, yet again,
a victim of gossip. But the world has always disliked its
victims who suffer in a proud silence. Vocal martyrs have
been longest remembered in history. It may have been
James's unlikeness to others that exasperated the furies,
or it may have been his inviolable restraint. Or, again, it
may have been the slow vengeance life reserves for those
who refuse to surrender their innermost sanctuaries. . . .

As the years went by, I heard that he was interested in
the legends of chivalry and of genealogy. Then, presently,
I heard of other interests which were quite as legendary,
though less literary, in character. "I have even been credited with murder, but I was not the philanthropist who
committed it," James wrote, to my unending delight, in
Special Delivery. For a man was killed, on a dark night,
in Richmond, and, for no better reason than close kinship, and the finding of the body on the pavement in front
of the Cabells' house, James was promptly, though secretly,
"credited with murder." The news was whispered to me,
one morning in the autumn of 1901, or so I recall, and
I scoffed, in reply, "Why, that is ridiculous!"

"I know. He wouldn't hurt a moth," my informant rejoined, with true Southern logic, "and, anyway, nobody
blames him." For, among the best families, there was a
generous code relating to justifiable homicide. "They say

the man was leading a most immoral life, and, besides, he was James's cousin. I hear the family are trying to hush it up. I don't mean James's family. I suppose they haven't heard that he is suspected."

For some weeks there was vehement public excitement. A Pinkerton detective, I was told, came down from New York; and then abruptly, in the midst of the gossip, silence smothered the mystery while it was still unsolved. Nobody blamed James, though most people believed he had been the private avenger of public morality. At last, however, the truth was reluctantly divulged, and for the second time, it was proved, James had been used as a vicarious sacrifice. It was revealed that the erring cousin had been struck down, in front of the Cabells' house, by the brother of a country girl who had been seduced. Morality was avenged, for it was generally thought that the family of the seducer had benevolently aided the slayer to escape.

But this was divulged, accurately or inaccurately, years later, and during all those years James was living as a hermit, burning his kerosene lamp in patience, and sleeping in his third-story room until sunset. When, presently, he married the woman who was designed to be his wife, his manner of living changed abruptly; and, at last, after long failure, with the fortunate suppression of *Jurgen,* he was elevated to a prominent, if insecure, seat among the indecorous literary gods of the postwar decade.

When Hugh Walpole made his first visit to America, before too much prosperity had changed disarming youth into pompous middle age, I asked James to go with us on a picnic, to Williamsburg. He had not been to the

College of William and Mary since the day he received his diploma, and he was greeted, with enthusiasm, as the long-missing heir of the College.

That was a day to remember, and, just for this once, James dropped his pose of detachment, and appeared only very moderately histrionic. We laughed and talked, and unpacked our lunch basket under the crumbling, ivy-covered wall of an old graveyard. . . .

TWELVE

The Shadow of the Wall

During the following winter and spring I spent several months in New York, and I went to a number of disappointing "literary" parties. My ears bothered me less in New York, because of the many vibrations of sound, and I had little difficulty in hearing, though I was still nervous when I met strangers. A few weeks before I left Richmond, Hamlin Garland, one of the first authors to congratulate me on *The Descendant*, came to see me on his way South. In one of his memoirs, he says, "but she does not seem as natural in conversation as she appears in her books." What he did not discern was my agonizing tension because his voice was not clear enough for me to understand what he said.

In those first few years of partial deafness, I would never see strangers, and not even my former friends, except in the presence of Cary, who would know by intuition the words that I missed and would hasten to snatch up the broken thread. For my sensitive shyness, my fear of betraying an affliction, was, in itself, an incurable malady. I stopped seeing my friends. I would go out of my way to avoid those I had loved rather than ask them to raise their voices. There was a man, I remember, who was beginning to interest me. I knew that he cared, and that I was hurting him, but I couldn't bring myself to tell him I could not hear all he said. Even after he suspected, and asked me frankly if that was the reason, I kept away from him. I could not bring myself to tell him the truth. He told me, with deep tenderness, that the affliction I dreaded would only bring me closer to him; but even when I opened my lips to confide in him, all I could force myself to speak was a mocking evasion. At twenty-two, I told myself that marriage was not for me, and I meant it more firmly every year that I lived.

But it was a blessed relief to find that I appeared to hear better in New York. Twice a year I went on to be treated by one aurist or another, and as soon as I received a sufficient income from my books, I began a pilgrimage all over the world, as patient as, and more hopeless than, the pilgrimages to shrines of saints in the Dark Ages. I went everywhere I could perceive the faintest gleam of light. I was treated, not only in America, but in Europe, by every specialist who had distinguished himself in work for the ears. And it was all as futile as the quest for miracles, and far more expensive. In my case, which was a common, and very simple, hardening in the Eustachian tube and the middle ear, there was no cure to be found anywhere. Science had failed my body as ruinously as religion had failed my soul. Both quests, physical and spiritual, had ended in disillusionment. My only prop, a strong one, was a kind of humane stoicism. I could bear what I had to

bear, but I could not pretend it away. I could not pretend
that my life had not been blighted before it had opened.

After this, my point of view changed so completely that
I was able to build a wall of deceptive gaiety around me.
There was a surer refuge in mockery, I found, than in too
grave a sincerity. It was then that I began to cultivate the
ironic mood, the smiling pose, which I have held, without
a break or a change, for almost forty years. "You are the
only one of my patients who is not depressed by deafness," one of the leading aurists in New York said to me
a few years ago. I smiled that faintly derisive smile. If
only he could know! If only anyone in the world could
know! That I, who was winged for flying, should be
wounded and caged!

I had been eager to see what I still thought of as "literary
life in New York"; but the mental climate in which I
presently found myself seemed scarcely less flat and stale
than the familiar climate in Richmond, where social
charm prevailed over intelligence. At the Authors' Club
I met the various authors who would soon become, by self-
election, the Forty Immortals of the American Academy.
They were important, and they knew it, but they were
also as affable as royalty; and no one who valued manners
could help liking them. Life had been easy for them, and
literature had been easier. They had created both the
literature of America and the literary renown that embalmed it. They constituted the only critical judgment,
as well as the only material for criticism. When they were
not, as Charles Lamb once remarked of a similar coterie,

"encouraging one another in mediocrity," they were gravely preparing work for one another to praise. For this reason, no doubt, they impressed me with a kind of evergreen optimism. They were elderly, but they were not yet mature. One and all, in their sunny exposure, they had mellowed too quickly. And this ever-green optimism spread over the whole consciousness of America. That, also, had mellowed too quickly; that, also, had softened before it was ripe.

For I had grown up in a world that was dominated by immature age. Not by vigorous immaturity, but by immaturity that was old and tired and prudent, that loved ritual and rubric, and was utterly wanting in curiosity about the new and the strange. Its era has passed away, and the world it made has crumbled around us. Its finest creation, a code of manners, has been ridiculed and discarded. Insolent youth rides, now, in the whirlwind. For those modern iconoclasts who are without culture possess, apparently, all the courage.

But I had broken through the crust of experience too often, and too dangerously, to be able to glide lightly over the surface. I was looking for a purpose, for a philosophy that would help me to withstand a scheme of things in which I had never felt completely at home. I wanted a reason, if not for creation in general, at least for the civilization which men had made, and were still making. The truth was, I suppose, that I still needed a religion. Though I was a skeptic in mind, I was in my heart a believer. I believed even in the art of fiction, and one who believes in that can believe almost anything else. My mind, how-

ever, was faithful to its disbelief, though I was living in a
period when nobody doubted but the damned and Robert
Ingersoll, whose benign features I had seen portrayed
among flames. I had never known a person, certainly not
in the Solid South, who believed as little as I did, for I
doubted the words of man as well as the works of God.

But the more I saw of these agreeable authors, the more
I liked them. The trouble was that I thought of them as
old gentlemen, and they thought of themselves as old
masters. There was an insuperable disparity in our points
of view. I respected Mr. Alden, of Harper's, as a benevolent purpose, but I could not salute him as an inspired
poet and prophet. Mr. Richard Watson Gilder, a younger
master, whom I saw once or twice, appeared to me to
possess a carefully studied charm, as if he were a pallid
understudy for Robert Louis Stevenson. I thought him
affected; but, then, if print were flesh, I should probably
consider R.L.S. affected. Hamlin Garland was the soul of
sincerity, but he was also young enough to become a disciple. His first volume of stories, *Main-Traveled Roads,*
showed an almost savage fidelity to life; but, when he left
the West and came to New York, he was tamed of his
wildness, as well as of his originality, by the civilizing
influence of Mr. Howells. I met Mr. Howells only once;
but I had watched him from afar, and I had determined
that, much as I respected him, I would not allow myself
to come within the magic circle of his charm and his
influence. For more than one full generation all the well-
thought of fiction in America was infected by the dull
gentility of his realism, and broke out in a rash of refine-

ment. Even Hamlin Garland's Western novels contracted
this sanguine flush. Only when he turned from fiction to
autobiography was he able, as a writer, to recover his
native soul.

And so, at the turn of the century, I owed less than
nothing to these creators. They dispensed their favors
only to disciples; and I had no slightest inclination ever
to become a disciple. I would write, as I had read, because
books were, for me, an essential part of both living and
dying, and writing was my natural form of expression.
It was the only method in which I felt at home, and free
to interpret some special aspect of experience. But the
aspect, and the interpretation, must be mine. Another's
way might be superior, but it was not my own. It was
not that particular truth which had been cultivated in
my garden. Though I conformed to no other creed, I
could still pledge myself to a faith in artistic integrity.

Well, they have had their day, those hopeful spirits,
and their day, as it happened, was long and sunny. It is
now a winding road from that past to this, our present;
and the way does not appear, in a reflective glance, to
have reached higher levels. For one thing, the literary
mind of that epoch was, by and large, an organ of benevolent motives.

Apart from letters, it is the vulgar custom of the moment
to deride the thinkers of the Victorian and Edwardian
eras; yet there has not been, in all history, another age,
with the possible exception of the Age of the Antonines,
and the more limited reign of the Emperor Asoka, in
India, when so much sheer mental energy was directed

toward creating a fairer social order. The thinkers of the latter part of the nineteenth century were no better satisfied with the world they lived in than the thinkers of today are satisfied with our declining civilization. It is true that the men behind us left much undone, but it is true, also, that they accomplished much we have not undertaken. They could not overturn a social system, and, dreading catastrophe, few of them tried to do so. But many of them worked, without reward, to make living conditions more tolerable for the dispossessed of society. If there were robber barons in industry, there were, as well, giants of good will in philanthropy. Nothing, as history proves, is so ungrateful as a rising generation; yet, if there is any faintest glimmer of light ahead of us in the present, it was kindled by the intellectual fires that burned long before us.

But to return to the American scene in the last years of the century. Literature, too, has passed on. I have watched so many literary fashions shoot up and blossom, and then fade and drop, that I have learned to recognize a new movement while it is still on the way. Yet with the many that I have seen come and go, I have never yet encountered a mode of thinking that regarded itself as simply a changing fashion, and not as an infallible approach to the right culture. For my part, I could observe and ponder, because I also was sure of my own special pursuit. I knew that I craved the best amid a chaos of second bests. What astonished me most, I think, was the general lack of disinterested effort, and the lack, too, of the feeling that one's work was something larger and more important than one's private aims or ambitions. It may be that literary circles are perpetually closing in toward the center of gravity. Log-rolling was a prevalent pastime then, as it is nowadays; for that is always the case, I suppose, where reputations are made easily, and without merit. Never, in all the years since then, have I lost that sense of unreality, of insincerity, and of time-serving, in much, but by no means the greater part, of American culture. I had no place in any coterie, or in any reciprocal self-advertising. I stood alone. I stood outside. I wanted only to learn. I wanted only to write better.

THIRTEEN

---◄◆►---

Wanderings

In the year 1899, my brother Arthur, ever the most generous spirit, sent the three of us, Cary, Rebe, and me, abroad for a long wandering. When he came over from England, the old gray house appeared as a tomb, and he hoped that an ocean voyage and a change to other countries might help us to escape from memories. Unhappily, Frank, who most needed change, could not leave his tedious round in the Tredegar Iron Works. All through my childhood and my early youth there existed in our family a curious delusion that only women suffered from grief or from maladjustment to circumstances.

We sailed early in January, and for nearly a year we wandered from country to country. I saw Egypt. I saw the Pyramids, at noon and at sunset, by moonlight, and at sunrise. I saw the Tombs of the Kings, and the great Temple at Karnak. I saw the lovely vanished Temple of Philae. I saw the coast of Asia Minor, and the harbor of Smyrna. I sailed on the Aegean Sea. I saw the Isles of Greece, and the Acropolis. I saw the Golden Horn in the sunrise, and the minarets and the cypresses of Constan-

tinople. I saw the island of Corfu at the season of flowers.
I saw the Alps. I saw Italy. I saw Switzerland. I saw Paris.
I saw London. I saw England in summer. I saw the frozen
lakes of Norway, and the midnight sun over the ice fields.

Many other persons, wiser or less wise than I, have seen
and described all these places. For me, they became, with
time, a part of the unchanging hills and valleys within
my mind. In long sleepless nights, I return to these scenes,
again and again, as if that special vision were carved from
some indestructible element. I remember Egypt undisfig-
ured by modern inventions, when the Sphinx and the
Pyramids were alone in the desert. I remember the deep
triangular shadow of the Great Pyramid cutting into the
bright distance; and I remember, too, the solitary stoop-
ing figure of an old water-carrier, his goatskin bag hung
over his shoulder, who passed slowly, as a heartbreaking
symbol of ages, between the gold of the sand and the
paler gold of the horizon.

We were the only guests, as I recall, on our first night
at the Mena House. There were no tawdry bazaars and
no baksheesh-begging donkey boys to spoil the divine
loneliness of sunset, moonlight, and sunrise. Even Shep-
heard's Hotel was not overcrowded that winter. We spent
a fortnight there before we went up the Nile; but, when
we returned, we stayed in the more fascinating French
Hôtel du Nil, down in the Arabian, or it may have been
the French, quarter of Cairo. In recent years, I have met
only one man, an artist, who had stayed at the Hôtel du
Nil, and he could not tell me whether the house was still
standing.

Our rooms opened on a high balcony, wreathed in gar-
lands of flowering bougainvillaea. Directly in front of us
there was a mosque, with a lovely greenish minaret, where
a muezzin chanted the hour of prayer at dawn, at noon,
at four o'clock, at sunset, and at nightfall. With the first
notes of the crier, the chanting chorus would respond and
float upward from the hundreds of minarets over Cairo.
Below us, we could see a mysterious closed house, with
a sculptured front and wide, dark windows of old lattice-
work. Over the walled garden in front, large gray and
black ravens, different alike from our crows and from the
English rooks, would flit back and forth, close to their
moving shadows. Occasionally, in the afternoon, the half-
veiled ladies of the harem would stroll in the early spring
sunshine, pursued by an aged crone bearing a tray of what
we imagined was syrup or sherbet or, perhaps, Turkish
Delight. Even now, the recollection reminds me of a romantic page from my child's copy of *The Arabian Nights;*
but I wonder whether the half-veiled ladies were as satisfied as they appeared, or whether the aged crone was, for
that matter. . . .

Other memories drift by, and fade, and disappear. . . .
The Isles of Greece under flamingo-colored clouds . . .
Sunshine flooding the Acropolis . . . Poppies blooming
amid the feathery grass by the Parthenon . . . Beauty
that is lost but eternal . . . They come and go, these
memories, and give place to others . . . Human memories among them . . .

Although I have never suffered, sentimentally, from the
maternal instinct, and I have cared little for children,

unless they were neglected or ill-treated, when my heart would go out to them, I have never forgotten a little cabin-boy, on our outward voyage. We sailed on the old *Aller*, of the North German Lloyd Line, and we stopped at several forgotten ports, before reaching Egypt, at the end of three weeks. While we were having tea on deck, we noticed a beautiful German child, in a blue sailor suit, who looked not more than ten, though the stewards told us he was twelve years old. At first, we gave him cookies, and then, as the slow days passed, we fell into the habit of bringing him fruit or candy from our cabin. One day, when we missed his shy greeting and expectant smile, we asked, "Where is Max?" and, after trying to avoid an answer, the deck steward told us that the child was in the ship's hospital, dangerously ill with pneumonia. When we sought the doctor, he said there was a bare chance of recovery, and that the boy, in case he was still alive, would be landed at Genoa. We begged to be allowed to see him, but no passengers, we were reminded, were permitted below decks.

The captain remained, and in response to much urging, he gave us permission to visit the hospital, where we found that the child recognized us, and was able to smile when we gave him an eiderdown pillow and the basket of oranges and grapes we had brought. I had never before seen a ship's hospital, and, nowadays, the *Aller* would be considered far from luxurious, even in the first cabin. The sight of Max, barely conscious, but smiling up at us, was intensely moving; especially when the doctor admitted that the boy would, probably, die before reaching Genoa.

That afternoon, we told the other passengers of the child's illness, and, together, we contributed a comfortable sum for him to be taken to the hospital. Though the doctor thought Max could not last through the night, he was alive when we landed, and we saw him carried off the boat over the shoulder of a friendly seaman. We spent our hours in Genoa in finding the Protestant Hospital, and it made me happy to see Max lying between spotless sheets, with a fresh slip on his eiderdown pillow, and a large, fair, motherly head nurse bending over him. Though he could not speak, he could still smile, though the nurse had no hope of his recovery. When we kissed his forehead, his smile did not fade, but the tears rolled down his cheeks as we turned to wave back at him.

Such recollections live, I suppose, as long as we do. Afterwards, I had letters from the boy's parents in Germany, for Max lived to go home again, and, in the end, he went back to the sea. The letters from his parents were touching. They found it hard to make a living in Germany, and they begged me to find a janitor's place for them in America. But life is full of hardship, and, after all, what can one do with one's world?

In September of that year we went to Yorkshire, and to the village of Haworth, because of our feeling for the Brontës, especially for Emily. We drove to Haworth, I remember, though I cannot recall where we spent the previous night. It was raining when, at dusk, we reached the steep street, paved with cobblestones turned endwise to help the horses in the long climb. In those days, the

place was desolate, yet, to us who loved the Brontës, it
was steeped in the poetry of place and in the loneliness
of Emily's spirit. Few lights were glimmering through the
murk (there is no other word for it) and when, at last,
we came to the Black Bull Inn, we found that every bed
was engaged by the neighboring farmers, who had gathered to sell their second crop of hay the next morning.
The pleasant landlady, much concerned for our discom-
fort, promised us a good supper, and brought us into the
old inn, still unchanged, and filled, for us, with reminders
of the pathetic Branwell Brontë. There was a bar at one
end; hams were hanging, overhead, from the smoky
beams, and in front of the glowing hearth, the Yorkshire
farmers were bargaining in their strange dialect. We listened to them, fascinated but without understanding a
word; and, after our supper of new-laid eggs and Yorkshire bacon (the best bacon ever provided by any hog),
we started out, led by a silent boy with a lantern, to seek
a night's lodging. This was not easy to find, for the farmers,
it appeared, had taken possession, but, at last, at the end
of our search, a kind-hearted woman who had a son in
"the States" proffered one single bed for three persons.
Here, lying across the bed, with our feet on chairs, we
spent a few sleepless hours, and, at the earliest hour, we
returned to the Black Bull for breakfast. After that for-
tifying meal, we walked in pale sunshine over the moors
that Emily loved, and saw the bleak parsonage, still unchanged, beside the forsaken churchyard, with its toppling
headstones. The place breathed the very essence of soli-

tude; yet she had loved it. I remembered what she had
written in homesickness:

> The house is old, the trees are bare,
>   Moonless above bends twilight's dome,
> But what on earth is half so dear—
>   So longed for—as the hearth of home.
>
> The mute bird sitting on the stone,
>   The dank moss dripping from the wall,
> The thorn-trees gaunt, the walks o'ergrown,
>   I love them—how I love them all.
>
> A little and a lone green lane,
>   That opened on a common wide,
> A distant, dreamy, dim blue chain
>   Of mountains circling every side.

In November we sailed for America, and after reaching
home I wrote the final chapters of *The Voice of the
People*. Though I was glad to wander, I was eager to
return to myself, and to my own work. In the overwhelm-
ing egoism of youth, nothing could be so important to
me as the world within and my own special act of creation.
That this was less than the tiniest whirling speck of dust
on the earth made no difference to me, or to the vast, be-
wildered reaches of my ambition. "But you have achieved
your ambition," someone said to me not long ago. I
laughed. "In the delirium of youth, my ambition lost itself
in the sky. No, I have failed, because I once hoped to be
another Tolstoy. . . ." But, instead, I began, in outline,
a novel of the Civil War, and my social history of Virginia since the decade before the Confederacy. For I was

born a novelist, and no matter how far I wandered, I would always return in the end. . . .

Change of scene may be a diversion, but it cannot ever be a cure for unhappiness. I felt that my deafness was worse, and the intolerable effort of pretending to hear had increased that morbid sensitiveness which has stalked me, in a panic terror, for the greater part of my life. Though it is true that I was a born novelist, it is true also that I flung myself into my work as desperately as a man might fling himself into a hopeless battle. For I was young; I was ardent for life; I was tremendously vital; I was wounded and caged. Recognition at this moment might have saved me from despair of achievement. But I waited and worked, and watched the inferior exalted for nearly thirty years; and when recognition came at last, it was too late to alter events, or to make a difference in living. Had I been born in New England or in the Middle West, I should have found, if not complete understanding, at least an acknowledgment. But I was born in the South. I was a part of the South. And, in the South, where conversation, not literature, is the serious pursuit of all classes, I continued to write as I must. . . .

How much my horror of deafness had to do with this, I shall never know. If I began as a novelist, I began, too, with a gift for living, and with that special charm which flames up with a vital warmth, or dies down and fades away, according to the responsiveness or the unresponsiveness of another. . . . But I am rushing too far ahead. . . .

———◄◆►———

FOURTEEN

Miracle—or Illusion?

Without warning, a miracle changed my life. I fell in love at first sight. Though I had had my casual romances, and even a rare emotional entanglement, I had not ever been in love with my whole being. One major obstacle was a deep conviction that I was unfitted for marriage. Loneliness had exercised a strange fascination; and I felt that I could not surrender myself to constant companionship, that I could not ever be completely possessed. It is true that I was both temperamental and imaginative, lightly disposed to cherish unreal and airy romances; but, apart from the lack in me of what people call the maternal instinct, I felt that my increasing deafness might be inherited, and that it would be a sin against life to pass on an affliction which, even while it was scarcely noticeable, had caused such intense suffering. . . .

It was the winter after our return from abroad, and Cary, Rebe and I were spending a few weeks in New York, in order that I might talk with my new publishers, Doubleday, Page and Company. While we were there we went often to the play and the opera; and, among our friends, one we loved very much would ask us to drop in for tea on our way home from a matinee. It was in her charming drawing room (how vividly I can still see it!) that the flash came from an empty sky, and my whole life was transfigured.

Like all other romantic episodes, great or small, in my life, this began with a sudden illumination. Or, rather, it did not begin at all; it was not there, and then it was there. One moment the world had appeared in stark outlines, colorless and unlit, and the next moment, it was flooded with radiance. I had caught that light from the glance of a stranger, and the smothered fire had flamed up from the depths. And this first love, as always, created the illusion of its own immortality. When I went out into the street, after that accidental meeting, I felt that I was walking, not in time, but in eternity. I moved amid values that had ceased to be ephemeral, and had become everlasting.

I remember shrinking back, as I entered the room; and when we were introduced, I scarcely distinguished him from the man with whom he was talking. Then, gradually, I noticed that he kept his eyes on me while he was speaking to someone else, and, in my shyness, I became faintly uncomfortable. Still, however hard I tried, I could not keep my glance from turning in his direction. I felt my gaze drawn back to him by some invisible thread of self-consciousness. I was aware of his interest, and I was aware, too, of his tall thin figure and his dark keen face, with hair which was slightly gray on the temples. What I did not know, at the time, for his name meant nothing to

me, was that he had been married for years, and was the
father of two sons, already at school or at college. What I
knew, through some vivid perception, was that the awareness was not on my side alone, that he was following my
words and my gestures, that a circle of attraction divided
us from the persons around us. Most women, I suppose,
have lived through such moments, but with most women
this emotional awakening, as intangible as air, and as life-
giving, must come, I think, earlier in youth. For I was
twenty-six, and my twenty-seventh birthday would come
in April. In the years before my youth was clouded by
tragedy, I had known an attraction as swift and as imperative; but not ever the permanence, and the infallible certainty, as if a bell were ringing, "Here, now, this is my
moment!"

Looking back, over the flat surface of experience, the
whole occurrence appears incredibly wild and romantic.
It does not belong to life; yet it remains, after all the
years between, intensely alive. It is the one thing that
has not passed; for not ever again, in the future, could I
see my life closing as if it had not once bloomed and
opened wide to the light.

After a little while, he broke away from the group, and
crossed the room to join me by the window. I remember
the window, the street outside, the carriages that went by;
and I remember, too, the look of the room behind him,
and even the shadows of firelight on his face, as he paused
for an instant on his way toward me. We talked first of
my two books, and, crude as they were, he liked them,
because, he said, "there is something, I don't know what,

but there is something." While I listened to him, not wondering whether I could hear his voice, I found, with a shock of pleasure, that his clear, crisp tones were distinct, without straining, without effort. The one tremendous obstacle to a natural association did not exist at all, or existed but slightly, when I was with him. Even when, as occasionally happened, I had to ask him to repeat what he said, he replied as if this touch of dependence were an added attraction. Out of the whole world of men, I had met the one man who knew, by sympathy, or by some other instinct, the right way of approach, who could, by his simple presence, release me from my too sensitive fears. I shall call him Gerald B——, because this name will do as well as another.

Of this, I knew nothing at that moment. All I felt was a swifter vibration, a quivering joy, as if some long imprisoned stream of life were beginning to flow again under the open sky. His eyes were gay, searching, intensely alive. Though I felt, or found, that we had scarcely an intellectual interest in common, the difference seemed only to increase his imperative charm over my heart and my senses. For, through that difference, he had recognized something in me—that mysterious something—which was akin to his own nature.

Months afterwards, an unsuspecting friend said to me: "One miracle in life I have seen, without knowing the cause. I saw your whole life change in a single spring. Everything about you, even the way you looked, came to life. I saw radiance stream under your skin. I saw the stricken look leave your eyes. I saw the bronze sheen return to your hair. No one could miss it who watched you. A month before you had been cold and reserved. Then suddenly, you bloomed again, and everyone felt your charm. I used to see people look at you, and think to myself, 'They feel something about her.' "

If these were not her exact words, they are near enough to express her meaning and her surprise. What she did not know was that this passionate awakening to life had restored my lost faith in myself. Love had proved to me that my personality, or my charm, could overcome, not only my deafness, but the morbid terror of that affliction, and, especially, of its effect upon others. . . . But of the many ties between us, I think the strongest was a kind of intimate laughter. It began at that first meeting, and it endured until the end of his life, seven years later. This laughter, springing from a kindred sense of humor, with a compelling physical magnetism, was to thrust itself, as a memory, between me and the fulfillment of any future emotion. . . .

On the way home that afternoon, Cary told me what she had heard of Gerald B——. Of all the incredible pursuits, it appeared that he was engaged in high finance, with a firm in or near Wall Street. Several times, rumor reported, his wife had been on the point of seeking a divorce, and had been prevented only by his devotion to their two sons. Now, though they occupied the same house, it was common knowledge that they were barely more than strangers to each other.

But all these truths, or half-truths, were without validity. The look in his eyes was the only reality. Some essence of joy had passed between us at our first glance; and I knew that he had perceived this more quickly than I. Only the old or the loveless, I told myself, could deny this affirmation of life. It must mean less to him, naturally, but it must mean something. Even if I never saw him again, I could hold fast to this one moment. Yet, deep in my unconscious mind or heart, I knew that I should see him again.

The next afternoon, before sunset, he came to see how we were settled, or so he remarked lightly. We were staying in an old apartment house, the Florence, and the rooms were large, with high ceilings and wide windows. A friend was in our living room when he came. I cannot recall how it happened, but when I left the room to find something, she showed him a photograph I had just given to her. She told me he looked at it until they heard me returning, and he had said then, as he gave it back to her: "She is so lovely, how could anyone help loving her?" The words shone in my mind, ringed with light, when they were repeated. Even now, they gleam with a faint incandescence, and I shall always remember and treasure them. For it was not until long afterwards that I made a curious discovery. Although I was not beautiful, I created the semblance of beauty for everyone who has ever loved me. This may be true of other women. I do not know. I know it has been true of me, not only with the men who have cared for me, but also with many of the women who were my closest friends. . . .

The next day I left off the half-mourning I had worn

since Mother's death, and I went out eagerly to buy dresses that were gay and youthful and becoming. There is much to be said, I feel now, for the modern fashion of taking death so simply that nobody stays at home, not even the corpse, which often stops in a funeral room on the way to the grave. But to us of Southern blood, in the eighteen-nineties, death and dying and burial were still solemn occasions. We could not put one we loved into the earth as soon as the heart had stopped beating, and the custom of mourning meant, for us, long remembrance. It was not reasonable, that lost habit of fidelity, but in its very unreasonableness it was impressive. I saw, now, that those years of prolonged sorrow were wasted years. They had helped no one, least of all the dead, for whom I went in black, and sacrificed, unconsciously, what should have been the happiest years of my youth. Mother would not have wanted this sacrifice, nor would Walter have wanted it; for both Mother and Walter wished us to be happy; and this pall of Cary's grief, and of mine, bore as heavily upon Rebe, who was just growing up into her saddened girlhood. She and I had always been inseparable, and we remained so until her marriage in December, 1906. Shadow, I had called her.

But now, in this lost and recovered April of my life, I longed for vivid colors, and, wearing them, I became, myself, vivid. I bought the smartest hats from Paris, and, as my books were bringing in a little money, I went, for my clothes, to fashionable dressmakers. In a few weeks, I was so changed that Rebe was writing home, "I wish you could see Ellen. I don't know what has happened to her.

After all those years in black, she is buying the gayest
and brightest clothes, and you can't imagine how becoming they are to her. She looks years younger. You ought
to see the admiring way people look after her."

Whether it was the gay clothes or the demolished in-
hibitions, I do not know; but that spring, for the first time,
I felt that it was possible to overcome what I had regarded
as an insurmountable impediment. The great discovery
that my own identity, that I, myself, could triumph over
brute circumstances, had destroyed and then re-created the
entire inner world of my consciousness. "I will make myself well," I resolved. "I will make myself happy. I will
make myself beautiful." For years, after that, I plunged,
once a day, into the coldest water, winter or summer. I
played golf, or walked miles, in all weathers. I slept, on
stormy nights, with the snow drifting in over me. Little
by little, I won back at least moderate health and nervous
equilibrium. I looked better than I had looked at sixteen.
"To me, you will always be the youngest thing in the
world," he said.

For the next seven years I lived in an arrested pause between dreaming and waking. All reality was poured into
a solitary brooding power, a solitary emotion. I use the
word "solitary" with meaning, because this intense secret
life was lived almost, if not entirely, alone, and under the
surface. So little happened in the concrete to exert so
tremendous an influence. We were apart so much, and
together so little. Several months each year, I spent in
New York; and then we saw each other in the evening,

whenever it was possible. But, in those seven years, though my two sisters must have suspected, I confided in no one.

It is more than difficult to write, literally, of those years. Yet no honest story of my life could be told without touching upon them, and the only reason for this memoir is the hope that it may shed some beam of light, however faint, into the troubled darkness of human psychology. Outwardly, there was little to record, little to keep for remembrance. Inwardly, the impression spread in my unconscious mind, like the circle made by a stone flung into deep water. Since I had absorbed it into the elements of my nature, not as a passion, but as a transfiguring power, I could escape from its control only by escaping from my own personality.

I cannot ever, at night, walk through the streets of New York without remembering and forgetting all over again. Forgetting and remembering! The little cares, the little anxieties, the little joys. There were dozens of small, foreign restaurants he had known of, or we had stumbled upon almost by accident. Sometimes, in summer or on mild spring evenings, we would take a boat to Coney Island, where we could lose ourselves completely among the four elements. Yet a few memories start out more vividly. Going out with him the first time he drove his small racing car. An evening in the country, when we sat on a bench before a tiny tavern, waiting for the car to be mended, and wondered what would happen if we never went back. And, more vividly still, the many dinners in an obscure Hungarian restaurant, tucked away at the end of a strange street smelling of crushed apples.

Again and again, we went there, urged by some instinct
for the alien and the remote. Over and over, a sad vio-
linist played a nameless Hungarian air; and this air is
woven and interwoven, like a thread of song, through
every recollection of those seven years. I never knew what
it was, yet I can still hear it, filled with longing and very
far-off in space. Like the "little phrase" from a sonata
that Proust recalls in *A la Recherche du Temps Perdu*,
this thread of song was wound, not through external
scenes and episodes, as in the life of Swann, but, deeper
still, through all the after memories of joy or of pain.
At the time I had never heard of Proust; but years later,
I discovered, with a startled surprise, that "little phrase"
from the sonata.

All that spring, and all through our other springs and
autumns, the nameless Hungarian air followed us; and,
frequently, I, who have no ear for music, would hear him
humming it, without words, as we sat together. Spring
passed. Time passed. Life passed. Then, suddenly, one
day, long after he was dead, when I was engaged to be
married to another man, I felt a quiver of desire, and I
heard again, rippling very faint and far away, scarcely
more real than a vibration of memory, that sad, gay, nameless little song. So closely intertwined was that music with
my emotional responses that a fragile wisp of sound could
rise from out the past, and hold me back from surrender
to another, and a newer, impulse. After those years, I felt
love again, but never again could I feel ecstasy, never
again the rush of wings in my heart. Several times I was
in love with love. Twice I was engaged to be married.

Always, when my senses were deeply stirred, some ghost of recollection would float between me and perfect fulfillment. I would feel a chill of disillusion; the joy would darken, the vital impulse would fail. "This isn't real," would whisper that malicious demon of irony, who had been driven but once out of my mind. "This is only pretending."

All this, it must be remembered, occurred, not in the mental upheaval of the Freudian era, but in that age of romantic passion, the swift turn of the century. If only we had read Freud and the new wisdom, we might have found love a passing pleasure, not a prolonged desire. Yet even this is uncertain. Of one thing alone I am very sure: it is a law of our nature that the memory of longing should survive the more fugitive memory of fulfillment. The modern adventurers who imagine they know love because they have known sex may be wiser than our less enlightened generation. But I am not of their period. I should have found wholly inadequate the mere physical sensation, which the youth of today seek so blithely. If I were young, now, I might feel differently. It is possible that I may have been only another victim of the world's superstitions about women. Perhaps. I do not know. Yet I am so constituted that the life of the mind is reality, and love without romantic illumination is a spiritless matter.

Since that decade, many standards have fallen, and most rules of conduct have altered beyond recognition. I was always a feminist, for I liked intellectual revolt as much as I disliked physical violence. On the whole, I think women have lost something precious, but have gained, immeasurably, by the passing of the old order.

From those seven years, I saved these two indestructible memories. Time has flowed over them, but they are still there, in the past, changeless, steadfast, hollowed out of eternity.

A summer morning in the Alps. We are walking together over an emerald path. I remember the moss, the ferny greenness. I remember the Alpine blue of the sky. I remember, on my lips, the flushed air tasting like honey. The way was through a thick wood, in a park, and the path wound on and upward, higher and higher. We walked slowly, scarcely speaking, scarcely breathing in that brilliant light. On and upward, higher, and still higher. Then, suddenly, the trees parted, the woods thinned and disappeared. Earth and sky met and mingled. We stood, hand in hand, alone in that solitude, alone with the radiant whiteness of the Jungfrau. From the mountain, we turned our eyes to each other. We were silent, because it seemed to us that all had been said. But the thought flashed through my mind, and was gone, "Never in all my life can I be happier than I am, now, here, at this moment!"

Another year, and another place. It is evening, and I am looking for a book in the library of an inn in Switzerland. The place is Mürren, a tiny village nestling on a crag in the Alps. My two sisters and I have spent part of the summer there, and it is, now, almost autumn. A chill is in the air, and a wood fire is burning in the fireplace, round which the English visitors, mostly middle-aged

ladies and clergymen, are gathered. I have known Gerald
for seven years, and in the past year I have felt anxious
about his health.

A complete Tauchnitz edition of Anthony Trollope is
in the library, and since coming to the Grand Hotel and
the Kurhaus Mürren, I have read over, or read for the first
time, ninety of these small red-covered volumes. Tonight,
I am looking for one of my favorites, *Framley Parsonage*.
The book is in my hand, I am still standing in front of
the shelves, when a servant comes in, and brings me a
letter. He goes out, and I open the envelope, after I have
seen Gerald's handwriting. As I read the pages, the sound
of English voices recedes, and I am alone again in that
unconquerable isolation. "I am in the hospital. They have
told me what I suspected. I have only a few weeks at worst,
a few months at best. I waited too long for the operation.
But what was the use? They couldn't cure me, and, God
knows, I wouldn't have lingered on as an invalid. My first
thought was of you. . . . It meant giving you up. . . ."

Many days later (I cannot be more exact concerning the
time) I went up on the hillside, and lay down in the grass,
where a high wind was blowing. Could I never escape
from death? Or was it life that would not cease its hostilities? If only I could lose myself in nothing or everything! If only I could become a part of the grass and the
wind and the spirit that moved round them, and in them.
I thought of the mystics, who had attained Divine consciousness through a surrender of the agonized self. By
giving up, by yielding the sense of separateness, by extin-
guishing the innermost core of identity. I tried with all

my strength to find absorption in the Power people called God, or in the vast hollowness of the universe. . . . Then, after long effort, I sank into an effortless peace. Lying there, in that golden August light, I knew, or felt, or beheld, a union deeper than knowledge, deeper than sense, deeper than vision. Light streamed through me, after anguish, and for one instant of awareness, if but for that one instant, I felt pure ecstasy. In a single blinding flash of illumination, I knew blessedness. I was a part of the spirit that moved in the light and the wind and the grass. I was—or felt I was—in communion with reality, with ultimate being. . . . But thinking came long afterwards. There was no thought, there was only blissful recognition, in that timeless awakening. . . . Then the moment sped on; the illumination flashed by me; the wind raced through the grass; the golden light shone and faded. Ecstasy born out of agony was as fleeting as the old delusions of mind or of heart. The vision was gone, and neither vision nor spirit ever returned.

Spirit? Matter? Imagination? Or a fantasy of tortured nerves? I do not know. But I do know that, for a solitary instant, on that golden afternoon, high in the Alps, I felt that blessedness, I saw that mystic vision, I found communion with the Absolute, or with Absolute Nothingness. I know, too, that the recognition was lost again in the very moment in which it was found, and that I never recovered the miracle or the delusion. . . . But there are no words to describe an instant or an hour that remains indescribable. . . . Words deal only with the semblance of truth, not with the essence, or the end, that lies beyond all semblances of reality. . . .

God must find the soul, for the soul alone cannot find God. All religion, for me, was a more or less glorified mythology, and, too often, a cruel mythology. Christ, I told myself, had been crowded out of Christianity. The inn at Bethlehem was the world's symbol. Divinity flamed up, here and there, like a wandering light; but underneath, there remained the unyielding heart of African darkness.

Gerald died before I sailed for America, and I knew it only from a newspaper (the Paris edition of the *New York Herald*) that I read on a train. So that was finished, that was over forever. . . .

In the next year I passed through a curious physical recoil from pain. I became insensible, not emotionally alone, not simply with an anaesthesia of the mind and the heart, but with a seeming loss of sensation in every nerve of my body. Of course I had not, literally, lost sensation. The idea was fantastic. Yet I would tell myself, over and over, that I could not feel anything, that if a pin were stuck into me when I was not looking, I should not be aware of the prick. I could taste nothing, and once I imagined that I could not smell the scent of gardenias when they were brought to me.

But nothing lasts. This passed with everything else. After a period of death-in-life, my mind slowly became alive again, and took up the old search for reality. Science had failed me. One could not build one's home in a skeleton. Religion failed me. One could not build one's home in a phantom. From the beginning, I had harbored a dual nature, for my reason and my emotion were perpetually in conflict. Emotionally, I was a believer; intellectually, I was a skeptic. Yet my essential problem had not altered since that moment of dumb fear, when I saw the face without a body looming toward me from the sunset. My necessity was what it had always been. How can an oversensitive nature defend itself against the malice of life? How can one learn to endure the unendurable? Not the cruelty of civilization alone, but the cold implacable inhumanity of the universe.

Part Four

THE IMPENETRABLE
WALL

———————◆▶—————————

FIFTEEN

The Search for Reality

In the seven years I knew Gerald I had published three novels, and I had planned the general outline of my social history of Virginia. My mind was engaged with this theme; but, in the long immobility that followed grief, I turned away from my real interest, and tried in vain to find an ephemeral distraction. It was then that I wrote *The Wheel of Life,* a book which I regarded, from every point of view, as a failure. I was seeking what I did not find, an antidote to experience, a way out of myself. I was trying to break the tight inner coil of my own misery. Emotionally drained, I had nothing to give. Yet I needed to live, and more even than I needed to live, I needed an escape into a world that could bear thinking about. . . . But this crisis in my life was not the result of one grief alone. I could have risen above a single grief, as I had risen before. All the piled up unhappiness of the years, beginning with my delicate and misunderstood childhood, had accumulated into a mountain of grief or despair.

I turned then to philosophy, not in the modern sense, but as the ancient decreed pursuit of the highest good.

Long ago, I had read Plato, and now I wandered, either by intuition or by accident, toward the Neoplatonists. I read eagerly, as one reaches out for an anodyne, the *Enneads* of Plotinus. Here, I found a certain assuagement of sorrow, and to that sublime mystic I shall forever be grateful. For a breathing space, he helped me to lose my troubled identity; but I lacked the spiritual wings for his flight of the alone to the Alone. One day, at this time of desperate need, I opened, listlessly, a small red-covered volume I had carried, in the pocket of my coat, from Egypt to Norway. A passage caught my eye, marked: "At the Temple of Karnak, March 7th, 1899," and a few pages beyond: "The Desert and the Sphinx, Saturday, February 25th, 1899." Then, again, the Acropolis, in April, and farther on, Hadrian's Villa, in May. And so, again, I looked for strength, and found fortitude, in the *Meditations* of the Emperor Marcus Aurelius. "Many grains of frankincense on the same altar: one falls before, another falls after; but it makes no difference."

In the following years, what I needed most was a positive rest for the mind. Pascal's God known of the heart was not enough. My Absolute must be known of the reason as well. I could be satisfied neither with spiritual yearning nor with hard-bitten fact. It was then, in those bleak years, that I studied Kant, and from Kant I passed on to Schopenhauer and Spinoza. Hegel, I could not read. It may have been that his stiff and involved German style defied translation. It may have been that I was irritated by vagueness even in metaphysics. Or it may have been that I was reading from the wrong motives. After all, what

I wanted was not to know, but to live. To live in the mind,
it is true, but to live with certitude and with serenity,
with reason in the ascendant, but still in sympathy with
all animate nature. This was the point where Spinoza
failed me. He may have been blessed, but he was not
human; and the God of mathematics must reserve his
heaven for mathematicians alone. In spite, or because of,
his embittered compassion, Schopenhauer was the more
human, and certainly the more satisfying to the mortal
seeker of wisdom. Moreover, alone among modern philosophers, if we except the incomparable Santayana, who
was then a stranger to me, Schopenhauer has a style that
can survive, not only translation, but critical violence.

Nevertheless, I remained, by constitution, imperfectly
philosophical. Longing rose strong and warm and flushed,
but more urgent than longing, ran the clear cold stream
of skepticism which warned me to doubt everything I
wished to believe. Many years later, when I discovered
Locke and Berkeley and Hume, I felt that I had merely
lost my way among other philosophers. By that time I had
traveled as far, and back again, as the great religions of
India. I studied the Upanishads and the Buddhist Suttas
in the plain and prosy English of *The Sacred Books of
the East*. These early teachings have not had, and now
cannot ever have, the benefits that attended King James's
Bible. "And, in any case, who remembers prophets?" in-
quires Lytton Strachey. "Isaiah and Jeremiah, no doubt,
have gained a certain reputation; but then Isaiah and
Jeremiah have had the extraordinary good fortune to be

translated into English by a committee of Elizabethan bishops."

In spite, however, of the numerous misconceptions, and the absence of Elizabethan bishops, Gautama, the Buddha, emerges as one of the two sublime figures in the blood-stained pilgrimage of mankind. As Mr. H. G. Wells has recently reminded us: "We must remember that in the time of Buddha it is doubtful if even the *Iliad* had been committed to writing. Probably the Mediterranean alphabet, which is the basis of most Indian scripts, had not yet reached India." Yet he adds: "The fundamental teaching of Gautama, as it is now being made plain to us by the study of original sources, is clear and simple and in the closest harmony with modern ideas. It is beyond all dispute the achievement of one of the most penetrating intelligences the world has ever known. . . . For Nirvana does not mean, as many people wrongly believe, extinction, but the extinction of the futile personal aims that necessarily make life base or pitiful or dreadful. Now here, surely, we have the completest analysis of the soul's peace. Every religion that is worth the name, every philosophy, warns us to lose ourselves in something greater than ourselves. 'Whosoever would save his life, shall lose it.' There is exactly the same lesson."

So, between 500 and 600 B.C., a Divine teacher came, and spoke and was misunderstood, and changed his world, and passed on; and the world that he had changed closed again in the old pattern. Then the Christ came, and spoke, and was misunderstood, and passed on; and Christianity settled back again into the old human pattern. Twelve

centuries went by before there came a man who has been
called "the only Christian since Christ." In the summer
of 1908 I made a pilgrimage over Italy, in the footsteps
of St. Francis. I followed the white roads, thick in dust,
from San Damiano to Portiuncula, and then, over white
roads again, to that pearl of all Italy, the Lower Church
and the Upper Church of Assisi. Here indeed was the way
of the heart as well as the way of the Cross! As I left that
sacred place, I felt that the memory of St. Francis flooded
my soul with a spiritual radiance. But I left the church
and passed on, and the radiance was blotted out by a dark
image of human nature. Going down the steep hill from
Assisi, we met one of the wretched "little brothers" of St.
Francis, a small skeleton of a horse, staggering under a
lash as it dragged several robust Franciscan friars up to
the church. And I saw then, as I saw again and again
throughout my pilgrimage, that St. Francis was one alone,
but the Franciscan Friars are a multitude. For he also,
though they made him a saint, had failed to change human
nature and human behavior. They built for the Little
Poor Man the most beautiful sepulcher in the Christian
world. But, for me, his spirit dwells, not in a great church,
but in the solitude, among the singing birds, of La Verna,
that soaring peak, green with the pines and the fir-trees
and the ancient beeches, within the rocky shelter of the
Apennines. . . .

They made him the kind of saint he was not, and had
never been; but "the first companions who did not suc-
ceed in flight had to undergo the severest usage. . . ."
I am quoting from *The Life of St. Francis,* by Paul

Sabatier, who gives his sources. "The first disciple, Bernardo di Quintavalle, hunted like a wild beast, passed two years in the forests of Monte-Sefro, hidden as a wood-cutter. In the March of Ancona, the home of the Spirituals, the victorious party used a terrible violence. The Will was confiscated and destroyed; they went so far as to burn it over the head of a friar who persisted in desiring to observe it. . . ."

It was all in vain. Like human nature, I remained intractable. What I found in Christ, in Buddha, in St. Francis, was not the miracle of Godhead, but a very special divinity. The spirit stirred me to the depths, yet, when the spirit passed on, the surface closed again and began, slowly, to harden. I had given several years to this search for some reality of the soul; but I could go only a part of that mystic way; I could love, I could worship; but I could not believe. On that road one could travel by faith alone, and there was no faith in the light that was guiding me. . . .

In the wilderness of metaphysics, I could at least discern the vanishing-point in the perspective. At a later period, I told myself that life had prepared me for Locke. Life had prepared me for Hume. Life had prepared me for the good Bishop who abolished both matter and the immortal soul. How, I wondered, had I missed them in my desperate search for reality, which might prove, after all, to be nothing more than perpetual illusion? I could not answer. But, by this time, I was reading, not in the pursuit of truth, but in the flight from remembrance. I was ready for the three of them, Locke, Berkeley, Hume. I was as

ready for destructive idealism as for destructive materi-
alism. *There is nothing in the mind except what was first
in the senses.* So be it. But *matter has no existence except
as a form of mind.* So be it. And yet *we know the mind
only as we know matter, by perception. Mind is not an
entity, but a series of impressions.* Well, so be it. Let all
go, knowledge, matter, mind. The lonelier the universe
became, the more at home I should feel in it. I could
hold out hands empty of both faith and knowledge, and
say: "I, too, am a part of you—of what was not, is not,
and never shall be. . . ."

Yet, strangely enough, golf helped me more than philosophy to bear life. The game meant little to me; but
two hours spent on the course, in the open world, with
a background of waving broomsedge and woodland, were
more exhilarating than two hours in a library. I enjoyed
golf, I think, more than any other means of flight from
the self within. When the Virginian background changed
to the far blue sea and the high rocks of Maine, I played
better, and I hoped that this one pleasure might last as
long as I needed it. For ten years, with a long intermission
after Cary's death, golf helped me. . . .

When my mood or my interest changed, I tossed philosophy into vacancy, and turned to pick up *Candide.*
Laughter was left. Laughter is an "ayrie spirit." Laughter
is eternal. One could still laugh after one had finished
with love. . . .

But was it possible that I had too hastily written my
epitaph? Though I had finished with love, it appeared,

presently, that love had not yet finished with me. While my emotions were absorbed in Gerald, I had kept wholly free from other romantic entanglements. If other men had felt an interest in me I had been unaware of it. Or was it true, as a friend used to say, "The only way to keep out of love, is to be in it?" I do not know. My experience of love has been deep rather than wide. Still, in spite of my sound conviction that I was not made for marriage, I became engaged, and the engagement, which, on my side, was honestly and frankly experimental, lasted for three chequered years. Everything in me denied it; for it was the wrong moment. Emotionally, I was exhausted and empty. Though I enjoy companionship, I have never known a companionship I could enjoy all the time. From my sad childhood, I had worn the protective coloring of gaiety, and this successful effort at dissimulation had consumed my small store of strength. Frequently, for days, I would find myself unstrung, quivering with sensitiveness, and vaguely exasperated with people or circumstances. But a great love had come to me (why, God alone knows!) and I might at last have found complete reconciliation with life. Here was everything my love for Gerald had missed. Not only freedom from other ties, but intellectual congeniality, poetic sympathy, and companionship which was natural and easy, without the slightest sting of suspicion or selfishness. Everything but the sudden light in the heart, the distillation of joy. It was the kind of love I had wanted all my life, the strong friendship, gradually unfolding into a deeper emotion; and it entered my life when I was trying in vain to lose the in-

tolerable burden of a divided self. Surely, one of the most
curious problems in human psychology is the intimate
relation between desire and the sense of inadequacy. Does
abundance ever inspire an intense longing? For the next
three years there came to me every morning the love letter
of a poet. These were the kind of letters every woman
dreams of, and longs to receive; yet they stirred in me no
emotion stronger than gratitude. Some years later when I
burned them, I felt that I was burning flowers, and I felt,
too, that flowers could suffer. But in that moment, so
vivid yet so fleeting, I was burning everything I associated
with my earlier youth. I was destroying the past. I was
flinging the whole of life into a solitary instant of time.

Beneath an ironic gaiety of manner, I have felt grateful
to anyone who has sincerely cared for me. But gratitude,
though noble in sentiment, is without madness; and madness is the very essence of falling in love. Had I failed
merely because I preferred the second best in emotion,
just as my fellow-countryman so often preferred the second best in literature? Or were the nerves of my memory
still vibrating from that old pain, from that old ecstasy?
Could the wisest of modern psychologists answer that
question? Not that any of that matters today, or will matter tomorrow. But long after that first love, and the regret
for that first love, passed out of my thoughts, something
lived on, more in the senses than in the mind, and a faint
whisper of emotion would start awake at a touch or a
breath from the past.

So, in the end, this experimental engagement was
broken, and I turned away from what might have been,

or might not have been, happiness. The most faithful of my friends and lovers went out of my life; but fifteen years afterwards he sent me a message from Europe, where he was living. "If ever you see Ellen," he said to a friend who ran across him in Paris, "tell her I still love her, and that it is exactly the same love." When his message reached me, I was ill, crushed, despairing, broken in everything but in that sardonic spirit which mocked incessantly: "I *will* not be defeated! I *will* not look defeated!" In that far distant future, thoughts of death, like crows in a frozen landscape, were flocking nearer and nearer. No sense of duty to the unseen, no superstitious feeling that I must allow myself to be tortured, restrained me. The common pathological horror of death had never entered my consciousness. Death appeared to me as Whitman called it, "lovely and soothing." To me, the noblest passage in modern literature occurs in Santayana's *Winds of Doctrine:* "Nothing can be meaner than the anxiety to live on, to live on anyhow and in any shape; a spirit with any honor is not willing to live except in its own way, and a spirit with any wisdom is not overeager to live at all."

Still, there was the small mocking voice repeating: "I will not be defeated. . . ." But I am running out of step with my time; for all this came long afterwards. We are, at the moment, living in pre-war America, and in the year 1909. . . .

I had just published *The Romance of a Plain Man,* a book which parallels *The Voice of the People* in my social history of Virginia. Both volumes deal with the rise of the workingman in the South, but the point of view is dissimilar, and the theme is approached from opposite directions. In *The Voice of the People,* I was writing, objectively, of the "poor-white" farmer in politics, and in *The Romance of a Plain Man,* I was treating, subjectively, the progress and decline of modern industrialism.

Though I had attained a still narrow but slowly widening success, I knew that, if I were completely unnoticed, I should still work on, in literary isolation, feeling my way toward the special form I required. I would work on, not because it was in my will, but, more simply, because it was in my nature to write. It is true that life had distracted me. Something, either joy or pain, had come between me and my single-minded devotion to craftsmanship. I was not ever free to make that "complete plunge." Without admitting it, I had felt, at times, that I was writing, not with the whole of myself, but with some second personality. When I was in love with Gerald, I used to think: "Some day, when I am older, and living is less intense, I shall be able to put the whole of myself into my work. Then I shall ripen into the artist I have it in me to be." Maturity might be late in coming, but some sure instinct told me it would come in its own season. . . .

For years, now, ever since my deafness had begun to come nearer, I had felt as if I were waiting for an impenetrable wall to close round me. Meeting strangers had become torture, and I would go blocks out of my way to avoid a person I knew. The hardest part of such an affliction, I think, is the wasted nervous effort of trying to pretend it away. I was social by instinct, and from infancy

I had been able to make friends with a word or a look; but, as my sensitiveness increased, I tried never to see anyone when my sister was not with me. As money came in from my books, we traveled from specialist to specialist in America and in Europe; but there followed only one disappointment after another. These men were all kindly and sympathetic; yet they gave the same verdict. So far, no treatment had been successful with my kind of trouble, and, yes, it might, or it might not, be inherited. Yet, at eighty-six, my father had no difficulty in hearing, and could read without glasses.

I have called my sensitiveness, morbid; yet it may have been merely natural. "I know it is worse for you," a specialist in Vienna had said to me, "because you are young, you are pretty, and you have great charm." Did that make it worse or better? Or was this kind old man, who was like an understanding father to me, only trying to help when he knew that he could not heal? Meanwhile, the wall was slowly but inevitably closing in. And there was no breaking through. Other troubles might be pushed away for a day or an hour. One might find distraction from grief, even from heartbreak; but not from that ever-present "wound in the soul" which is deafness. The voices I could hear clearly were becoming rarer and rarer; yet whenever I asked a person to speak louder, my hands would turn to ice and a cold sweat would break over me. Some physical pride drew back, and continued to dodge questions, though, like so many Southerners, I had been born with the gift of talk, and enjoyed mingling with people. But even my trips abroad every summer were spoiled because I dared not go out alone, or even sit alone on the deck of a boat. Instinctively, I was running away from the ignorant kindness of human beings. During all those years, the friends I made were those who came close in spite of my shrinking from them down into myself. They were either attracted, as Gerald was, by what appeared to be shyness, or they felt, intuitively, the reason, and knew that I needed them. At first my deafness had been barely perceptible; but when I was thirty-five or forty, I forced myself to use an electric device; and the effort turned from seeking a new aurist with an improved method to finding a new and a better hearing machine. . . .

Cary was living with Father and me in the old gray house on the corner, in a neighborhood that was already forsaken. It was a house of memories; and in the last year Frank, the best of us all in so many ways, had found life unendurable. Because he had gone so quickly, so quietly, we could scarcely realize that he was not among us; and it seemed to Cary and to me that we could still hear or feel the echo of his footsteps going up or coming down the long staircase. Father was growing old, and old age was making him more irascible and dictatorial.

Only a gentle Irish terrier named Joy, and his inseparable companion, Littlest, a beautiful gray terrier, part Skye, with an angelic disposition, contributed an illusion of brightness to our life. Eight years before, on the night Joy came to us, I went down into the garden, at three o'clock, to ease his loneliness, and to bring him upstairs. As we were entering the house, Littlest ran out from a tangle of honeysuckle and joined the procession. We never learned how he got there, but the two of them, Joy and Littlest, added greatly to our happiness. It is amazing how large a place even a very small dog can make in the heart. They were with us for eight years, but by 1910 we had them no longer, and we could not bear to replace them. . . .

SIXTEEN

———◄♦►———

Heartbreak and Beyond

In the early autumn of 1909, I returned from a summer in Colorado to speak the first word ever uttered in Virginia in favor of votes for women. My interview in the newspapers started an incredible storm of protest, which did not subside until the suffrage was finally won, at the end of the First World War. It was that year, I think— though I am seldom certain of dates—that Miss Laura Clay, of Kentucky, came to Richmond, and Cary and I asked a group of women to meet her at tea. Nothing could have been more ridiculous than the timid yet courageous air with which the few bold spirits arrived, glancing round, as they ascended the front steps, to assure themselves that no strayed male was watching them. Several days after this tea, the first suffrage meeting in Virginia was held, among carved rosewood furniture, in the charming Victorian drawing room of Mrs. Clayton Glanville Coleman, the mother of my lifelong friend, Caroline. Mrs. Coleman was one of the loveliest elderly women in Richmond, and in her youth she had been the beauty of Winchester. In her house the Virginia League for Woman

Suffrage was organized, and the next day I went with Cary to ask Lila Meade Valentine to become president of this frail undertaking. After long hesitation, the group had decided that Lila was the one and only woman who combined the requisite courage and intelligence. Her health was delicate, but a pure white flame burned within her, and she possessed the inexhaustible patience of which victors and martyrs are made. When she had carefully weighed the many obstacles, she at last consented to serve, and from that moment she never faltered in what, for so many years, appeared to be a forlorn hope. By the time success came, she was in her last illness, and the registrar carried the ballot books to her bedside, in order that her name might stand first on the list.

My own interest in that struggle, or in any struggle, was ended by the crushing blow of Cary's illness and death, in the year 1911. Like every other movement of my time, this fight for the suffrage had come, for me, at the wrong moment. My enthusiasm had flowered and dropped long before. When I was eighteen, and an ardent disciple of John Stuart Mill, I might have thrown myself into the cause; but the intellectual ardors of the 'teen age seldom linger on into the thirties. It is true that in London, in the early spring of 1909, I had marched, with May Sinclair, for a part of the way in one of the great English Suffrage parades. But she had made me drop out, because she thought there might be arrests at the end; and my heart was too heavy with grief for Frank, who died that April while I was abroad, for me to share either the courage or the exaltation of those militant suffragists.

In Richmond, as long as Cary lived, or was well enough, we attended the meetings of the League, in an old-fashioned parlor in Franklin Street. Cary was whole-heartedly loyal; but, with her long illness and death, my own feeling for every cause on earth, except the need to prevent or alleviate mortal agony, was extinguished.

Stronger hearts than mine, however, were ready to devote themselves. For years that valiant spirit, Mary Johnston, gave herself, in mind, in heart, and in soul, to an impassioned propaganda, and she endured an unbelievable amount of public abuse, which, occasionally, lapsed into the gross obscenity of falsehood. All that, I must admit, was far beyond me. Like Voltaire, "I am an ardent friend to truth, but in no sense a friend to martyrdom." Moreover, except in my youthful homage to John Stuart Mill, I have never believed that either woman's acknowledged intuition or woman's unacknowledged intelligence would change so much as an atom in man's practical politics. If women wanted a vote, I agreed they had a right to vote, for I regarded the franchise in our Republic more as a right than as a privilege; and I was willing to do anything, except burn with a heroic blaze, for the watchword of liberty. What I secretly felt, though I did not offer this as a reason for lukewarmness, was that, so long as the serpent continues to crawl on the ground, the primary influence of woman will remain indirect. . . .

Cary had been closer to me than anyone else. She was the only one of my elder sisters who had cared for me when I was a child and Emily, Annie and Cary were all grown girls, interested in love and in lovers. After Mother's death, when I was rewriting *The Descendant,* she was the one person I confided in, and her sympathy and criticism were of inestimable value. I used to think that I could never write another line if I were to lose her. Yet it is one of my deepest regrets, and there are many, that she died before I was ready to do my best work. *Virginia,* the first book of my maturity, was written in the bitter years immediately after her death. A tragic irony of life is that we so often achieve success or financial independence after the chief reason for which we sought it has passed away. Mother died before my first book was published, and had she lived but a little longer, I might have made her future life so much easier. Even now, after so many years, the sharp pang of that regret will sometimes awaken me in the night. But, so long as Cary was with me, I read my manuscripts aloud to her, chapter by chapter, and we would discuss the characters as if they were actual persons. She had the most brilliant mind and personality I have ever known; yet she could fling her whole interest into something outside herself. . . .

Before Rebe's marriage, the three of us would go abroad every summer; and then, when Cary and I were alone together, we spent, in our restless wanderings, the increased income that came from my books. In this spring of 1910, we sailed for a visit to a new but dear friend, whose husband was in the English Embassy in Constantinople. We were much interested, Cary especially, because they had promised to take us to see some recent excavations of Troy. But when we reached Naples, my sister was seized with a mysterious illness, and we gave up our visit, and started back to America. On the way home, after a rest in Italy and in Switzerland, she seemed to recover, and on board ship, for she loved the crossing, and was never seasick, she became, as usual, the life of any group that gathered about her. She had inherited Mother's gifts of friendliness and of animation. I have heard many able conversationalists, but never one that could equal her in wit or vivacity.

A few days after our return to Richmond, she was taken to the hospital. When the carriage came for her (there were very few motorcars then), I looked down from the window, and saw that it was drawn by a pair of pure white horses, with flowing silvery manes and tails. In that instant, I, who had escaped from the world's superstitions, felt the clutch of a sudden chill, as if I had walked over a grave without knowing it. The carriage with the white horses was the carriage of death.

The next day there was an operation. I was told it had been successful, until Emily, my eldest sister, who was living in West Virginia, burst into my room, and cried out, through her tears, "Do you know that Cary is dying? Dr. Willis said I wasn't to tell you, but I have to tell somebody." That was the way death was broken to me, and I turned on her furiously. What was Cary to her? What was Cary to anyone else?

For three days, I let grief have its way with me. All the other sorrows in my life dwindled in memory. I saw no one. I could not touch food. I was too shattered, too despairing, to go to the hospital. If only I had done more for her! If only I had not so often sacrificed her to others

I loved! If only . . . On the third day, Roberta Wellford, her closest friend, came in and warned me that I must think first of keeping the knowledge from Cary. Not that she feared death; but she had all the horror Mother and so many other women felt, of this particular malady. But for this instinctive horror, as several physicians told me afterwards, she could easily have been saved in the beginning. Now, when it was too late, there were only two choices for us who loved her. Either we must tell her the truth, and leave her absolutely free to take her own way out, or we must hide from her, at any cost, the true nature of her illness. "How can we keep it from her if you look like this?" Roberta asked.

"But I shan't look like this tomorrow. Give me one more night. Give me only one more night. I shall not break down again."

For hours we discussed the possibilities; and, at last, we decided that the truth should be kept from her until she began to suffer great pain. When this happened, we would tell her and let her make her own choice.

"I will not break down again," I had resolved; and I never did. She lived thirteen months longer, and she never knew that her condition was hopeless. No one, except the doctors, the nurses, and Roberta Wellford, knew the whole truth, for even Emily, who had stumbled upon it, believed a change for the better had set in after the operation. I had determined, right or wrong, that no other person should learn a secret about Cary of which she herself was ignorant. When she left the hospital, she wanted to go to the Warm Springs; and I rented the old "Rose Cottage" there. My

one feeling was that she must have one last pleasant summer of life before she left it forever. My one endeavor
was to leave her free, to give her anything that would
please her. I took charge of her meals, and I bought the
wines she had most enjoyed when she was abroad.

For six months she lingered on, as an invalid, very weak
but without pain. Then she slipped, slowly, into unconsciousness; and for seven months after this, she slept away
the end of her suffering. If she had suffered, I could not
have borne it. Anguish had worn on my nerves, until I
felt as if they were harp-strings, played upon, day and
night, by stumbling fingers. Hour after hour, day after
day, week after week, month after month, I sat here, in
this upstairs study, where I am sitting now, absolutely
alone, but for the nurses, in a house of sorrow. I could
talk to no one. I had no wish to see any human being.
Roberta Wellford and the nurse, who had been a stranger
to me, became my only support. Anne Virginia Bennett,
the nurse, had come home in the ambulance with Cary
when she was brought from the hospital, and, today, Anne
Virginia is still with me, as my beloved secretary and
companion.

I lived through those thirteen months; but, even now,
I cannot think of them except in my troubled sleep, and
after nearly thirty years, they will not bear writing about.
It was then that *The Miller of Old Church* was published;
and, to this day, I am unable to read that book without
anguish. The dedication was the last thing Cary read before she became unconscious; and I seem to see the printed
page through her tears. Strangely enough, the fifth volume

in my history of manners, *Virginia,* a book she would have loved, pushed its way into my distracted mind while I sat, waiting in agony, for an end without hope.

I bore it out to the end, though I have no endurance, only a kind of defiant courage, only that blind instinct toward life: "I will not be defeated."

Fortunately, I was able to give her everything that she needed. Physicians came and went constantly. Two nurses watched over her. I bought lovely gowns and bed-jackets of lace and tea-rose chiffon. Her changeable beauty never varied while she lay there, slipping on into eternity. She was so thin and frail that she seemed scarcely more than a child asleep. Her small child's face was of a delicate pink, and so transparent that it was like porcelain with a light shining through. Her lips were vividly red, and her lashes cast twilight shadows on her cheeks. She felt nothing, the doctors said, neither mental nor physical pain—but did they really know? I often asked myself. For her breathing, so soft that one barely heard it, Roberta told me, fluttered, occasionally, as if she were dreaming unhappily. Then, one hot close August night—the nineteenth of August, 1911—while Roberta and Anne Virginia and I were sitting beside her bed, she died without a sign that she was passing away. . . .

Of what was I thinking, through all those weeks and months, while I sat beside Cary's bed, or, alone, upstairs, in my study? For the past six months, I had seen no one but Roberta and the nurses and doctors. Father, I met only at meals. Most of the time, since he had retired from the Tredegar, he sat, reading or doing accounts, in the library. Though his mind was as clear and strong as it had ever been, his memory, at eighty-one, was stored from the past, not from the present. I could not tell him of Cary's fatal illness, because I feared he would forget the secrecy, and confide in the first casual acquaintance who called on us. He appeared content, and I suppose he must have led a sufficient inner life of his own. The loss of his son, who was sacrificed to his iron will, appeared to have left Father unchanged. At Frank's death, Father had seemed stunned, they told me (I was in England at the time), but all he said was: "He was always with me. I don't see how I can go on without him." I could not see that the shock and the great loss had, in the very least, softened or altered him. Only one of my sisters, who lived near, had come to us in Cary's long illness; and this sister, Annie, stayed only a week away from her children. All three were married and living in other cities, and they were all absorbed in their own families. . . .

After that first convulsion of grief, though I had reached, and passed, the breaking-point, I did not again break down. Instead, I grew harder; I grew embittered against life. Sitting there, with trembling empty hands, I told myself, not in self-pity, but in a kind of mortal enmity, that one human being could bear so much, and no more. Was I never to have a breathing space while I lived? Was my whole life to be smothered in tragedy? When I looked round me, I could see happy persons. Many of my friends had never looked on illness and death; some of them had never lost a being they loved. Why was

I, with my frail body and damaged nerves—why was I, alone, called upon to endure the unendurable?

I could not read any longer. I could not work. I could do nothing but sit there, alone, and let misery wash over me. But I cannot bring myself to live over that old anguish. . . .

After Cary's death, I left Richmond, hoping and thinking that I should never again see the city and the old gray house, behind magnolias and boxwood trees, on that forsaken corner. In that agonized recoil, my flight was the instinctive flight of a wounded animal from the trap. Almost blindly, I went, with Caroline Coleman, my most faithful friend, to New York; and, in an utterly vain effort to forget, we tramped for miles, in that August weather, over the scorched pavements. We were looking for an apartment, and, finally, I leased one, with a beautiful view, high up on Central Park West. I did not want people; I did not want sympathy. I wanted only to lose myself in a strange place, where nothing would remind me of grief or of joy or of any life I had known. The past had become my present enemy, and my flight, I felt without thinking, must be toward the unseen future. To drop back would mean, simply, annihilation. At the moment, I told myself, all that was vital and profound in my nature had fulfilled itself, and was over. For months I wandered along the streets I had never known. I was so safely hidden that even my few close friends in New York did not know where to look for me. I had lost myself, and I hoped my sorrow, in the midst of a crowd. . . .

But this could not last. In the autumn my mind awakened from sleep, and, strangely enough, I found that my imagination was more active than ever. The long vacancy, the fallow season, had increased its fertility. The idea for *Virginia* pushed its way to the surface of thought; but I soon discovered that the characters would not come to life in New York. They needed their own place and soil and atmosphere; and after a brief and futile resistance, I went back, for a visit to old Petersburg, which is the Dinwiddie of my novel. There, I found not only Virginia herself, but the people and the houses, and the very essence of time and place. My social history had sprung from a special soil, and it could grow and flower, naturally, in no other air. For the same reason, perhaps, I could not write in New York. So I lived there for a few months at a time. Then, when the mood for work seized me, I would go back to the upstairs study in my old house, where I would stay hidden, until the mood for work changed into the impulse to wander. Most of my summers were spent abroad, but wherever I was, whether in the actual world or in the old world of imagination, I was driven, consciously or unconsciously, by my old antagonist, a past from which I was running away. But, even then, there was no escape from that closing barrier of deafness which held me, imprisoned, with my sorrow and my memories. Not for a solitary minute in time could that wall of silence be broken through or pushed back into nothingness.

SEVENTEEN

England and America

In 1914 I spent a part of the spring and summer in England. I remember perfect weather, and for the first time, I met those living English authors whose work I could admire without reservation. The American authors I admired so heartily were all dead; for it was impossible for even the most sanguine imagination to restore Hawthorne, Thoreau, Emerson, or Poe to the ungrateful flesh. Even Hawthorne's fame was slightly dimmed, because, it was felt that, after all, he was deficient in "brightness." In the case of Emerson, there was also a lack of "brightness," though there remained, oddly enough, an abundance of light. At this time, or a little earlier, one of our most respected critics was declaring, "In my opinion *The Awakening of Helena Richie* is a greater book than *Anna Karenina*, because it presents a higher ideal of womanhood. . . ."

Early in June I spent some unforgettable hours with Thomas Hardy and his fine young wife, to whom he owed the subdued tranquillity of his later years. My friend Louise Collier Willcox was with me, and, in response to an invitation from Mrs. Hardy, we drove out from Dorchester to tea at Max Gate. The afternoon was brilliant with one of those rare English days in which heaven appears to touch the earth. Our reception was charming, and I had no difficulty in hearing Hardy's voice. Somewhat to my surprise, for I had heard that he could not be made to speak of his work, Hardy talked to me, freely and frankly, about his books. His poetry would outlive his novels, he believed, and he gave the impression of caring little for the Wessex Tales, which had brought him fame. He did not hesitate to say that he considered *The Dynasts* his greatest work (he may have said "best") and he was pleased when he found that I had read it all, and was able to repeat from the "Semichorus of the Years":

> O Immanence, that reasonest not
> In putting forth all things begot,
> Thou build'st Thy house in space—for what?

Hardy smiled. "Not many have read that."

His reticence was attractive to me, for it made whatever he said well worth the saying. He was small in stature, and, unlike so many other old men, especially old men of letters, he was immaculately neat in his appearance. His face was small and worn to sharpness, but the skin was singularly clear, with a tinge of red of the cheekbones; and in both his expression and his manner there was the quality of wistfulness, as if he wished to be kind, but was not quite sure he was going about it in the right way.

I told him I thought "A Blinded Bird" the most beautiful of his shorter poems. He replied that he liked it, too,

and that it was written to a real bird. When we talked
of his novels, I confessed that I could never decide whether
I cared most for *The Return of the Native* or for *Jude
the Obscure*. He told me with pride that his wife had read
all his novels when she was twelve years old. His face
lighted with pleasure, as if he were relating something
extraordinary. Of all the human beings I have known,
none could have been more natural or less pretentious.
From the beginning, it was easy to reach an understanding. In our philosophy of life we soon touched a sympathetic chord; for he told me that he also had suffered all
his life over the inarticulate agony of the animal world.
"I have often wondered," he added, with that wistful
smile, "whether I'd choose the lot of a wild or of a do-
mestic animal; and I think, all things considered, I'd
choose the lot of the wild."

His wire-haired terrier Wessex, afterwards famous in
literary biography, never left his side, except to jump up
in a chair at the table when tea was brought in. He was
a very attractive little dog, not yet a year old, and as his
master remarked, affectionately, "always ready for his tea."
As we drove away from the house, in the late afternoon,
I looked back and saw Hardy standing in the doorway
with Wessex in his arms.

A world war and a personal life and death came and
passed before I saw him again. I could not have believed,
on that cloudless day in June, that thirteen years, of anxiety and horror and a little joy, would go by before I
spent another spring and summer in England. Nor did I
suspect that this second visit would be my last glimpse

of Hardy, who died a few months after my visit. In London, in 1927, I had hesitated whether or not I should go down to Dorchester. "I shouldn't go, if I were you," Hugh Walpole had said to me. "I haven't seen him since the war, but I hear he is much changed."

Still I hesitated, but, in the end, I wrote to Mrs. Hardy, and I received, by return post, a cordial note asking me to stop for tea when we were motoring by Dorchester. She wrote that Hardy had been ill, but he was now much better, though he was able to see very few visitors. And she added: "How kind of you to remember our dear old Wessex. He died of old age just three months ago. Somebody has given us a Persian kitten, but it can never fill the place of Wessex in our hearts." Few incidents have given me a more vivid sense of the relentless passage of time. Only a short while before, I had seen Wessex as a puppy, and now, after so brief a period, he was dead of old age.

There were two other guests, the Tomlinsons, father and son, at Max Gate that afternoon in 1927, and the conversation was more general. But Hardy himself had not changed. He was still gentle, considerate, with a poetic fire in his glance when he spoke of something that moved him. They had a handsome blue Persian kitten, but he told me he missed Wessex more and more. "Wessex was so fond of the wireless," he said, "that I used to get up early in the morning and come downstairs to turn it on for him." And, presently, he took me out into the garden, and showed me the little grave where Wessex was buried.

Then we talked of Stonehenge, and the way it had still preserved its ancient air of sacrifice. When I spoke of his novels, he dismissed them with a gesture, and replied that he was interested, now, only in verse. His poetry he appeared to love deeply, and I have come to wonder whether he was not right, after all, in his estimate of his own work. It is possible, since poetry has an enduring fiber, that some of his poems may outlast his great fiction.

I was glad that I had not taken Hugh Walpole's advice, and that I had come again to Max Gate; but, as I left, I had a premonition, stronger than certainty, that I should never see Hardy again. In the autumn, after I returned to America, his death was announced, and I read, then, among other appraisals of his work, an article, by "a distinguished American critic," which contained a strange comment upon Hardy's personality. It seemed that this man of letters had called on Hardy some months before his death, and after this visit, when the convenient reporter had asked the American critic his impression, he replied in the single word, "stony." Well, if I had been asked my impression, I also might have replied in a single word, but that one word would have been, "sympathetic." . . .

But we must go back thirteen years, to the summer of 1914. Another perfect day was the one we spent with Joseph Conrad and his family at Capel House in Kent, where they were then living. Although Conrad's work, with the exception of *Heart of Darkness,* has not, in my

judgment, lasted so well, at the time of my visit to him
I was familiar with every book, and with almost every
line, he had written. And I found the man very attractive,
with a lovable personality, capricious and fascinating. His
dark, animated face, with the prominent cheekbones and
the narrow chin, held a shy woodland charm of its own.
He had a strong foreign accent, and his occasional slips
in English idiom increased the impression of other-world-
liness. Yet he was a brilliant talker, and he was never at
a loss, apparently, for a word or a magic phrase.

From the first instant of meeting, I felt we were friends,
and I was gratified when he told Louise Willcox that he
thought I was doing better work than any other American
woman novelist. He showed me some of his manuscripts,
with scarcely a word left unchanged, for he was a patient
and precise craftsman. "I'll come back next summer," I
said, lightly, as we parted; but I never saw him again.
Within a few months, England was at war, and my summers abroad came to a sudden pause. After that one day
in Kent, I have always loved the memory of Conrad; and
when he came to New York to visit his publishers, I had
a characteristic letter from him, telling me that he had
hoped to see me in Richmond before he sailed; but his
chronic malady, the gout, had attacked him, violently,
since he came to America, and he was compelled to bring
his visit to an abrupt close. It was for him, I heard, an
unhappy visit; and before I again saw England, he had
died and was resting in Canterbury. But I shall always
think of him as a lost friend, with a natural innocence
of heart which left him too utterly at the mercy of circum-

stances. One longed to defend both him and his fame from
unscrupulous exploitation.

A few evenings after we had been to Capel House, we
dined with the Galsworthys, and I remembered that Conrad had told me that he was the first person to see John
and Ada after they went away together. It was a happy
evening. Mrs. Galsworthy had (and, I suppose, still has)
a most appealing personality. She seemed to me to be the
woman he had idealized in *The Patrician*, lovely and pas-
sive, with the consecrated air that so frequently invites
martyrdom. When I looked at John Galsworthy, I reflected that it is a minor tragedy to be born either before
or after one's proper time in the world's history. He was
one of the most distinguished men, both in appearance
and in manner, whom I have ever known; and though he
was no longer in his youth, he had the features and the
bearing of the lost ages of chivalry. For he belonged, essen-
tially, as his art belonged, to the rapidly disappearing era
of the gentleman. Even before the First World War had
swept out the gentleman, as an institution, and had swept
in "the tough guy," as an authority, the foundations of
the moral order were beginning to crumble.

Much as I loved *The Country House*, I said to John
Galsworthy *The Man of Property* would always remain,
for me, his finest novel. Though the whole *Forsyte Saga*
came afterwards, I have never changed my opinion; and
I am glad I met him in 1914, when I could speak with
entire sincerity of my great admiration for his books. The
books he wrote during the war, such sentimental romances

as *The Saint's Progress* and *Beyond* appeared to me to be
obviously second best. So long as he was faithful to his
greatest creation, Soames Forsyte, he was a superb novelist; but in his later middle age, he allowed himself to
become preoccupied, in a literary sense, with the trivial
problems of the young girl. Like his central figure in *The
Dark Flower,* he was unable to divorce sex from sentimentality. But I met him before his work had softened
and thinned, and I was completely under the spell of *The
Man of Property* and *The Country House.* As a man, he
seemed to me, that evening, to represent the best example
of what English tradition could attain, aristocratic, distinguished, humane, and compassionate.

The next day he sent me an autographed copy of *The
Country House* and a copy, too, of Hudson's *The Purple
Land,* which he extravagantly overestimated. . . .

When we told the Galsworthys that the Arnold Bennetts
had asked us to tea the next afternoon, Mrs. Galsworthy
remarked in her pensive voice, "I wonder what you will
think of him." She added that she liked and admired him,
and so did John, though there were persons who considered him—I cannot recall her exact expression, but it
meant, in English idiom, "a bit of a bounder." There was
little doubt, I felt, of my liking the man who had written
The Old Wives' Tale, which I still regard as one of the
very greatest of English novels. Yet every other book by
Arnold Bennett seems to me to be as dull and thick in
texture as the novels of H. G. Wells.

So the following afternoon we were prepared to find
that we both liked and enjoyed Arnold Bennett, and that

we were agreeably diverted by his handsome, dominant, and very French wife, whom he called Marguerite. As a person, apart from his work, I found him curiously interesting; but it did occur to me that the hypercritical might consider him—well, just "a bit of a bounder." Yet, notwithstanding the controlled stutter in his speech, I could have talked with him interminably, because of the scintillating audacity of his wit. When I told him I ranked *The Old Wives' Tale* among the six greatest English novels, he promptly rejoined, "Now, let's decide on the other five!" As our choice of the other five proved to be in agreement, he began to show an increasing appreciation of my compliment; the next morning I received a copy of *The Old Wives' Tale,* with an unusually charming inscription. He basked, as most of us do, in admiration; and because of my personal feeling for that one book, he exerted himself to be brilliant and sympathetic, and to be tactful, after the usual English manner, when I did not hear. But I felt with him, as I felt with every other British author I have ever met, with the possible exception of Joseph Conrad, who was not British, that he was trying to overcome an inherent condescension toward all things American, and, especially, toward American letters. I have never met a British writer who had ever really read American literature. One and all, they appeared to regard our prose or poetry as of a single piece. Wherever we went that summer, my friend Louise Collier Willcox, a brilliant woman who wrote able criticism, was addressed, respectfully, as "Ella Wheeler Wilcox." "If only," Louise wailed at last, in desperation, "I might enjoy Ella Wheeler's international reputation, without being held responsible for her verse!"

It is true, of course, that the pre-war English novels were superior to American novels; but, then, the English had had an immeasurably longer time in which to improve the pattern and build up a tradition. What annoyed me, however, was the calm assumption that America was there, chiefly, as a clearing-house for British mediocrity. A just preference for the greater English authors, I could understand perfectly, because I shared it. But I have always resented (though resented is, perhaps, too strong a word) the ease with which English men of letters have passed over to us any inferior novelist who was unable to make a living within the boundaries of Great Britain and her Colonies. During my stay in London a farsighted poet had confided to me that he had declined to write a preface for the uniform American edition of a British novelist who did rotten work, but was such a worthy character that he had to be looked after. "Of course, anything goes in America if you send it over with the right introduction," he observed shrewdly, "but it will be a sad day when you cease to act the fairy godmother over the water."

"It will be a sad day indeed for somebody," I assented.

In the early summer of 1914 we had not turned our friends into creditors by becoming the world's pawnbroker. True, the British might condescend, but that was more an international habit than a point of offense. Louise and I went here, there, and everywhere in England, and we liked all that we saw. She had grown up in England,

and her brother, Price Collier, had left many devoted
friends in London. Henry James, for one, spoke of him
with deep affection. For, among authors great and small,
we met Henry James, now and then, in the best houses.
My dear old friend, and the friend of all the world, Mrs.
W. K. Clifford, introduced us—or so I recall. Through
her we received invitations to a reception given by the
Ranee of Sarawak, and the three of us went together. To
our great delight, we met Henry James almost as soon as
we arrived, and the ever kind Mrs. Clifford drifted off,
and left us to talk with him. Whenever we happened to
meet him, he was, invariably, imposing, urbane, and delightful; but it was a dubious pleasure to have him begin
one of his hesitating, polysyllabic, and endlessly discursive
soliloquies. Unfortunately, we saw him only in crowds,
and we were always pushed on and swept away by gathering streams of people, before he had found the exact right
beginning, middle, and end of the involved sentences he
was laboring to utter. He was, I felt, a kindly soul, but,
even in those too brief meetings and too sudden partings,
I felt also that there was a hollow ring somewhere. In
looking back, I recall that I had seen him only in the
houses of my wealthiest or my most important acquaintances. He had, I suspected, little use for the lowly; and
when one industriously sifted his moral problems, there
was little left but the smooth sands of decorum. Amiable
as he was, he seemed to me (and this may have been entirely my fault) less real in substance than the great English novelists. Placed beside Hardy or Conrad, Henry
James would have appeared, in spite of his size and his

dignity, slightly foppish in manner. Some years later, when his letters were published, I searched in vain for an intimate note addressed either to the obscure in station or to the impecunious in circumstances. Nevertheless, he was a great artist; and I have no doubt that, at heart, stripped of his punctilios, he was a simple man. We were grateful for the pleasant words and pauses he wasted upon us.

Our opportunities for observation were unlimited that summer. My brother and my sister-in-law had lived for many years in London, and they had made hosts of friends. Their charming house in Berkeley Square was gay and bright with window boxes of running pink geraniums. How lovely were the window boxes in London before the First World War! In June 1914, Mayfair was a place of abundant bloom and fragrance. Mr. Walter H. Page had been one of my close friends ever since he had discovered *The Descendant,* and he and Mrs. Page made a homelike atmosphere in the Embassy in Grosvenor Square. We dined there frequently, and met many British and American authors. I have not forgotten an amusing lunch with lovely Mrs. Stillman, no longer young, but still a veiled Pre-Raphaelite beauty. "Oh, do come again," she said, when we left. "We love to have Americans. They make such a cheerful noise in the house. . . ."

As I look back, it appears incredible to me that we should have heard no rumor or prophecy of war with Germany. Everywhere we went, people were talking, anxiously, of a possible uprising in Ulster. Ireland held the attention of the British Empire, and there was much bitterness on both sides of that forgotten dispute. Though

I talked with hundreds of well-informed men and women, not one of them alluded to the threatening war cloud over Europe.

We sailed for America the first of July—or it may have been toward the end of June. I cannot recall the date, but I remember that our boat was the German *Imperator*, and that our western voyage was unusually pleasant. Colonel Roosevelt was returning, as I recall, from his last African trip. The Walter Pages had asked him to look out for me, and a day or two after we sailed, he invited us to tea in "the imperial suite" which he occupied. "You must not think this magnificence is owing either to my affluence or to my merits," he remarked gaily. "The Hamburg-American line is still dazzled by the past glories of the Presidency."

I had not met him until this crossing, and though I was prepared for the vital charm of his manner, I had not expected his intuitive and unfailing tact. Never once, on the several occasions when I was with him, did he forget, even when he was speaking to another person, to turn slightly in my direction, or to place his voice at exactly the right pitch, neither too high nor too low. It was agreeable, of course, to find that he had read my books, and could discuss them convincingly; yet it was to his human magnetism, not to his dubious literary insight, that I surrendered. I had not wished to like him, for my particular abhorrence is the roving barbarian of the West who goes to Africa to kill animals. Had anyone told me I could ever really enjoy and like "a big game hunter," I should have laughed at the ignoble charge. Nevertheless, in spite of his savage methods with his lesser brethren of the plains and hills, I did like Colonel Roosevelt. What he needed, perhaps, to make him a great human being, as well as a great leader of men, was simply not to have been born a Roosevelt—or, failing this, another incarnation or two in some less fortunate lot. . . .

When I landed in New York, we were planning to spend the next summer abroad; but within a few weeks the First World War broke out in Europe, and life in England, as we had known and loved it, was never the same afterwards. In the summer of 1915, Carrie Duke and I went to California, and though it was beautiful, and we enjoyed it all, the impressions merely skimmed over the surface of living. Then, suddenly, New York became intolerably irksome. I had never stayed there longer than five or six months at a stretch, and my wanderings were now over. So I gave up my apartment, and returned to the old house in Richmond. Father was eighty-six years old, and old age, even the old age of the stoic heart, has its pathos. My sister Emily had died, and the splendid nurse, Anne Virginia Bennett, who had been with her as well as with Cary, had stayed on to look after Father, who, in place of personal attachment, had a strong sense of patriarchal responsibility.

When I left Richmond five years before, I told myself, passionately, that I should never return. But there is, I had learned, no permanent escape from the past. It may be an unrecognized law of our nature that we should be drawn back, inevitably, to the place where we have suffered most.

Part Five

THE YEARS OF THE LOCUST

EIGHTEEN

———◄▸———

Fata Morgana

If a note of hesitation or reluctance has crept into these memoirs, it can mean only that I have come to the one episode I dread most to live over again. If it were possible, I should wish to erase the recollection as completely as I have tried to remove all outward reminders of the incident. But one remembers, not with the mind alone. One remembers with the nerves, and the arteries, and the bloodstream long after the mind has defeated and banished the visible images. There are nights, even now, when I am awakened by a drumming along the nerves to the brain, not, it seems, from the brain downward, but in an upward march from the quivering muscles of my body. Then, while I am half-unconscious, the ghost of some old unhappiness will rush into my thoughts.

At last I recognize my dream for a buried reality, and I understand why I was in pain before I fully awakened. And, then, I ask myself, awake or asleep, how I, who worship reason, could have remained, for almost twenty years, an unwilling prisoner of unreason. How? Why? I can find no answer. We boast of our discoveries in psychology, of our arbitrary laws and inelastic categories; but all that we have acquired is a general framework for the more obvious reactions. Of that finer essence, by virtue of which one individual differs from another, which responds and recoils, not according to scientific rules and measurements, but in obedience to its own special nature, which arouses unreason in the reasonable, and enkindles hatred from the waning embers of love—of all these secret sources of behavior, we know as little in this epoch of electricity as we knew in the candlelit ages of faith.

Month by month, I have put off the moment of recognition. But fidelity to life is the sole merit I can attribute to these more or less incoherent memoirs. Their value as psychology depends upon their unqualified truth as autobiography. From the beginning, I resolved that the appeal of this book, whether or not it was ever published, should rest upon intellectual and emotional veracity, and upon that basis alone. One phase, it is true, may drain illumination from the other, and may appear to be, temporarily, in the ascendant; but the inevitable change will recur with the seasons, and then the darkened stage will recover its brightness. Never in my long experience have the dual aspects shone with equal light at the same instant. My best books have all been written when emotion was over, and the reflected light had passed on. My deepest feelings have responded only when my intellect was obscured.

But is this wandering merely an excuse for evasion? Well, no matter— In the end one must come to the point if one continues to follow the beaten path. Although this comedy of errors consumed twenty years of my life and all my illusions, including the illusion of my own disillusionment, I shall try to treat of it as briefly as possible. It killed my spirit, but it taught me much of the vast geography of human nature. When it was over, if it were ever over, I could travel, by instinct alone, through that "dark wood" of the soul, where "the straight way was lost."

It was, then, in the early spring of 1916. The war had come in Europe, and because of the war and the restlessness in New York, I had come home again. I had come back to the old gray house on the corner, where the great tulip poplars were slowly dying from the wounds at their roots and the electric wires in their branches. In that year my father died. At eighty-six, he had died, like a Roman, superbly, without fear, without reluctance, but without haste, as if he were starting off on an expected journey. I was alone, now, in the house where so many of us had once lived together. My brother Arthur was having the house restored, redecorated, and supplied with all those comforts (I remembered this with an aching heart) Mother and Cary had never known, not even when they were dying. Electric lights dispersed the thronging shadows on the staircase, and white tiled bathrooms were added to all the rooms. Yes, I was back again in the place where I had started, and in all my search, far and near, I had found nothing to which I could hold fast and say, "Here, at last, is reality."

My only companion was my secretary, Anne Virginia Bennett, who, as a trained nurse, had watched two of my sisters and my father die. She was, and is, a woman of much character, and of great natural intelligence; and since she had taken a business course before she entered a hospital, it was not difficult for her to learn the work of a secretary. But nursing was her real vocation. As soon as she put on a cap and a uniform, her talent asserted itself; and a year or so later, when America went into the war, she volunteered for the Red Cross service, and went over to nurse in France.

More than anyone else since I lost Cary, Anne Virginia has had my interests at heart; and she has shared my compassion for all inarticulate creation, and even turns that compassion upon me. For, in all the years she has lived with me, she has never really regarded writing as anything more serious than "a way." Few persons have ever felt less interest in, or respect for, the profession of letters; and, as with the other inhabitants of Richmond, some of them almost as dear to me as Anne Virginia, she has always looked with suspicion upon the "people who write." To another, and a more unreserved person, such an association, however helpful in other ways, might have appeared lacking in congeniality. But I had always done both my reading and my thinking alone. I have known intimately, in the South at least, few persons really interested in books more profound than "sweet stories." My oldest and closest friends, with the exception of James Cabell, still read as lightly as they speculate, and this description applies as accurately to the social order in which I was born, from which I had escaped, and to which I had at last returned from a long exile. Nevertheless, as I had discovered in

New York and in London, the social levels are very much the same everywhere.

I had learned of life in too hard a school to treat it flippantly. My chief concern was with the things of the mind, and, so far as I have been able to observe, the things of the mind have never, not in any place or age, received a welcome in the highest circles. When I went out to parties in Richmond, I talked of Tom, Dick, and Harry. Even if I had never heard of them before, I still talked of them. I talked of whether they were engaged or were not engaged, of whether they were to be married or to be divorced, of how much they had paid for their curtains, and whether marquisette was really more fashionable than the Brussels lace our grandmothers favored. The talk had not changed, I imagine, since our grandmothers' time; yet our grandmothers would have felt a vast difference. What had gone forever was, to them, a native element, dearer than Brussels lace, since the whole structure of their lives depended upon an invulnerable sense of reality in an illusion. Nowhere in the social life of Richmond would they have found the old inestimable air of exclusiveness. Even in the Richmond of my childhood certain imponderables were more precious than wealth. But there was only one key to unlock modern Richmond, and that key was golden. Anybody from anywhere who could afford to give a larger party became automatically, as it were, a "social leader."

There were, of course, many Virginians of the old order still living in Richmond. Here and there, one might discover an authentic antique among all the varnished repro-

ductions scattered to the far end of Monument Avenue.
Yet even in a rapidly increasing retirement, the ancient
tradition was not wholly discredited. More than one
middle-aged member of the Westmoreland Club, had remarked, over the frosted silver brim of a mint julep, that
not a single name among the dancers of the minuet at a
recent "Colonial Ball" would have been received in society
even so short a time as a few decades before. Yet, speaking truthfully, that may prove anything—or it may prove
nothing. The only point I wish to make is that, even before the First World War, elegiac airs were played out in
Richmond, and the lament for the dead was already succeeded by the regimental bands of the living. Few qualities
were more admired in the South than a native gift, however crude, for getting somewhere. Imponderables might
be respected, but possessions were envied.

Among the more recent examples of modern glaze, the
most perfect specimen in Richmond was, unquestionably,
the man I shall call "Harold." I shall call him "Harold
S——," first because Harold was not his name, and, sec-
ondly, because it was a name we used in play at the beginning of our long association. An astrologer had predicted
that under those auspicious syllables his life would be fortunate, and at the same time, a less happy selection, the
"psychic name of Varda" had been conferred upon me.
It all began in a jest, and when the jesting was over, both
names were discarded.

For many years I had heard Harold S—— criticized, not
without an acid drop of envy, I suspected; and I had con-
sistently avoided a person who appeared to combine so

many of the thriving attributes I most heartily disliked. It was related that he had sprung from a vigorous stock in Southside Virginia, that he had worked his way through the law course at Washington and Lee University, and had come, in Richmond, to a boarding-house kept by a decayed gentlewoman. A man of outstanding ability and tireless energy, he was, in that period, so eager to arrive somewhere that he injured his eyesight by studying all night in his hall bedroom and even, or so his landlady recounted, rose from a severe illness, against the orders of his physician, to attend the first important party to which he was invited. All these acts revealed a forthright spirit and a commendable zeal. When this same landlady added, however, that he always kicked away every rung of the ladder he mounted, and especially that he had never recognized her in the street since he had been able to afford a car of foreign make—when one heard these complaints, one, not unnaturally, reconsidered one's judgment, until one discovered that he was painfully nearsighted. . . .

In later years, long before I knew him, he had reached the top of his ladder and the ground below was liberally strewn—or so malice remarked—with the rungs he had kicked aside. If there is any social top in Richmond, he was standing upon it. People might laugh at him, but laughter, even satirical laughter, is an endearing impulse to any Virginian. They might ridicule his English accent (the round "o" and the long "y" had never passed his lips, they said, since his first visit to England). They might ridicule his slightly pompous manner and his too punctilious way of living. They might ridicule his English clothes, his valet, his footmen in plum-colored livery; but it was his accurate boast that only death kept them away from his dinners. An unusual intellectual endowment, a constitution of iron and an infinite capacity for taking advantage, had enabled him to attain the highest peak but one in his profession. Only the Supreme Court was denied him, and delegations of prominent Virginians soon attacked Washington, in the hope of correcting, during President Taft's Administration, that error of circumstances. Had not Harold S—— played golf with President Taft at White Sulphur Springs? Did not a more than life-size portrait of the President preside over the soft Du Barry rose curtains and cushions in Harold's well-furnished library? But it was whispered, also, with a serpent's tongue, that the chief impediment in his way to the Supreme Court arose less from the open hostility of his enemies than from the secret animosity of his friends. It was one thing to feast on diamond-back terrapin at a man's table, and quite another thing, argued the serpent, to provide the missing rungs for his ladder. Meanwhile, Harold still mounted securely. Rumor, with or without foundation, insisted that a long friendship with an Englishwoman of title had polished off the provincial edges of Southside Virginia. Certainly, some alien influence, people said, had selected the right furniture for his house, and the right vintage wines for his dinners, while it insured an endless supply of perfectly trained English butlers. At least one ancient product of chivalry, who missed no opportunity to sample either terrapin or champagne, had observed, with sprightly offense, that an older Virginia idiom still kept up a guerrilla warfare against a newer Oxford accent; and, inspired by indigestion, no doubt, he had muttered under his breath, as he nodded in his chair, before the last toast was drunk: "A pluperfect snob, sir!" . . . But all this was in Harold's earlier life, before his Red Cross activities had taught him that royalty may be democratic, though never republican, and before he had come home determined to push his way into national politics through the popular front.

Like so many witty sayings, however, this particular *bon mot* contained, not a truth, but a half-truth. The man was not incapable of perception. He was, on the contrary, made of sensitive fiber. His too rapid climbing was little more than a successful struggle to overcome an early unwarranted sense of inferiority; and though he used people a little too obviously, he used them less for selfishness than for self-improvement, a different, and not an ignoble, pursuit.

It is easy, now, to look back and to see how utterly illogical was the situation in which I presently found myself. At the time I saw only my desperate need of something—of anything to save me from the inescapable past. I felt only that an unconquerable isolation was closing in. Once I had loved loneliness, but it was loneliness of the spirit in freedom. The utter desolation of the present was different. This was a loneliness peopled with phantoms. Shade after shade, they passed before me in that first year of my homecoming. Shade after shade, they approached, looked at me, without stopping, and vanished into complete darkness. Time curved back on itself; all the years I had lived flowed into a single year. The past was the present, and past and present were equally haunted. Mother, Walter, Frank, Cary, Emily, Father. The house belonged to the dead. I was living with ghosts. They were the ghosts, too, of all I had known and loved in my life. One after another, they went continuously by me in the lonely evenings—Mother, Walter, Frank, Cary, Emily, Father—but the only shades that stopped the beating of my heart were those of Mother, Frank, Cary. Whenever I remembered those evenings with Gerald in New York, they seemed to have occurred, not in New York, but in another life, on another planet. That summer morning in Switzerland, we might have looked on the mountains in the moon instead of the Alps. All was gone now. There was nothing left of the past. There was nothing to expect in the future. What I failed to consider was my own inexhaustible vitality. Whether I desired it or not, life, in its constant renewal, would flow again in my mind and heart.

Even the creative impulse was disintegrating within. I knew that it was dead, but I did not know that when the resurrection came, that impulse would arise stronger and more vital than ever. A really fine novel, *Virginia,* had passed almost unnoticed, though it is still being discovered, but a lesser work, *Life and Gabriella,* had an unusual success. Yet I had not put my heart into that book. I knew that I had never written with the whole of myself, and I felt, now, that I should die with the best still unuttered. Philosophy, which had served me in the past, was a frail defense against phantoms. Was it not, I asked now, a phantom itself?

I was still in mourning for my father when a friend asked me to lunch on Easter Sunday. There would be only my brother and three others, she said, so it "wouldn't be a party." "I am asking Harold S——," she added, "because he wants to meet you. He is bringing Lady So-and-so and her daughter, whom he met at Palm Beach. He has known them only three days, but they are now visiting him."

I laughed. "Well, I don't care. I don't like big brothers to the rich. I don't even like the rich in any special sense."

"But he reads," she returned, impressively. "I mean, he really does."

"Oh, he reads!" Hadn't one of my best friends remarked as she kissed me good-by, at the station: "Ellen, I was crazy to read your book; but I never found anybody I could borrow it from!"

In the end I promised to go, for I reflected that few books have been written by either the rich or the titled, and any reader must have at least a bowing acquaintance with people in my own circumstances. The next day, as I walked up Franklin Street over the pale shafts of sunshine (I can still see the spring sunlight; I can still feel the air), I laughed again to think that I was really going of my own free will to meet the kind of person I had always avoided. "Oh, but the past!" I cried inwardly. "Anything that will set me free from remembrance!" If only I could forget for a moment, I might find the courage to go back among shadows.

I was early, and a little later, Harold S—— came in with Lady So-and-so and her daughter, a pretty girl, who was wearing the latest thing in orchids. Oddly enough, I noticed carelessly and recalled afterwards, that Harold had learned to enter a room, very slowly, as the leading actor walks on the stage awaiting applause. They were all animated and gay, laughing, apparently, at some secret jest which they did not divulge. I observed him for an instant over my cocktail, wondering whether he could be used effectively in a comedy of manners. My curiosity flagged. What on earth could I find to talk about to a person like that? For three days he had been enormously impressed by Lady So-and-so; and the impression, which was still visible in his face, reminded me of patterns the waves make in sand. On that morning, after a vacation in Florida, under a sun that showed obvious favoritism to the idle rich, his skin was burned, like his hair, to a deep sand color.

Let them laugh, I thought, and then: "I knew I shouldn't like him. He is merely a posture, and he thinks he is impressing me." But I knew what he didn't—that nothing really impressed me. Not since the Pyramids, anyway, or Plato, or Shakespeare—or—oh, well, certainly I was not going to be impressed by a posture. Yet, even then, I knew that all their secret merriment could not equal, for sheer audacity, my own protective ironic coloring.

The lunch was merry, and suddenly in the midst of it I realized that something had happened. Once again in my life, the unexpected had overtaken me; once again,

I was surprised by the attraction of opposites. The man I should have disliked by intuition had become the only other person in the room, and I felt, through some warning sense-perception, that, for him also, this mysterious communion, which defied analysis, had occurred. Often since then I have tried to puzzle it out, and, as often as I have tried, I have failed hopelessly. I was the last woman in the world who should have attracted him at a first meeting. All the things he respected most, I looked down upon. Trivial honors, notoriety, social prominence, wealth, fashion, ladies with titles, an empty show in the world—all these rewards of his unceasing homage left me indifferent. On his side, what was there in me to make an appeal? Nothing more, perhaps, than a defiant gaiety which piqued interest. Because I mocked at the things he worshiped, he assumed, with insufficient evidence, that I was more important than the objects of his veneration. Odd as it sounds, considering how they have invaded every class and province, authors were more unusual in his rise to place than were wearers of titles. For the moment at least, until a more important personage—a queen, perhaps—appeared on his horizon, I held undisputed possession.

For my part, I was warmed and thrilled by the man's vitality. Here was life itself, solid, eager, active, confident, undefeated. Here, if anywhere, I felt (since I had turned from Plotinus or Spinoza to Locke and Hume), is all that we can ever know of reality. And above all, here was release from the past; here was something new in experience. It is only for an hour, I thought. I have known many men, but I have known none quite like him—for a few days or weeks we may amuse each other, and after that—well, no matter— Doesn't all experience crumble in the end to mere literary material?

When we parted I knew I should see him again. What I did not suspect was that the association we were beginning so lightly would cover, with the exception of several vehement interludes, a period of more than twenty-one years.

In a few days he telephoned to ask if he might come in the evening, and when he came, the whole atmosphere of the house responded to his animation, his buoyancy, his light-hearted strength. In later years he grew heavy and somewhat pompous and repetitious, but in that first spring I responded to his mere physical presence. It was pleasant, I thought, ironically, when the latest thing in orchids bloomed elsewhere than on that English girl's shoulder.

He was writing some addresses, and we went over them. Before three weeks had passed he had fallen into the habit of coming down several evenings in the week, usually to a late supper, either in the cool dining room or by candlelight under the clustering vines over the back gallery, or porch, overlooking the garden. And gradually, with this new rush of vitality, the past loosened its chill clutch on my heart and, finally, dropped away and dissolved into itself. I ceased to fear loneliness, but I ceased also to love it. I was not myself; my very identity was altering; after a brief period of restlessness, my creative faculty sank into a trance. Was my search for reality succeeding at last? Or was the way leading only into a blind alley? My will was

flowing out again toward life. The tomb of the past had
opened. Phantoms no longer came and went through the
endless nights. True, there was none of the illumination
Gerald had cast upon people and objects. First love was
utterly different. But there was a closer touch with the
actuality. There was warmth, substance, solidarity. I had
touched the earth again, and my strength was renewed.
Harold's physical presence brought reassurance. For seventeen months out of twenty-one years we were happy together.

Although, in after years, this whole episode exercised a
profound influence over my work, in the immediate present my creative mental processes remained in a trance.
If I do not linger over this, it is because I have deliberately
avoided the current patter of Freudian theory. Instead of
molding both causes and effects into a fixed psychological
pattern, I have tried to leave the inward and the outward
streams of experience free to flow in their own channels,
and free, too, to construct their own special designs. Analysis, if it comes at all, must come later. I am concerned,
now, only with the raw substance and the spontaneous
movement of life, not with the explicit categories of science. But when I reflect that I may have included too
much, I remind myself of the rest—of all the things I might
have included—and did not. For this association taught
me much that I had not learned, not even from Gerald,
of emotion, and also of mutability. While those first years
may have turned my erratic mind toward the political
scene, quite as irrationally, they made of Harold a poet.

Once, after a sharp rift in our friendship, he, a product of the judicial sense, sat up all night to write a poem in Spenserian verse. . . .

He possessed—I have never doubted this—extraordinary ability and a sound historical judgment. Where he was not superficial, he was broad, and even fine in grain. When I met him, however, he was drifting in purpose, unsatisfied by his hard-won success in his profession; and much of his sudden interest in public affairs was directly owing to me. Yet I felt, even then, the truth of what one of his political associates said of him afterwards, that he would never win any place or any honor depending upon a popular vote. As Walter Bagehot sagaciously remarked of Gibbon, "He had arrived at the conclusion he was the sort of person a populace kills." But a populace, we must remember, often kills the wrong person.

Though, instinctively, I side with the oppressed, I am, quite as instinctively, against the victorious mob. My natural sympathies are with the underdog, right or wrong. But I could not fail to see that Harold appeared at a disadvantage among even the flimsiest democratic institutions. A background of monarchy would have enhanced his appearance, and he would have done well, I imagine, under Queen Elizabeth, who had a firm yet tender hand with her favorites.

Our differences, however, made our companionship the more interesting. It is true that both conscience and reason warned me against marriage; but it is true, also, that conscience and reason are not inflexible motives. If the First World War had not come, the shape of our lives would have been different. But the war came, and it was war that divided us. To me, though not invariably the worst choice, war is always an obscene horror. To him, though he felt the horror, no doubt, this particular war was not only a patriotic adventure, but a new and higher ladder to eminence.

NINETEEN

On Falling Out of Love

When America entered the First World War, Harold threw himself ardently into the Red Cross, and presently he led bands of eager young women in white veils marching up Franklin Street. He collected, I believe, a prodigious sum, which was all as it should have been to a humane spirit. As a reward, some envious persons hinted, the title of Colonel was bestowed upon him by the Red Cross, and he was appointed Chairman of a Commission to the Balkans. He sailed from Seattle on the first of August, 1917, and one of those clairvoyant insights, so unreasonable and so infallible, told me that something had died at our parting. Yet we were never nearer in spirit than at that moment—for we were engaged to be married. We were looking ahead to a future together—though, because of my terror of deafness, I knew then, as I had always known in my rational mind, that marriage was not for me—that so close a possessiveness was not, and could never be, what I needed from life.

On the voyage he wrote almost every day, in a kind of diary, free, natural, filled with excitement over his plans, and an unaffected longing for home. From Japan, from Russia, and farther on, I heard frequently. Then he touched the Balkans, and vanished into the silence of Rumania. After months I had my first letter from Jassy. "Since we arrived we have been very busy with work and social affairs. On Friday the Queen received the entire party at 11 A.M., and at 5 P.M. the King received all except the nursing unit. They were most cordial. I understand quite unusually so. Yesterday they entertained the Commission at luncheon. The Queen has also attended a number of private parties in our honor, granted us one private audience, and has asked me to come tonight for a private talk over work." After that, there was only the silence and darkness of war. Yes, he was undoubtedly a born executive.

In October there came word (I saw it first by accident in a cable to the *New York Times*) that the majority of the Commission would sail home, but Colonel Harold S—— had decided to remain for the winter in Jassy. A few members of his staff would stay with him. They would be surrounded by armies and no letters, barely a word of news, would be able to come through. Then, little by little, as the other members of the Commission drew nearer we heard rumors of disaffection. The Colonel was suffering, they whispered bitterly, from delusions of grandeur. He had organized the whole unit on a military basis, and had treated civilians as important as himself, if not more so, as if they were raw privates. Tales were told of . . . Oh, well, tales were told. . . . At home, gossip was seized upon, avidly; for it was more Harold's misfortune than his fault that he should invite gossip and enmity. Much was exaggerated, much was, no doubt, malicious; and all of it, when it reached America, was retold and retouched by friends who could be more dangerous than enemies. Yet, beneath the injustice, there was a grain of reason, if not of right. He could inspire respect or win admiration for his abilities, but he lacked the common humanity that sustains friendship. His fine qualities were impersonal. Men who worked with him spoke of his consideration for them, but, oddly enough, they spoke without warmth and without affection. My chief wish is to be fair, and to acknowledge whatever was just and strong and true in his character. The world of the egoist is, inevitably, a narrow world, and the boundaries of self are limited to the close horizon of personality. . . . But, within this horizon, there is room for many attributes that are excellent. . . .

Nothing else came, that winter, out of the frozen silence —nothing except rumor, except another fragment of gossip hidden among war news—or another vague innuendo. One insinuation hinted that more than a liberal share of the Red Cross money was given to Rumania. Another correspondent reported, indefinitely, that it was whispered the gallant Colonel S—— had attempted to rescue the Queen from both the Germans and the Bolsheviks. All incredibly foolish, of course. Harold was a superb organizer, and I knew, wherever he was, he was not sparing himself. But why was he fated to meet every crisis with a spectacular gesture? Afterwards, when I read, in the "Life Story" of a Balkan Queen, that, as she said farewell to a Southern Colonel, he had fallen on his knees before her and kissed the hem of her skirt, I recognized the last act of chivalry. So Harold had parted from me when he sailed for the Balkans.

When I look back on that winter, it is like a frigid nightmare, an allegory of doom. As I lay, sleepless, in the dark hours, I seemed to see the *danse macabre* whirling over the battlefields, over the dead and the dying, over all the bleached skeletons that had danced as gaily when they were clothed with flesh. In the beginning, I had shared the general hysteria, but this passed quickly, leaving me with a poignant disgust, more sickening than pain, for a world I would not have created. Camp Lee was near, and many of my friends were entertaining the officers. Several women told me it was the gayest winter, in little ways, they had ever known. On with the dance! Faster! Faster! The worst thing about war is that so many people enjoy it. And as long as so many people enjoy it, there will always be war. For the cause and cure lie not in diplomacy, but in the dark labyrinth of subconscious humanity.

Night after night, I saw, in imagination, the gangrened flesh on barbed wires, the dead, stiffened in horror, the eyeless skulls and the bared skeletons, the crosses and the poppies, the edge of the universe. Night after night! How common soldiers felt, I have never known. The privates could scarcely have enjoyed the trenches. Still, war went on and on, and, as usual in human society, the few reaped the benefits. I knew of persons who made great fortunes in the war, but they were not ever the fighters.

What I hated even more than the conflict was the lurid

spectacle of a world of unreason. I hated the black witches'
brew of intolerance and cruelty. The wisdom, or what
was left of wisdom, in the creature ironically known as
Homo sapiens, was directed toward mass murder. And
this mass murder was to make the world safe for democ-
racy. As if murder had ever made the world safe for anything but other murders! And the unconscionable stupid-
ity of it all, the prolonged boredom of a state of mind
that had sunk back into savagery. It is true that I felt
these things. Yet it is true, also, that if the evil I hated
most, if naked inhumanity had pushed its way into my
area of vision, I should have fought it with all, or with
any, weapons at my command. Only I would not kill for
diplomacy, for nationalism, for abstract idealism. Surely
the human heart is a bundle of contradictions. And the
coming generation will say, "You had your war. Now we
will have ours."

In March, Anne Virginia Bennett left with the McGuire
Unit to nurse in U.S.A. Base Hospital 45. My closest
friend, Caroline Coleman, spent the nights with me, but
I was alone all day, and my imagination could not detach
itself from the horrors in France. Of all the misery of my
life nothing has surpassed that desolation, in which my
mind lay like a drowned corpse in my body.

Then June came, and Harold returned to America. But
he remained only a short time, for his real interest was
still in Rumania. The first night in Richmond he came
down in his colonel's uniform, glittering with decorations.
"I thought you would like to see me as I looked abroad,"
he said, with innocent vanity. But at my first glance I saw

only the difference; I saw only that nothing would ever be again as it was before he had gone to the Balkans. Something had intervened. I could not give this something a name, nor even a habitation; but I felt it as one feels a foreign substance beneath the familiar earth in one's garden.

Whatever the reason, the harmony was ruffled. He could talk of nothing but the Queen and, occasionally, of the Princess Ileana. "And I said to her, 'even though you are royal, your Majesty, and I am not, I think I can understand you.'" Oh, well, I felt no interest in queens, especially in this queen, who seemed to be, as Goethe remarked of the assassination of Julius Caesar, not in good taste.

For hours—or so it seemed—we wandered round and round, in a circle that led nowhere, and avoided always the center of gravity. I, who had stayed away from the war zone, had had, in the current idiom, my "nerves shot to pieces," while he, who had spent the winter walled within a starved country, appeared well, vigorous, and eager to return to his prison. In spite of his protestations, I felt that he was not here in the present. Even when he was with me, I had that curious sense of remoteness and unreality, as if only the shell of him were moving or speaking beside me. Everything was different—but why? Why?

Right or wrong, all this may appear irrelevant; yet when the crisis came suddenly, it precipitated one of the most thrilling adventures of the mind. And because these memoirs are concerned with my inner life alone, this episode,

however incredible, cannot be omitted. As intangible as
a dream, it is still vividly real and alive in my recollection.

It was the evening, several weeks later, that we had our
first quarrel. The air was close and heavy, or it may have
been merely the emotional climate that seemed so oppres-
sive. I cannot recall the weather out-of-doors, though I
remember that it was the third of July in 1918. Harold
was to make a patriotic address the next afternoon, and
he had to read to me a carefully prepared speech. He had
invented a phrase, which, I think he told me, had made
a fine impression upon the Queen of Rumania, and he
was preparing now to test its potency upon the Virginia
patriots. *"Happiness comes only from the sacrifice of self
in the crucible of service."*

On this note our discussion ended, and we parted with
friendliness, even with my old provocative coloring of
gaiety. "Don't I always come back?" he said, as he went
out. "Aren't you the greatest thing in my life?"

Then he was gone, and looking after him, I felt, with
sudden insight, that the fault—or was it only a failure in
adjustment?—was mine alone. The shadow of my childhood was still over me. Those early bodiless fears had never
dissolved. I could not break away from that conflict of
types, of hostile elements, of long buried yet living antagonisms. In the resilience of early youth, I had tried to
make myself into something else; but I was a woman now,
not a girl, and I could not begin life over again. I had
no wish to begin life over again. Not in this moment of
searching regret for that something I had lost but had not

ever possessed. Yet, even then, it was not my own personal suffering, it was the suffocating anguish of a world at war, and never at peace, within or without, that closed over me. . . .

Every reflection of that night was bitten into my memory with acid. And, in looking back months afterwards, I asked myself if I was not being unjust. For it was true Harold had not spared himself. He had fulfilled a difficult task with honor, and with great ability. If he appeared to enjoy the war, that was a charge one might bring against many celebrated noncombatants.

But, so inconsistent is the human mind or heart, that, alone in that haunted house at midnight, I looked out upon a world from which the last tattered rag of illusion was stripped. With or without reason, the bold mortal sickness of the spirit, black, malignant, unutterably hideous, curved toward me, engulfed me, and scattered through the room, the house, the world, and the universe. Nothing, I felt, was left, not so much as the merest glimmer of faith or of desire. There was no help in religion; there was no help in philosophy; there was no help in human relationships. Ghosts were my only companions. I was shut in, alone, with the past.

This is not rhetoric. This is what I thought or felt or imagined, while I stood there, in that empty house, with the few strident noises floating in from the street, and my eyes on the darkness of the garden beyond the thick leaves on the porch. I felt, literally, that I was attacked by fear, as by some unseen malevolent power. Material or spiritual, it made no difference. I had fought long enough.

I was no longer in arms against life, or fate, or myself. Nothing mattered, nothing that came or that did not come. I did not care, for I had finished with living.

I remember that I turned off the lights in the drawing rooms, but not in the hall. I remember that I closed the blinds and bolted the French window. Presently, Carrie Coleman would come in, and tomorrow, before coffee was brought to me, she would leave to spend the day and night of the Fourth at Beechwood, her old home in the country. I remember that I went upstairs, very slowly, step by step, and I remember, too, that the past followed me, step by step. Locked in my room, safe from everything but myself and the dead, I thought only of sleep. Sleep, I must have . . . sleep, after sleepless nights, in this haunted house. Sleep, not death, was in my mind as I undressed and put out the lights. I had found some sleeping tablets left over from a last illness, and I swallowed several of these by the electricity from the street. Then, when sleep did not come, I swallowed more tablets, and still more. Now, at last, it was over, for a night or a lifetime. Sleep or death did not matter. . . .

What followed, in spite of its vividness, was merely a dream. I know that the intense vision was nothing more than the effects of a sedative, or an overdose, on the mental anguish of an overwrought mood. It was the revulsion from protracted despair, the sharp relief, the sudden cessation of torture. How soon it began, or how long it lasted, I cannot recall. All I remember is that time was, and then time had an end. One instant I was thinking that living, for a few hours at least, would be over. The next instant

I had ceased to think at all, and my bodiless fears had dissolved into vacancy. In place of thought, I felt that waves of unconsciousness, not dark and obscured, but as light and transparent as foam, were lifting me upward, were bearing me onward. A tide of blessedness was rising, was ebbing, around me. Blessedness. Once again in my life, when I thought, or felt without thought, that death was approaching, I have known this sensation, this utter awareness.

Then slowly, as the tide receded, I seemed to be stranded alone in a dream that was more real than dreaming. I was under a strange sky with a strange light flooding down on a country that was without end or horizon. On each side, spreading fanwise, were fields of luminous green starred with small flowers, like the pale spring flowers Botticelli paints in his landscapes. In the middle of these fields, which seemed infinite, a straight road ran on and on, as far as the eye could see, through the shimmering radiance of that place without end. Over this road, cut out of light, without nearness or distance, in the midst of transparent spears of grass, all the beings I had loved and lost on earth were approaching me. On they came, walking singly or in twos and threes, and as they drew nearer the distance changed from light into ecstasy. Mother, Cary, Frank, Walter . . . then my childhood's "Mammy" . . . and then Emily, Annie, Father. And running beside them in the fields, there were the familiar shapes of every dog, and every bird even, flying high overhead, that I had lost in my childhood. Nearer, nearer. Then, suddenly, as is the way with dreams, the light changed, and flickered, and died.

Pain was returning. After hours or days I could feel pain crawling over me. I could feel pain drumming back into my brain and my nerves. Nausea gripped me, like a black chill, in the pit of my stomach, and the violence was renewing consciousness, identity, utter despair. "No, no!" I cried out, thrusting off recognition. "No! No! No!" But it came on in spite of me. The old enemy was tracking me down into prison. I was caught again. My brief freedom was over. The dream, for ecstasy was a dream, had vanished forever. Still, I cried in a passion of terror and anguish, "I will not come back! I will not come back into life!"

Yet life would not release me. Though I struggled, like a small trapped animal, life would not release me. The slow drumming grew louder, grew closer, grew more insistent. . . .

The dream was gone, but it came again, at least once in the future. This, to me at least, has been the strangest part of the hallucination. Once again, when I was in unbearable physical pain, and a sedative—or it may have been a narcotic—was given to me, I had this dream repeated in every remote outline, in every unforgettable feature. . . .

We were, then, still in the horrible second summer of the First World War. For the war went on, life went on, death went on. In those months personal identity shrank to a kernel; but it was a hard, not a soft, kernel of anguish.

What did individual pain matter in the midst of a world's misery? Yet no agony is impersonal, and all suffering must be measured in the end by the individual capacity for a sense of pain. After those intolerable years, all my best work was to come. They gave me, when they had passed, a deeper source of creation, a more penetrating insight into experience, a truer knowledge of what the human heart can endure without breaking. Beneath dead and dying illusions, *Barren Ground* was taking form and substance in my imagination.

In November, Harold S—— was sent back for more relief work in Rumania. It was, I knew, what he had hoped for, and he sailed with a high heart, I imagine, on the very day the Armistice was signed. Though the war was over, our moral obligation to make the world safe for Balkan kingdoms had not ended. And what better investment could one find for easy American millions? Had not the starving peasants of Rumania (as Harold described with the right emotional tone) knelt in the road, whenever he speeded past with the Stars and Stripes floating above him?

He was so fortunate as to spend Christmas in Rome, and his letters were gay with accounts of dances and receptions. He was invited everywhere, and had met the Roman aristocrats; but he hoped to enter the Balkans as soon as he could handle his vast store of supplies. Then, abruptly, silence fell, and I knew that he was back at last in Rumania. But the needs of devastation were even more vital than the needs of war. Mystery and darkness were more impenetrable than they had been on his first expedition. In the outside world postwar rebellions were already beginning; but the Balkan kingdoms were still enshrouded in the funereal pall of an embalmed royalty.

Influenza, more fatal than war, had ravaged America. On every side people had fallen, especially the young, the hopeful, the inheritors of the future. In my house, it attacked every servant, and Carrie Coleman, who was married in January, was severely ill. As for me, I had learned that, frail as I had been from birth, I could endure anything. Only an act of God, I was convinced, could ever kill me. For months, after Carrie Coleman left me, I lived alone, except for my servants.

This also passed. Late in the summer, letters came through from Harold. By an ironic accident, two letters arrived on the same day, one telling me that he could not leave while the starving peasants in the country were still eating grass and roots, and the other letter describing a ball he had given in honor of the Queen of Rumania. The guests were all in masquerade; the illumination in his gardens was wonderful; the scene was indescribably beautiful.

In October, he returned to America. The Red Cross had withdrawn its activities, and he was returning, as he wrote, to begin again a career which had been wrecked by the war. He looked well, glossy, robust, a trifle stouter, and, as usual, immune to disaster. It was, he confessed, a little difficult at first to feel at home out of uniform. In his bountiful luggage he brought a second profusion of decorations, a half-length portrait in oils of Queen Marie, innumerable generously inscribed photographs, taken in every imaginable costume and pose, a painted miniature framed in semi-precious stones, several sentimentally inscribed and handsomely bound copies of her literary efforts, and a forlorn and pathetic Russian wolfhound from the royal kennels. Though I smiled over the inscriptions, I wept over the sad wolfhound.

It was not easy, one may suspect, to find room in a narrow house for this embarrassment of honors. Only after frequent consultations with an interior decorator in New York, did the stars and crosses find a last repose in a coffin-shaped spinet, with a glass top, which Harold placed on view in his formal and well-furnished drawing room. Upstairs, in his library, an appropriate change passed over the Du Barry rose complexion of the brocade, for the brazen stare of a President yielded precedence to the indulgent smile of a Queen.

Although we saw each other at first constantly, and then, at the end of fifteen years, more infrequently, the glamour had passed away, and life was dying in a shell that was still unbroken. Several times in those years we parted forever, as we thought, but from some obscure cause the parting was never final. Always, the tie drew us together again. For twenty-one years, the bond held.

Gradually, as this grasp weakened and relaxed, all the other parts of my nature, all that was vital and constructive, returned to life. Creative energy flooded my mind, and I felt, with some infallible intuition, that my best work was ahead of me. I wrote *Barren Ground,* and immediately I knew I had found myself. Recognition, so long delayed, increased with each book. After more than twenty-one years, I was at last free. If falling in love could be bliss, I discovered, presently, that falling out of love could be blissful tranquillity. I had walked from a narrow overheated place out into the bracing autumnal light of the world. Earth wore, yet once again, its true colors. People and objects resumed their natural proportions.

There was one more sad, gay last parting. I could look, now, into his head and see his thoughts as clearly as if they were exotic goldfish swimming, round and round, in a glass bowl. Years ago, he had longed to achieve, permanently, something outside himself; he had had his moments of greatness. At sixty-six, all that was left of a devouring ambition was a passionate desire to stay young; and with that curious illogic of so many logical minds, he had persuaded himself that to chase in circles after immature persons would restore, miraculously, the youth he had lost. It was absurd, but it was strangely pathetic. Time alone, left to its own malice, had solved both the first and the last of our difficulties. There could be no reproaches. In our tangled lives we had cared, but we had not cared enough—except, perhaps, in that cloudless harmony the First World War destroyed. After that, there was feeling, there was even happiness, but never again was there harmony. The difference, though we had not recognized this in the beginning, was fundamental, for it was rooted in the very sources of personality. We wanted to make each other over, not to accept, and abide by, the same values. True or false, we did not worship the same gods. . . . So we parted for ever, and within six months he came back with an able address he wished to read to me before he spoke at some public meeting in New York. Nothing, apparently, had changed—nothing, except that I was free. The obscure instinct that had warned me, in my early life, against marriage, was a sound instinct. I could even feel thankful, not that the First World War had come when it did, but that, in coming, the larger conflict had taken my small decisions forever out of my hands. I am now watching my niece make a valiant adjustment to that partial deafness, which, in my father's family, passes over the generations, but returns at long intervals to blight a life or a hope; and I marvel at the patience with which she appears to bear her affliction. "I have shed many tears in the darkness," she will say to me. "You know . . ." But she has both courage and endurance, and I had courage alone. . . .

Yes, it was true. I was free from chains. I belonged to myself. There was nothing to take the place of emotion, however temperate, not even hostility, not even dislike. There was, moreover, no cause for reproach against anyone in my life. Not ever, except in rare moments of futile anger against cruelty, have I been able to dislike any person I have known well; but, then, no one I have known well has been willfully or deliberately cruel. Dislike as an active motive lacks finality. One is too apt to discover some hidden reason for sympathy, or, it may be, for pity. Still, the wonder grows that love, unless it is first love, the biological imperative, should be so magnified in a life.

It was a man called Edwards who remarked to Doctor Johnson that he too, in his time, had tried to be a philosopher, but somehow cheerfulness was always breaking in. Though my quotation may not be precise, in much the same flippant manner the unruly spirit of comedy has insisted upon breaking into the tragic mood of this episode. I have tried to be grave and kind; and in spite of my effort to avoid the critical note, an irresistible sense of irony has defeated my purpose. But there is no sting in the humor. It is pure humor, inherent in the subject, and the laughter is light and gay, perhaps too light and gay, yet it is innocent of either mockery or malice.

In those years, Harold S——, who had given me so much for which I was grateful, gave me at least one perfect treasure. On Christmas Eve in 1921, he came down with a basket in his hands and told me he had just been to New York for my present. The basket, when it was opened, revealed an enchanting prize Sealyham puppy, of seven months, with a flawless head and marking, and with eyes like brown diamonds. His name was Llangollen, and I called him Jeremy, because I had always felt a liking for that name.

From the first moment, when Jeremy jumped down from Harold's arms and ran from me to Anne Virginia, and then again to me, asking if we would like him, he won and kept a special place of his own in our hearts. For the eight years he lived with us, he was a thing of joy and life in the house. Every guest who came told us that, for the first time, the old rooms appeared bright and cheerful. I doubt whether any other living creature ever came quite so close to me. His natural intelligence taught me much of both human and animal psychology, and his grasp of words and power of communication never ceased to amaze us and our friends. Sometimes, I still dream, as I dreamed every night after his early death, that I have lost him in an empty universe, and that I am searching for him through infinite space. Few persons will be able to understand, but these few will have learned more of the universal soul of things than the mass of mankind will ever imagine.

After his first year with us, Jeremy met in the street a small white poodle, who had a sunny temper but an unhappy home. They came in together one morning, running in with Anne Virginia, and going into every room in the house, upstairs and downstairs, and then out into the garden. For months after this, Jeremy would sit at the window and watch for Billy to go by in the street. Then he would bark a welcome and dash downstairs to make us open the front door. They became devoted companions, and when the year was over, we were able to buy Billy, and to rescue him from the home where he was not happy. Billy was the only dog Jeremy ever liked, or with whom he would allow even so much as a speaking acquaintance. They were never apart, but after Jeremy's death, Billy, who lived on for eight years longer, would not take the slightest notice of any other dog. He never forgot; and once, some years after Jeremy had died, when he looked through the hall and the front door, and saw us patting a white dog in the street, he became almost frantic with excitement and the hope of a return from the lost.

Not long ago, I discussed the subject of animal psychology with a physician who had risen to the peak of his profession. He agreed with me that, at its best, the attachment between a man and his dog may become a rarer and a more disinterested tie than one finds in the bond between two average human beings. I had thought him a hard man, but, to my surprise, he told me that he had never been able to recover from the loss of his dog a few years before. It is true that this dog had given more than love and loyalty, he had given his very life for his friend. "Of all the creatures I have known," this man said to me, "he is the only one I have never wanted to change. Only this morning, when I looked at his photograph, and remembered what his loyalty had cost him, I felt the tears in my eyes."

Well, so much for "the anthropomorphic delusion of grandeur."

Part Six

WHAT ENDURES

———————◄•►———————

TWENTY

England Again

"And all this beauty was in the world, was here, in England, while I looked on Main Street, and dreamed of the ugliness that is war!" The year was 1927, and the day was of that opalescent loveliness that comes only to Yorkshire in August. Caroline and I were gazing on Fountains Abbey under scattered flowers of sunshine and low drifting clouds. "All this beauty!" we repeated, together, and fell into each other's arms in sheer ecstasy. At that instant I understood why Shelley fainted when he came too suddenly upon a field of poppies.

After a visit to London, where we had stayed with my brother and my sister-in-law in their charming Moncorvo House, we had come up to Harrogate, because I had suffered a nervous breakdown, and the doctor had told my brother that I must have "the lowest blood pressure in London." Now, in the midst of drinking the waters, we had broken away, and were motoring to the ruined Abbeys and to the cathedrals of the North. When the "cure" at Harrogate was over, my sister-in-law, who was making her annual visit to Marienbad, lent me her car and her very intelligent chauffeur, for a motor trip over England. We drove slowly, lingering for a day or two wherever there was a cathedral, a ruined abbey, or an ancient almshouse; for early English almshouses have always held a strange fascination for me. "All this beauty!" we would repeat again and again. "We had forgotten that all this beauty was still in the world!"

On our way south, we stayed for several days at Ferne, with the Duchess of Hamilton, a great woman, and a great humane spirit, who is doing a wonderful work for animals. From Ferne, we went on to Salisbury, where we spent the night in order to see, yet once again, the Cathedral in the sunrise, and then, after an early cup of coffee, to drive out to Stonehenge, before the coming of day, while the Plain was still lonely. . . .

I loved the Abbey Church of Sherborne, with the Almshouse of St. John Baptist and St. John the Evangelist nestling close under the walls. This Almshouse was founded by Henry the Seventh, and the severe rules of another century are, apparently, still enforced. As we came out of the Abbey, I saw, in the cloisters, several old women wearing attractive red capes, and stopping before the archway, we asked the name of the building.

"This is the Sherborne Almshouse," replied the liveliest of the old women. When we begged leave to come in, she called the Prior, Mr. Phillips, a distinguished-looking old gentleman, in a long blue coat, with large and shining buttons, which I recall but vaguely as silver or brass. He had a charming manner, and he was, probably, Thomas Hardy told me later, a retired clergyman or a schoolteacher. In the chapel, he showed us the original altar-piece, and the pewter service, given, I think, by Henry the Seventh. Before we parted, the Prior gave me a little crystal bowl from his own chest of drawers. I kept this gift for years, and it was broken only a week ago, by a careless maid.

We talked, for a while, to the old women, and when I said to the liveliest one, "I wish I had a red cape like yours. It is very becoming," she retorted, with spirit, "You wouldn't want it if you were made to wear it!" This, I admitted, was certainly true, and even more certainly human.

After lunch, before motoring on, I found a shop near by, and I sent sweets to all the old women, and to the old men I sent enough tobacco to last them for a month. But the tobacco appeared to me to be of poor quality, so, in the autumn, after I returned to Richmond, I sent the Prior as much Virginian Edgeworth tobacco as a friend who sailed that week for England was able to take. My friend wrote me that he had paid the duty, and that he had put the tobacco safely on the train for Sherborne Almshouse. A month later I had a pleasant letter from Mr. George Phillips.

When I told Thomas Hardy of my special interest in old almshouses, he said he understood, because he had always felt the same way; and he urged me not to miss the Dorchester Almshouse, which was founded in the thirteenth century. I may not recall the date accurately, but I remember very distinctly our visit the next morning. It was a dismal and dreary place, with a moldering look

to the high projecting arches, which hung over the street.
Dickens might have written of the one old woman and
the seven old men that it sheltered. The old woman held
us in endless talk, shivering from dampness, while she
abused the seven old men as heartily as if she were married to each and all. Not only did she have to do their
washing, she told us, but they were so lazy they would
not even get up to fetch their own pipes. The worst one,
she added, was a retired sea captain, huddled, at the moment, on a stone bench in the gloom of the entrance.

I can write of the almshouses and of their inmates; but
I cannot write of the cathedrals. When I say that, for me,
the English cathedrals are the most satisfying of all Christian churches, there is nothing more I can add. The world
of beauty, as we knew it, as the Egyptians and the Greeks
knew it before us, is becoming a lost world to our younger
generation. In the things we thought grotesque, the ape-
like female figures, the bulging breasts and hips, the pro-
truding mouths, the grossly primitive gestures—in all these
things, they are able to discover new forms of beauty,
though, inconsistently, it would appear, they continue to
demand flatness in the figures of living women. But the
gospel of an industrial age is not confined to the primitive.
"There is more real art in a railway track," a modern art
critic remarked, recently, "than there is in a cathedral
spire." Well, well . . . We have had our day, and it was
a long day. As I look up from my desk, my glance falls
on the divine head of Nefertiti. . . .

But we are still talking of almshouses. On our last afternoon at Glastonbury, when we lingered on, for hours of

parting, at the Abbey ruins, we stumbled, quite by accident, upon a row of tiny cottages beyond a crumbling
stone archway. This was one of the delights of finding old
almshouses. We never looked for them; they came as an
unexpected blessing wherever we found them. Entering
the archway, we found that each cottage had in front of
it a special doormat garden of flowers. One of these gardens, scarcely larger than a single flowerbed, was planted
with roses, which bloomed gorgeously, as fine as any hot-
house roses we have in America. While we paused to admire them, an old woman came out of the one-room cottage, and introduced herself and her daughter. She was
a Mrs. Curtis, and her daughter, a frail pretty girl, who
limped after her, was suffering from tuberculosis of the
hip. They told me what had brought them there, to the
bleak poverty of that English almshouse. The husband
and father, a good carpenter, had died in an accident;
for a time Mrs. Curtis had tried to make a living by sew-
ing; then, after the war, things had become rapidly worse
for them; and, at last, the girl, who was a fine seamstress,
had become too ill to work. The neighbors had tried to
help; but they also were poor; and, in the end, there was
nothing left but the almshouse and the meager dole it
provided. They were allowed a few shillings a week. They
told me the sum, but I have forgotten. What I can never
forget is the vital personality of that old woman, and the
courage that looked out of her eyes into mine. She was
small and plain, with reddish gray hair and bowed shoulders; but she made me ashamed, not only of myself, but
for my world. The cottage was spotlessly neat, and she

must have spent hours of toil over her roses. She had raised all her roses from slips, and when I was leaving, she asked what color rose I loved best. I said, "Yellow roses are mine," and she told me she would raise a yellow rose from a slip, and name it "Ellen Glasgow." The next Christmas I sent her a present; but, after that, my own despair of life overwhelmed me, and nothing is more self-sufficient, or more selfish, than despair. Some years later, when the friend who was with me in 1927 went back to Glastonbury, she stopped at the almshouse and asked for Mrs. Curtis; but only one old woman remembered her and her roses. The roses were all gone, and her cottage was occupied by a stranger.

We had fine weather that summer, and a glorious trip over England. I loved it all, except the industrial towns, and the misguided effort in a few parts of England to copy the worst of America. My shock was great when I found American service stations approaching Canterbury; and I reminded Caroline that President Alderman, of Mr. Jefferson's University, had called American filling stations "the painted harlots of architecture, open day and night to all comers. . . ." But more of this after my last visit. . . .

There was an August afternoon, alone with Caroline, on Dartmoor, that we shall always remember as one of the most beautiful of our lives. We had driven out from Tavistock, where we were staying, and after leaving our car in the road, we wandered, on and on, for hours, in a glow that transfigured the earth. I have always loved moorland country, and Dartmoor, like the moors of Yorkshire, was akin to something, deep and inarticulate, within myself. In the sunset and the afterglow the whole world looked as if it were created of light. And we were absolutely alone with the earth as God made it, alone in that stillness and color and illumination. . . .

Among other unforgotten days of that summer, I recall one we spent, at Long Barn, with the Nicolsons. I admired their work, especially V. Sackville-West's poem, "The Land"; and it was pleasure to find her both beautiful and charming. After lunch, we walked, through the woods, to Knole, and went, at our leisure, over the house and the grounds. Harold Nicolson remarked, "This is the servants' day off," which sounded quite homelike, while he reached for the bunch of huge old keys by the door. I have wondered since why they should have taken so much trouble for strangers. Our only bond was the same publisher; yet they cheerfully gave up a whole day to us; and we saw Knole at its finest and its loneliest, with V. Sackville-West, who knew and loved every nook and cranny of the wonderful place. On the drive back to London we asked each other, to the amusement of Mr. Evans, my publisher, if English people were, after all, more hospitable than Americans—or, even, than Virginians. . . .

There was more, much more of that summer; but I must leave it, where it still lingers in a glow of memory. We sailed for home in September, and life began again, without a break, as I had known that it would.

On the fifth of September, 1929, Jeremy died, and, for months afterwards, I dreamed every night that I was try-

ing to find him, and he was trying to find me, in a vast
emptiness. Night after night, we were both lost in a black
universe, without moon or stars, alone with the wind. It
was Caroline, I think, who persuaded me to go back to
Harrogate, in 1930. The treatment there had been good
for me three years before, and I had loved Yorkshire.
This was to be my last English summer, but I was too
ill, nervously, to do more than enjoy it in snatches. In
London, where we spent a week, I forced myself to keep
up, and there were several bright and happy occasions.
I met, for the first time, Radclyffe Hall, whose *Adam's
Breed* I admired tremendously, and she asked us, after
one of those sudden friendships, to visit her in Rye, when
we returned from Harrogate. We found, too, our dear
friends, Carl Van Vechten and his enchanting wife, Fania
Marinoff, and they took us for an interesting day to the
Caledonian Market. The scene mingled Dickens with
Hogarth; and we went early enough to pick up a dog in
old Staffordshire ware for my collection. But my strength
was not equal to my enjoyment of London. A week later,
when I reached Harrogate, my doctor insisted upon my
going straight to a nursing home.

The modern hospital was crowded, so I engaged a room,
or my good Dr. Watson engaged it for me, in an attractive
old stone house, which must once have been some kind of
cloister. I lay in bed, in a damp room, with an open fire
in July, and looked out on a deep garden, where rows of
tall pink foxglove were blooming against a dark wall. In
the afternoon I watched the nurses, in their blue veils,
having tea in the center of the flower-beds, indifferent

alike to the beauty and the dampness and an occasional silvery shower. Only in England, I imagine, could one find such a place, and had I ever been warm and dry, I should have enjoyed the change. I became, as usual, quite attached to my nurses. The night nurse—there was only one for the entire house—would run in for a chat, between bells, from midnight till dawn, when my private nurse was off duty. What irritated me, however, was the fawning subservience of all the nurses, from the matron down, toward any doctor. When I asked my special nurse why they trembled with fear or with respect whenever a physician appeared, she smiled sweetly, and replied, "It's the way English doctors like to be treated."

That was a rainy summer, and in other ways disappointing. When we went out for our glasses of hot water before breakfast, we wore high galoshes, and at last I put on the first raincoat I had ever owned in my life. Many plans had to be abandoned, for the rain never stopped, except for a few hours at a time, and the continual dampness brought on one of my worst attacks of neuralgia. We saw Fountains Abbey, more beautiful than ever, through a silver film, and when we tried to walk at lovely Mount Grace Priory, we sank knee-deep in water. Yet whenever a pale finger of sunshine pointed down on the lawns of the Hotel Majestic, we would see a dozen variegated sunshades open, like flowers, over smooth British heads.

After a month with the waters of Harrogate, we went up to Scotland and saw, at Edinburgh, the only modern war memorial that has ever deeply impressed me. The Duchess of Hamilton asked us to spend several days at

Dungavel, and we found there, to our great pleasure, the splendid Miss Lind-af-Hageby, whom we had known and loved at Ferne, in 1927. We had fine weather, too, in Scotland, and this stayed with us until autumn.

Our visit to Rye will always remain among my happiest memories of that summer. Radclyffe Hall and her friend Una Troubridge lived in a fascinating Henry the Eighth house, which had been, they told me, recently excavated. They were, like all our other English friends, hospitable in a way that approached genius. We felt that we had known them all our lives, and we liked, too, Sheila Kaye-Smith and her husband, Penrose Fry, who dined with us the first evening. Radclyffe is an extraordinary woman, with a sensitive, humane, and lovable nature. She has had, in many ways, a tragic life; but I have never known greater courage, and few human beings can equal her in charity, in loyalty, or in magnanimity.

So ended our last summer in England. My sharpest regret was that I had not met Virginia Woolf. I had a pleasant greeting from her, but I had sailed before she returned to London in October. There was something else that troubled me, and this was my feeling that the English themselves were doing their best to spoil the beauty of England. I had seen the slaughter of trees; I had seen a quick and flimsy American style of architecture (if it may be called that) springing up like toadstools after a rain; I had seen Stonehenge threatened, and the approaches to Cathedral towns made unsightly. "If you love the English countryside don't go back," Clare Leighton

warned me as early as 1927. "Everything is sacrificed to
speed and to the ugly coast to coast roads."

Before sailing, we spent several weeks in Paris, where even
the sunshine held a September chill, and the leaves were
changing to a pale sad yellow in my favorite Parc Mon-
ceau, with its absurd monument to another favorite of
mine, Guy de Maupassant. Caroline had known a different, and a more modern, Paris than mine, for she had
been with friends who offered her, not history, but spring
or autumn displays of fashions, champagne cocktails at the
Ritz, and delectable luncheons or dinners in expensive
places. Although I was attracted by dresses and hats, my
chief interest was in the older background of Paris, and,
for me, the two most exciting, if not the most important,
events in history were the massacres of Saint Bartholo-
mew's Eve and the French Revolution. So the next morning we went, first of all, to the Church of St. Germain-
l'Auxerrois, whose bell once rang the tocsin of death, and
tried to imagine La Reine Margot in the ancient château
of the Louvre. The past came to life for us, and we
breathed the close, decaying, vaguely sinister atmosphere
which seems still to cling about the sudden arches and the
crooked streets of old Paris. Every morning we lost ourselves and wandered for hours. We made no plans; we
consulted no tourist guide; we strayed down any street
that tempted us, retracing my walks in other years, when
Caroline was not with me. Since she had always associated Paris with the immediate present, she was fascinated
by the vivid drama which was now finished, and all but

forgotten. A few memories glow with light in the dimness.
. . . A soft golden afternoon within the high walls of the
old Carmelite Convent. We had seen the corridor and the
door through which a hundred and twenty priests were
flung down to be butchered. Looking, through the trees,
on the scene of the massacre, we saw, outwardly, a quiet
garden sleeping under a slow rain of leaves. A priest and
a little girl were sitting on a bench in the sunshine. Otherwise, the only life in the garden was the stir and fall of
a summer that was now over. . . . Another afternoon,
still faintly golden and autumnal, in a place of poignant
memories. We are in the little Cemetery of Picpus. Again
life has hidden death, we think, in the Martyrs' Field of
the convent chapel. Lafayette is buried here, but, for me,
Jean Valjean, who was never buried, lives more vividly.
. . . Long mornings in the Louvre . . . The hour before sunset in the Luxembourg Gardens . . . Yet one
more memory. The gate of the Conciergerie is opened for
us, and we give our card to a man in a small dark room
where a bird lives in a cage. The bird in the cage is the
first thing I notice; for whenever anything is caged, either
in the prison of facts or the prison of memories, I am
there. Years before, I had seen the Gothic hall and the
dismal cells; but this was Caroline's first and only visit,
and she was interested and excited. As we went on, the
guide and I talked of the Revolution and, presently, we
fell to discussing the figures in that splendid and sordid
drama. A small curious crowd of visitors gathered about
us in the cell of Marie Antoinette; but we thought nothing of this until, as we were leaving, the guide left his

fresh group of tourists, and ran after us. "Will you tell me," he whispered to Caroline, "the name of that American lady? She knows more of the Revolution than any American I've ever taken over the prison. She was really a help to me." And this proves not how much I know of history, but how little the other Americans had even suspected. Still laughing, we passed from those dark towers into the sunlight on the quai de l'Horloge. . . .

At the end of our summer in England, when we decided that a glimpse of Paris was necessary, I felt a sudden pinch of economy. After the surface gaiety and, for me, the unusual extravagance of the Hotel Berkeley, in London, it was restful to sink into the faded background of the old Wagram in the rue de Rivoli. We had large old-fashioned rooms on the unquiet third floor, but we found the perfect treasure of a room waiter, who made, especially for us, delicious American coffee, which he served in an American percolator of plentiful size. Five days before we sailed, I was caught, in a cold driving rain, on a refuge between the rue de Rivoli and the rue de Castiglione, and when at last I reached my hotel, I was seized with an attack of French influenza. During the whole of my illness, and I left my bed only to take the boat, our excellent waiter cooked for me appetizing little dishes, when he found that I could not relish the table d'hôte. He was sympathy itself, and though I have forgotten his name, I still recall his untiring service, and I should be more than glad to hear that he has survived the worst hardships of war and famine. Even in time of peace, the lot of a waiter in Paris is far from easy. Though I tried to show my appreciation, I wish it had been possible to do more. He was young and thin and pale, and he told us of his home on a farm in the country. . . .

Between two world wars, I went for a third visit to Europe, but never again to England, the country I love best after my own. Years before, my friends, Mr. and Mrs. John Kerr Branch, had bought the Villa Marsilio Ficino, at Fiesole, and Mrs. Branch, now a widow, asked Caroline and me to spend with her the month of June, in 1937. This villa, which was, originally, a gift from Lorenzo de' Medici to Marsilio Ficino, after his translation of Plato, had been restored to its charm, and the gardens were, once again, a paradise of flowers and fragrance. Every evening we dined on the terrace overlooking a hillside of olive orchards, and while I undressed by moonlight, I could follow the white road, bordered by cypresses, which ran on to Fiesole. We had landed at Naples on the twenty-fourth of May, and though I had never cared for Naples, either dirty, as it used to be, or clean, as it is now, I adored Ravello, where we spent two days at the pension Caruso, in the old Afflitto palace.

All Italy appeared happy and prosperous that summer, for the Second World War was still below the horizon. There were no beggars with sores, and indeed there were no beggars at all. People were smiling as they worked, and there were so many children, all plump and rosy brown, that we could barely cross the street without stepping on one of them. Yes, everyone appeared happy, except the wretched half-starved little donkeys hauling stones to build the steep roads in the Apennines. In spite of Christian tradition, which is so often at war with Christian conduct, I suppose the overladen and ill-treated donkey will be the last creature to find justice, or even mercy, in the Catholic world.

Every morning we went into Florence, and I saw again, after many years, the galleries and the churches. When I spent an hour before *The Birth of Venus,* and the entire morning in that unchanged Botticelli room, I felt that all the years and even time itself were a fantasy of the mind.

But our day of days came when we motored up to La Verna, in the high peaks of the Apennines. Here, in the greatest of the Little Poor Man's monasteries, among the blessed ever-singing birds, we shared the Friars' soup, and spread on the refectory table the abundant lunch our kind hostess had brought for us. The Friars received gladly the sandwiches and the salad and the sweets, and especially a basket of fine cherries, which, they told us, were the first cherries they had tasted that season. After lunch, the organist, Padre Virgilio Guidi, who reminded me of the monk in Giorgione's (no, never Titian's!) *Concert,* played, for us alone, in the deserted church, among the sacrificial gifts of artists, who had loved, though they had not followed, St. Francis.

Of all these things, I am able to write; but I cannot write of the green solitude in the midst of those gray rocks, nor can I write of that deep cleft in the mountain's side, where the Little Poor Man made his bed on the moss and ferns, with the dark pines standing above him. . . . I cannot write of the bliss and the agony through which

the human soul must pass in its supreme hour of miracle—
or of illusion. For the air in that solitude was still brushed
by the passing, centuries ago, of that miracle—or of that
illusion. Outward or inward vision? What does it matter?
In that place, at that unforgotten moment, "the only
Christian since Christ" had found his Christ. Or had he
found, instead, "the flight of the alone to the Alone"? . . .

At the end of June I left Italy and Europe forever. . . .

TWENTY-ONE

Rootless Years

The nineteen-twenties were rootless years in American literature. They began well, those years, with an earnest revolt from parochial smugness and village *mores*. But it was not long before the rebellion broke away, also, from reason, broke into a desultory guerrilla uprising of the primitive, and into a final tremendous assault upon the intellect, along the popular front. The war had been the great liberator of instinct, and by the time the war was over, the new prophets of Freudian psychology were crying aloud to the multitude. All the bold young men, from the Middle West, were learning about America on Paris boulevards; and Bergson's theory of the *élan vital*, evolved, rather than formulated, in the early years of the century, was now filtering down into the lives of people who had never heard of Bergson, or indeed of any wiser philosophers. Sensation was so effortless, so unbridled, so direct in motive, and so democratic in method. Intellect, on the contrary, was a difficult master. Sensation was a lavish gift at birth, while only the minority, at any age, were endowed with the faculty of intellect. Moreover, it was flattering to discover that everybody possessed philosophy without knowing it. Monsieur Jourdain had become, overnight, the pattern of an age. The intellect, with its record of long service and of rigid systems, was condemned even by its former disciples. Sitting on the boulevards, the young men from the Middle West looked beyond the honest realism of *Main Street* and of *Babbitt* into the distorting mirror of America seen from abroad. One need not make an effort; one need not apply one's mind to a problem. Novelists and critics alike were tumbling, head foremost, into the soft modern theories. Nothing, any longer, was complicated. Everything was made easy, and intuition was sounder than reason. Acceleration, the mania of the period, set the pace of the movement. The more shallow and formless and flimsy a book appeared, the more certainly it would prove to be a work of effortless genius, predestined to reach a vast audience, which also was effortless. There was a wide rebellion against sentiment, but not against sentimentality, so long at least as its object was estranged from standard rules of behavior. Gamblers in liquor and nymphomaniacs in green hats met and mingled and hilariously populated whole areas of American fiction. The cult of the hairy ape and the "mucker pose" came later, in the nineteen-thirties, when the most casual reader of murder mysteries could infallibly detect the villain, as soon as there entered a character who had recently washed his neck and did not commit mayhem on the English language. The attraction of horror is a mental, or even an intellectual, excitement, but the fascination of the repulsive, so noticeable in contemporary writing, can spring only from some rotted substance within our civilization. . . .

Yet what a relief for tired minds! What a comfortable breaking down of invisible barriers! Sensation alone was enough. In sensation there is movement, speed, action, while reason, like Rodin's thinker, is confined, eternally, in an attitude of repose. . . .

When this book is published, if that ever happens, the name of Freud may have been long, or perhaps latterly, discredited. One thing we may be sure the time element will exact of the future, and that is an ultimate penalty for unbalanced fame. It may be that dreary Behaviorism will have triumphed. It may be that some newer prophet will have refuted all the present high-sounding theories. Nevertheless it is true that the novel, as a living force, if not as a work of art, owes an incalculable debt to what we call, mistakenly, the new psychology, to Freud, in his earlier interpretations, and more truly, I think, to Jung. These men are to be judged by their own work, not by the excesses of a secondary influence. For my part, though I was never a disciple, I was among the first, in the South, to perceive the invigorating effect of this fresh approach to experience. That the recoil went too far does not dishonor its leaders, for it is a law of our nature that every dynamic recoil should spring too far backward. Moderation has never yet engineered an explosion, and it requires an explosion to overturn a mountain of prejudice. Meanwhile, what had once been the profession of letters became, overnight, the practice of journalism. . . . And still I waited. . . .

My mind was thronging with ideas. My imagination was more vital and urgent than it had ever been. I felt that a tombstone had been lifted; but, even while I felt this, I knew that my health was lost, and forever. I had never been strong, except in will, and I knew that many of the past twenty years, though not all of them, had been wasted. Yet, in spite of the physical odds against me, I had begun to write my best books in the middle of the nineteen-twenties. After *Barren Ground,* which I had gathered up, as a rich harvest, from the whole of my life, I had written and published two comedies of manners: *The Romantic Comedians* (surely, as many critics have said, a flawless work of its kind) and *They Stooped to Folly.* In the early nineteen-thirties, I wrote *The Sheltered Life* and *Vein of Iron.* As a whole, these five novels represent, I feel, not only the best that was in me, but some of the best work that has been done in American fiction. Though, in these memoirs, I may appear to pass but casually over my books and my methods of writing, I have treated both these subjects with complete candor in a book of self-criticism called *A Certain Measure.*

If only I could keep my health, this, I felt, was the beginning of my really significant novels. If only . . . At sixty, I was hopelessly frail, yet, in some incredible way, I was more vital than ever. My physical weakness, after the heartbreaking strain of a divided life, appeared to lend light and warmth to my imagination. Pain had not defeated me. It had made me defiant and more confident of my inner powers. Though it sounds absurd, it is true to say I felt younger at sixty than I had felt at twenty.

Perhaps my belated youth may have prolonged my maturity. I do not know, nor do I know whether it is a blessing or a curse to have the life within more vigorous and enduring than the fortitude of the body. "Take my word for it," Dr. James Southall Wilson wrote to me at this time, "you have something that you can't know yourself which will make even a Modern Language meeting you take part in come alive."

I was no longer searching for a philosophy to live by. Years before, when I began *Barren Ground,* I knew that I had found a code of living that was sufficient for life or for death. It was a matter so purely personal that I was never able to formulate it, explicitly. The nearest I came to doing this was in a brief essay I once wrote for a book called *I Believe,* a symposium of personal philosophies.

A sensitive mind would always remain an exile on earth, and regarding life itself I had preserved no illusions. But there was something within my own consciousness—some apprehension of truth or pity—to which I owed loyalty. Although I felt no obligation to endure the unendurable, I had long ago decided that it was easier to suffer than to make suffer, and my nerves more than my will shrank from any act that would increase the sum total of pain. I loved happiness, and I hated cruelty, and it was my unhappy lot, or perhaps merely my too acute perceptions, that found cruelty more common than happiness. It is true that I recognized no obligation toward an unknown and invisible Power. I had ceased to believe that ideal goodness, or indeed anything ideal, existed as an abstract Reality in the universe. Yet within myself I found a sense of justice and compassion that I could not betray. The pious might receive this as moral evidence of the Divine nature. The skeptic would, no doubt, ascribe it to the long result of evolution. For my part, I had no quarrel with either, or with any other, interpretation. The question of whether or not a God ruled the universe had no bearing whatever on my private belief that it was better to be humane than to be cruel.

In one respect, growing older was a complete disappointment. I had hoped—and this expectation was founded on literature and philosophy—that time would act as a sedative on my nerves, and my imagination would become less sensitive to the horrors of a world I would not have created. But I appeared to be, as usual, a solitary exception.

Shreds of horror remembered from a newspaper would become entangled in my thoughts, and I would live them over and over at night, awake and asleep. A man arrested for stealing a loaf of bread, and hanging himself in his cell. A child kidnaped and murdered. A lost dog hounded to death. For months, even for years, I was tortured by a fire at the Stockyards at Richmond, where a hundred and fifty horses were trapped and burned. Then the fire at the overcrowded Ohio State penitentiary. Politicians might rest easily after refusing to build a modern prison, but I endured the torment, vicariously. And all the primitive cruelties of hunting and trapping. All the unspeakable horrors of vivisection. All the hopeless misery of animal lives in a hostile world. All the Pharisaical righteousness of civilized man. "Your skin is too thin to protect your nerves," a physician once said to me.

But in this later period my life was expanding. Between fifty and sixty I lived perhaps my fullest and richest years. Though my deafness still tortured me, and I could never overcome that raw, aching sensitiveness in the presence of strangers, I was able, in appearance at least, to rise triumphantly over misfortune. I made many friends. Whenever I went to New York in the spring and autumn, I fell into the habit of seeing people who spoke my own language. In Richmond, it is true, I was still socially submerged in personalities, like everyone else; but in New York, I formed gradually a wider circle. Cocktail parties, I persistently avoided (in my whole life I have not been to more than five or six literary teas); but my own friends would come to me, and very slowly, at long intervals, I selected the group I found most congenial.

Still, in New York, as in Richmond, my friendships are enduring. I have an unchanging warm affection for Irita Van Doren, for Stark Young, for Donald Adams, for Henry Canby and his lovely Marian, for Eleanor and Van Wyck Brooks, for Bessie and Howard Jones, for Norma and Herschel Brickell, for Fania Marinoff and Carl Van Vechten. Another dear friend, lost to me now, was Sara Haardt, the wife of Henry Mencken. I loved her, and I like and enjoy him.

I have admired few women so fervently as I have admired Irita. Beautiful in body, and invincible in spirit, all her defeats in life have been victories. If one is condemned to serve a life sentence on earth, I am fond of saying that one should ask to be born either like Irita or like Caroline Duke. As my old colored mammy would have said of them, "When you're marked for happiness, your spirit will never be broken."

When I first met Eleanor and Van Wyck Brooks, I felt that this also was a predestined friendship. They have that rarest of gifts, the faculty of mental and emotional insight. I had, for many years, admired Van Wyck Brooks's work, and I feel that he stands very nearly alone as a critic of American life and letters. Eleanor has extraordinary charm tempered by understanding. I can think of no marriage that has been more successful; and I wonder how much of his sanguine outlook is owing to his marriage? How important, after all, is marriage, for good or bad, in the life of a writer?

"You are wise," I sometimes say to Stark Young; "a writer, especially a novelist, should stay unmarried." But, when I pause to reflect, I think of the many satisfactory marriages I have known among writers in New York. It is true that they seldom move in circles, for whatever marriage may do to one's inner life, I am convinced that coteries are destructive. But happiness is something apart from the crowd; and I cannot think of Henry Canby without Marian, just as I cannot think of Van Wyck without Eleanor, or of James Cabell without Percie. . . .

James, who has survived the blighting frustration of every artist in the South, is absurdly spoiled by the efficient and practical Percie. He is so dependent upon her that he cannot be persuaded to go out to dine when she is ill, and he refuses obstinately to make a trip to New York unless she is able to drive. They are today what they have always been—kind, tolerant, civilized. James and I share the same sense of wit, though not precisely the same sense of humor. Our laughter at fate and at ourselves may be equally sardonic, but mine, I think, is more human, while his remains the disembodied mirth of Olympus. Never, at any time, he remarked somewhere, has he wasted an hour either deploring or resenting the universe, or suffered a pang over any mortal happening, however tragic, that he could not prevent. . . . Yet one never knows when it is wise to discredit an artist in words. Only a few evenings ago, this Olympian cynic confided to me that he awoke every night, at the exact hour of three o'clock, and moaned aloud over some act he could not remember, though it filled him with remorse. "And then, when Percie tells me to stop moaning, I take a pink pill from my bed-table."

"I also wake engulfed in horror," I said, in my turn, "but mine are all horrors with which, even in my dreams, I had nothing to do. My soul is the last unwilling scapegoat of Predestination."

The gift of imagination has been, with me, a divided endowment, and has run in two separate and dissimilar veins. Whenever I have worked one vein to the end, I find myself recoiling upon the other and seeking a fresh stimulus. This double system has prevented my "writing out," as so many novelists, particularly American novelists, have done after their earlier books. *Barren Ground* left me drained, but only in one capacity. Immediately, my imagination reacted from the novel of character into the mood of polite comedy. It required three comedies of manners to exhaust this impulse toward ironic humor, and not one of these books betrays, I think, the slightest sign that I had burned up my energy. After the long emotional strain of *Barren Ground,* my first comedy, *The Romantic Comedians,* seemed to bubble out with an effortless joy.

Although the primitive in art may be both interesting and impressive, as portrayed in American fiction it is conspicuous for dullness alone. Drab persons living drab lives, observed by drab minds and reported in drab writing—what other impression will be left in the memory? "An undistinguished victory," a critic, writing in 1935, has called this rising tide of uniformity. And he continues: "The outstanding characteristics of this literature seem to be that it deals only with the most ordinary people and things, and that it speaks a language scrupulously devoid of distinction. Because it is worded as the street talk of the uneducated it has a novel flavor, and because it is sordid it holds a gloomy fascination. Also, in its implication that nothing can be special or splendid, it is as depressing as the grave. . . . No critic would dare to be harsh with it, for it may be the literature of tomorrow. That makes it even more depressing."

Not that it matters. As long as one hated dullness and refused to be drab either in fact or in fiction, one might cast one's lot with a small but gallant band of irreconcilables. Mediocrity would always win by force of numbers, but it would win only more mediocrity. And this, also, would pass. Pollyanna and proletarian—were both protesting merely "the right of the ordinary to occupy the spotlight"? Yet, depressing or otherwise, we may make, even in the nineteen-thirties, another choice. In the midst of a colorless flood there are lighthouses. Virginia Woolf and Santayana are still writing—and there are others. Within the present decade, perhaps within the present year, which is 1937, the greenness of the moron may become as little sought after as the ripeness of the wise. . . .

An unsentimental republic might have discovered the moron, as it discovered sex, with more understanding and less romance. But America has enjoyed the doubtful blessing of a single-track mind. We are able to accommodate, at a time, only one national hero; and we demand that that hero shall be uniform and invincible. As a literate people we are preoccupied, neither with the race nor the individual, but with the type. Yesterday, we romanticized the "tough guy"; today, we are romanticizing the underprivileged, tough or tender; tomorrow, we shall begin to romanticize the pure primitive.

The result of this tendency has been, of course, the general softening and weakening of our national fiber. One may share the generous wish that all mankind should inherit the world's beauty, without consenting to destroy that beauty because it is beyond the reach and the taste alike of the vast majority. For beauty, like ecstasy, has always been hostile to the commonplace. And the commonplace, under its popular label of the normal, has been the supreme authority for *Homo sapiens* since the days when he was probably arboreal.

After thirty years collectors and colleges are asking me for my original manuscripts; but they are asking exactly a generation too late. When I left home, as I thought for-

ever, in 1911, after the tragic death of my sister Cary,
I left all my manuscripts, in my own handwriting, and
a number of letters I valued, put away on the high top
shelf of a deep old closet in the upstairs hall. In my absence Emily, another sister, the eldest of us all (and divided by an uncomprehending generation from Rebe and
myself), came, with her husband, to live with Father. In
1916, I returned to find that my housekeeping sister had
burned every manuscript and every letter, and that the
highest shelves of the closet had been scrupulously
scrubbed and cleared of all literary associations. . . . At
the time I was too ill to care or to feel annoyed; but I
can wonder, as the years pass, whether that particular incident could have occurred anywhere except in the South,
where, throughout the centuries valuable records and innumerable interesting diaries and letters have been treated
as so much waste paper. I smile when I recall that the
Indian basket which had been filled with autograph letters, many of them valuable, and all of them interesting,
had been turned into a receptacle for the intricate para-
phernalia of Red Cross knitting. . . .

Nothing is more consuming, or more illogical, than the
desire for remembrance. I have few romantic illusions,
and none concerning posterity. I can see no reason to
assume that the literary judgment of the future will be
superior to the literary judgment of the present. Not all
the works that survived the past were written by Shake-
speares. Many of them, indeed, have seemed to be mere
monuments to superfluity. But, so paradoxical is human
vanity, that I, who have avoided contemporaneous noto-

riety, would exchange immediate recognition for the sake of becoming a name to generations which I could never know, and to which, no doubt, I should be supremely indifferent if I ever encountered them in the flesh. Absurd and incredible, yet very human. I record this, in passing, though I have never thought of future appreciation as an incentive. On the contrary, I am inclined to agree with Bagehot, "In general, posterity is most ungrateful; those who think of it most, it thinks of least." I have friends who keep their manuscripts in iron safes, for the benefit of collectors now unborn; but such prudence has always seemed to me to be at best too dubious a venture. I know others who assume permanently a waiting, not to say expectant, attitude. The briefest of their notes are addressed, primarily, to posterity. These model letters may in time, and possibly by accident, reach their destination. One never knows. He who bargains for the future must play a long hazard.

Meanwhile, there is the world of nowadays. Human nature as a spectacle has interested me in every period. It is true that I have been an exile; yet is there an age recorded in history when I should not have felt myself to be both an exile and a stranger? In ancient Greece, perhaps, had I been born a man and a peripatetic philosopher. Or in the Italy of the Renaissance, had I been born an artist and a poet, with nerves steeled against man's inhumanity. But my quarrel, as I have said, was less with the world than with the scheme of things in general. I had never, like Margaret Fuller, made the great acceptance. Ridiculous or not, I was still in arms against the universe.

Only the inevitable is worth fighting, I had declared rashly in youth.

Nevertheless, the conflict, however unequal, was not without interest. Though I lacked fortitude, I possessed the immoral courage of the heretic. In my earliest youth, I had found it easier to break with tradition than to endure it. I still found it easier. It was less difficult to forgive contemporary opinion than contemporary behavior. I condemned the reproach to virtue less than I condemned the praise of brutality. For men's minds are filled again with the lust of killing, and we think in terms of war while we are arming for peace. Science, the promised savior, may become, in the end, the destroyer of man—and of the awkward pattern Western man has agreed to call civilization. It is a civilization built on science, that has discarded philosophy. Yet fewer scientists and more philosophers, less knowledge and more wisdom, might, whether we are saved or lost, at least make us worth saving. And it has always been a vital question in the human mind whether it is better to be saved unworthy, or to be lost but worth the saving. That has been man's eternal choice, and, right or wrong, he has had to abide by his answer.

But all memories return, especially the sharp-set memories of youth. For more than twenty years I had not thought of Gerald. He had ceased, even as a recollection, to have a part in my life. He was gone. He was finished, with my first love, with my girlhood. If he were to come back to me, I should scarcely recognize him, for he would be old. Once he had meant to me all the youth of the world; and, now, he would be old, and forgotten by time. So much had happened since I had known him. So much substance and illusion, so many figures and shadows, had come and gone in my mind, in my heart. . . . Then, when I was nearing sixty, I went out, one evening in New York, to a foreign restaurant in a strange street, which was yet vaguely familiar. I smelt the scents of crushed apples and crowded places; and, suddenly, I remembered. I saw him again, clearly; I heard again, from very far off, that little nameless Hungarian song. For one moment alone; not ever, not ever again, after that evening. . . .

It was nothing. It meant nothing. But that Hungarian air was the only music that I, who am not musical, have ever remembered. Or did I remember it? How can one tell where memory ends and imagination begins?

TWENTY-TWO

Epilogue: Present Tense

In the past few years I have made a thrilling discovery, and in the past year I have had an even more thrilling adventure. My discovery was that until one is over sixty one can never really learn the secret of living. My adventure led me to the utmost border of death ("the ragged edge of eternity," my doctor called it) and kept me lingering, wholly conscious, without fear or reluctance or hesitation, in the kind of peace (or was it spiritual affirmation?) that passes both understanding and misunderstanding.

With the sardonic twist of circumstance, so prevalent in human affairs, I had no sooner learned how to live than the threat of death struck me. Only an Act of God, I used to boast, could ever kill me; but the one end I had not ever foreseen (for I had always said jestingly that my heart was too hard and cold to give way) was now approaching. Pain was barbed with surprise, because this particular pain was the last thing I had ever expected. "You have had no mercy on your heart," the specialist remarked solemnly, and I retorted, lightly, "My heart has never asked me for mercy."

It had taken me sixty years to discover that there was nothing to be done either about my own life or about the world in which I lived. All my fighting courage had brought to me was a badly damaged heart, yet a heart that was still undefeated. When the doctor told me this, I had a sudden uplifting sense of inward peace, of outward finality. I had done my best, and I could do nothing more. I had finished my course. I had kept the faith.

Youth is the season of tragedy and despair. Youth is the time when one's whole life is entangled in a web of identity, in a perpetual maze of seeking and of finding, of passion and of disillusion, of vague longings and of nameless griefs, of pity that is a blade in the heart, and of "all the little emptiness of love." Then the soul drifts on the shallow stream of personality, within narrow borders. Not until life has passed through that retarded channel out upon the wide open sea of impersonality, can one really begin to live, not simply with the intenser part of oneself, but with one's entire being. For sixty years, I was learning this elemental truth; and in the very moment of my discovery, I found also that the shadow I had imagined my own was the shadow of death.

Not that I greatly cared. Pain I had feared, but not death. The keenest pang was in the thought that I had fought all my life, and changed nothing. My old antagonist, inhumanity, was still victorious. All I had left behind me in life was a single endeavor. All the insurgent

spirits that had so foolishly dreamed of destroying one
evil or a multitude—what had they accomplished?

Two things had never failed me: my gift of friendship
and my sense of laughter. In the tranquil years that followed, before the outbreak of a second World War, I filled
my days with work, with friendship, with the familiar
round of winters in Richmond and summers in Maine.
It is true that I had never owned what I most wanted—
a farm on which I could live through all seasons. I had
never done what all my life I had wished to do—travel,
alone, round the world.

But, if my traveling was over, I had seen, in the past,
the world's lost age of beauty, before science, the soulless
mother of invention, had devised the motor car, the tank,
the diving bomb, the machine gun from the air, and all
the barbarian mockery of a total civilized war. On some
inward horizon, in immemorial loneliness, uninvaded by
tourists, untroubled by motor horns, the Great Pyramids
and the Sphinx stand forever against the blue noon, the
flushed sunset, the silver night, and the paling sunrise over
the desert. I had traveled for so many summers, in so
many years. Everything I remembered was still my own.
I had only to sink back into myself, to slip through some
green door in the wall, and I could wander from Egypt to
Greece, and over the Aegean Sea, in a cloudless dawn, to
the glory of Smyrna. . . . I could ramble in the past for
hours at a time. But I remind myself that, in autobiographies, I unfailingly skip all wandering parts.

I had nearly completed the first draft of my novel,

which I had named *In This Our Life,* when the second
World War broke. I cannot write of this war. I have tried,
and I cannot. . . . The cruelty is too near. This cruelty
is now in my mind. This agony is now in my nerves.

After both world wars are over, we shall still be fighting
an eternal conflict between human beings and human nature. When this immediate evil power has been defeated,
we shall not yet have won the long battle with the elemental barbarities. Another Hitler, it may be an invisible ad-
versary, will attempt, again, and yet again, to destroy our
frail civilization. Is it true, I wonder, that the only way
to escape a war is to be in it? When one is a part of an
actuality does the imagination find a release?

It is strange—or, perhaps, it is not strange—that war
should reanimate the cruder, and more primitive, religious
instincts. Someone, somewhere, is singing the hymn I
hated and Father loved—poor Cowper's hymn—"There is
a Fountain Filled with Blood." Over, and over, and over,
until I shut out the sound by turning off my hearing device. . . . The blood symbolism in religion has always
sickened me, in defiance of that stalwart breed, my Scottish forebears. I can feel this presence in the external atmosphere of a place, or, more vividly, through the air of
my imagination. It is not alone the killing from which I
recoil. I know that there are occasions when killing is
necessary. But there is never a time when God or man,
or the god invented by man, requires a libation of cruelty.

At the very beginning of the war in Europe, I did not
feel the fullness of its impact, all at once. Emotion, in
common with all other mortal states or facts of nature,

has an ultimate margin; it has an ebb and flow; it possesses the long finality of the dust. I had saturated my mind with the disturbed mental and emotional climate of my novel. I had completed, after my usual habit, the whole skeleton frame of *In This Our Life*. I had written this rapidly, passionately, straight from experience inflamed by imagination. Of all my later books I had written three drafts, the first for vitality and vividness of theme and of characterization, the second, for arrangement and balance of scene and of structure, and the third, for style and manner and the effort toward an unattainable perfection. By December, 1939, the first, and most difficult, writing was over, and of the second writing there remained only a short portion unfinished. After this, would come a careful revision, and then the longest and final rewriting. Only a writer, it may be only a novelist, can understand how close this book, my last novel, had come to my heart. *In This Our Life* would bring the history in my long sequence of novels from 1850, the period in which *The Battle-Ground* opens, to the autumn of 1939. I was, moreover, approaching my subject, not from the single or even the dual point of view, but from the diffused mental and emotional outlook of a whole community. I felt that I was welding together, in this one symbolic expression, all the varied themes in my earlier and later interpretation of life.

I had reached this point when, in December, 1939, without warning, my heart failed, and a mortal illness attacked me. I might, with care, I was told, live on for some years, or I might drop away in an hour, in a day, in a month, or in six months. Well, no matter. I might still have time to finish my novel. I might even finish my autobiography. And so, as soon as the pain was over and I was able to sit up, I went back to my desk and my typewriter, and to four dozen new pencils with sharpened points. Though I had no fear of death, I did not like the thought of leaving a piece of good work, the topmost block in my building, unfinished.

For months I was able to work for only fifteen minutes, and a little later, half an hour every morning. Because this was not so much an act of creation as of rearrangement, enlargement, or elimination, the vitality of my novel would not, I felt, be impaired. By this time, the scene was permanently set; the living figures were all moving, and speaking in natural tones. This special effort, all the vital energy and motive power which a first writing exacts, would have been too much for me to demand from a failing heart. But I was dealing now, not with dim outlines, but with well-rounded characters, as vigorous and alive as the human beings who went by in the street.

The winter passed, and I had completed my second writing, when I started for Castine, Maine, where I was spending my summers. When I reached New York, the heart specialist there ordered me to a hospital.

I went reluctantly. "If I do not go, shall I have time to finish my book? I never like to leave work unfinished."

"How long will that take?"

"Until next winter. Maybe until November."

"You may and you may not. You may have six months. On the other hand you may have only three weeks. . . ." He had known me long enough to know that I wanted the truth.

So I left him to go to a gay and delightful luncheon in Emily Balch's apartment on the East River. Later in the afternoon I went up to Doctors' Hospital, where I spent an endless month in all the intolerable sultry heat of New York. All through that July, I lay watching, from a high window, the slow boats and the misty green and the colored lights on the river.

For the first three weeks I was not allowed to see my friends; but they kept my room bright and fragrant with flowers, and for one week before I left, they came, in spite of the torrid weather, to spend hours by my bedside. "I may not like human nature," I would repeat, laughingly, to my delightful and devoted nurse, "but I like human beings."

At the end of the month I left for Castine. There I began to work again, and gradually to drive a little way, and then to walk, with Anne Virginia Bennett, for a quarter of a mile in the woods. But those heavenly rambles along the Indian trails were now over. In other years, after working from two to three hours every morning, I would start out and tramp in the woods until lunchtime. These walks had been my chief pleasure, and I began to hope that I might smell again the balsam over my head, and feel again the moss under my feet. But I had not been at Castine for more than three weeks when I came down with my worst heart attack, a coronary thrombosis. . . .

It is not possible to express, and especially to express in writing, the most profound experience that one has known:—the recognition of death as another aspect of life. Millions of words have been written of dying; yet it is

beyond the power of speech or of intelligence to describe
the indescribable. Never again can I come so near the end
of life without passing on into death. For nearly half an
hour the Maine doctor watched, with his finger on my
pulse and his stethoscope on my heart, and for every minute of that time I was completely conscious, but too weak
to move my lips or flutter my eyelashes. I could see, fading
slowly away, features of a kindly Roman senator bending
over me. I could hear the voice of Anne Virginia calling
to hold me back. I could see the face of my sister Rebe
between the bed and the window. I could see the doctor's
lips whispering, and though I could not hear his words,
I knew that he said: "She is on the ragged edge. All we
can do is to wait." Afterwards, they told me he feared to
give a second hypodermic, lest the shock of the needle
might send me over that edge. . . . These things I remember or heard later; but these things are no more than
the surface awareness, the thin shell of the moment. In
my mind a single thought was repeated: If I cannot finish
my book, I want to go quickly. After pain, there was no
shadow of fear, of shrinking, or of reluctance. While an icy
chill ran from my feet upward, it was, strangely enough,
a chill that seemed the other side of a glow, of a warmth,
as of an unutterable sense of fulfillment. I had never believed in a limited personal immortality, in a narrow margin of eternity, or of the separate ego. The peace I felt,
was not the peace of possession. It was—the fleeting essence
escapes whenever I try to confine it—a sense of infinite
reunion with the Unknown Everything or with Nothing
. . . or with God. But whether Everything or Nothing,
it was surrender of identity. . . . By surrender, I do not

mean extinction of identity. I mean, enlargement and complete illumination of being. In my death, as in my life, I was still seeking God, known or unknown. . . .

Days afterwards, I promised myself that I would never try to speak of what I could not put into words. All I knew was that I had looked at death, which is the other side of life, and that death was "lovely and soothing . . ." When I thought of dying, in those weary months of convalescence, it was not of dying as a cold negation, but as a warm and friendly welcome to the universe, to the Being beyond and above consciousness, or any vestige of self. . . . But to feel is one thing, and to write of feeling is yet another thing. Solemn words may wear on paper a look of shallowness and complete insincerity. . . .

For two months after this I was not allowed to go downstairs, and all I saw of Maine that summer was a single tall pointed fir against a sky of crystal blue, or under swift scudding clouds. As soon as I was able to sit up, I went back to my book, for by this time I had reached very nearly the end of my second writing. At first I worked only fifteen minutes a day, but after six weeks I could hold out for half an hour. From far away the reverberations of war shocked my nerves; but the barbarians had not yet concentrated upon the British Isles, the spot of earth I loved most after my own country. . . .

In those weeks and months I never lost a piercing sense of unreality, as if the world around me, and even the thoughts in my own mind, were as insubstantial as mist, and might vanish at a breath, and leave me suspended in hollowness. Although I knew the sensation resulted from

physical weakness alone, I seemed to be perpetually waiting for a distant call, or for the sound of a bell ringing
somewhere, very far off, through the mist. To the people
about me, the appearance was simply one of abstraction
or absorption in work. But I could not rid myself of the
feeling that there was some connection between my present detachment from living and that hour when I had
hesitated, without fear, upon the brink of some deeper
awakening. I had felt then that I was borne outward by
a strong current, and I felt still the vague murmur of that
tide as it receded. Weakness again, or merely the heightened consciousness of finality . . .

I did not walk in the Maine woods that summer and
autumn of 1940. When I came home the first of November
I was ordered to bed until Christmas; and when Christmas
came and went, I was not allowed to get up. Death, I had
turned into a friend, just as I had made a friend of life,
notwithstanding my deafness, my frail health, and my
nervous maladjustment to circumstances. But I feared
pain with an unspeakable dread, and I was now oppressed
by the thought that I should never be able to write over
my book. Almost the whole of the third draft was still
ahead, and my strength had ebbed so low that I was not
equal to writing a note or a letter. To be sure, the difficult
part was behind me. I had finished everything but the
last corrections and eliminations, and the final, if vain,
search for some austere perfection. Now, I envied those
writers who had acquired the habit of dictation. But I had
never dictated. I had never written a line, except when I
was alone in a room, with the door shut.

James Cabell would come to spend hours by my bedside, reading chapters, and assuring me that this book did not require the usual third writing. His visits braced my will to hold on; but my book, with all the world, appeared to me to be shrouded in that mist of vagueness, of unreality. My publishers, too, came often from New York; and they also insisted that my novel could stand as it was. But I had always written a book three times, and ill as I was, something told me that I was not satisfied, that the work must be done over again. In the end, when my publishers left, and James went to Florida for the winter, I gathered my strength and wrote over the whole novel, chiefly for style and manner, in proofsheets. Only when it was finished to the last paragraph, and the final page proofs had gone back to the printer, was I content to lie back and listen to what my good doctors said to me. And, even then, I felt that I might have done better, that I had not given my novel a fair chance. . . . Perhaps . . . Perhaps not . . . The reception should have settled my doubts. This proved, at least, that in my last book there was no letting down of vitality. There was scarcely a review that did not praise the freshness and the vigor of the characterization. . . .

If I obeyed my doctor, now, and stayed in bed, it was because I was too frail and tremulous to put on my clothes and cross the hall to my study. Slowly, little by little, a measure of strength came back to me, and I was allowed to see my friends for a few hours in the afternoon. The rest of my winter, indeed, was one of the gayest I have ever known. Streams of visitors came to sit by my bedside, though I was permitted to see only one or two at a time. The friends of my childhood were the friends of my latter years. Caroline Duke and Elizabeth Crutchfield, the very Elizabeth Patterson with whom I had stayed in the immense old nursery at Reveille, would flit in for a minute, and flit out again. There was Julia Sully, who had wandered with me over Dinwiddie, when I was in search of a background for *Virginia,* and Roberta Wellford, who had stood by me when Cary was dying. . . .

Many others stopped over, going or coming from Florida. People I had forgotten dropped in to see me. My room was gay with flowers. I did not, they assured me, look as if I were ill, or, in fact, any older, they added cheerfully, if inaccurately. There was good talk and laughter about my bed, which was festive with presents of lace blanket-covers or pillow-slips or bed-jackets. Stark Young came from New York to spend a few hours with me. Eleanor and Van Wyck Brooks came from Alexandria, where they were spending the winter. Norma and Herschel Brickell came, and Margaret Mitchell, and Marjorie Kinnan Rawlings. . . . Harold came again, bringing me flowers. . . .

Marjorie Rawlings and I were immediately drawn to each other, but after her visit, when she sat by my bedside for several hours, I heard, for months, nothing from her. After publishing *In This Our Life,* which she liked and understood, as deeply as I loved and understood *The Yearling,* I sank down into an icy vacuum, that living death, when I told myself that, within, I was caught in

the midst of frozen fields, and could not escape. Then, last
night, I had this letter from Marjorie telling me of her
singular dream:

July 19, 1941

My very dear Ellen Glasgow:

I had such a vivid dream about you last night, that I must
write you—which I have been meaning to do ever since our
delightful brief visit together. The reality of a dream can
never be conveyed to another, but you came to live with me.
I was away when you came, and on my return, to one of those
strange mansions that are part of the substance of dreams,
you were outside in the bitter cold, cutting away ice from the
roadway and piling it in geometric patterns. I was alarmed,
remembering your heart trouble, and led you inside the man-
sion and brought you a cup of hot coffee. You had on blue
silk gloves, and I laid my hand over yours, and was amazed,
for my own hand is small, to have yours fit inside mine, much
smaller. You chose your room and suggested draperies to sup-
plement a valance. The valance was red chintz and you showed
me a sample of heavy red brocade of the same shade. I told
you that from now on I should take care of you, and you must
not do strenuous things, such as cutting the ice in the roadway. James Cabell came into the room and asked what the
two of us were up to. (As of course he would!) My memory
of my time with you is quite as vivid as the night's dream. . . .

Coincidence or telepathy? I cannot explain it. One can
never explain such things; and the extraordinary part of
it is that the dream bore, in every detail, the accent of
reality. I am not psychic; I am not superstitious; I seldom
dream significant dreams. Yet, now and again, in my life,
I have known such occurrences.

There was that occasion long ago, with another friend,

in Dorking, England. . . . I may have written of this, I cannot remember now. . . .

And all it meant is that with faithful friends I had come over the last hill into the endless valley. The friends were faithful, and I can say little enough about them, who, like Carrie Duke and Anne Virginia, I could count upon. The endless valley. I asked nothing more. I wanted nothing more. I could laugh at the end, because I had had my life. . . .

After resting in bed all winter, I had come to Castine for the summer. Maine is never lovelier than it is in June. The unmown meadows were running, in waves of bloom, white and green, red and yellow. The lilacs had not fallen, and the big bush at my side door was covered with rich purple sprays. It was all so beautiful, if only beauty were everything! If only beauty were enough for the mind or the heart!

But I was in almost constant pain, and I felt that my inner springs were exhausted. Always, or frequently, I had felt this; but, now, there was a deep physical cause. Yet I did not wish to live on after I was drained of that life-giving impulse. I began, from the moment I came, to do everything the doctors in the hospital had warned me to avoid. But, oddly enough, I appeared only to release some last rush of energy. My rebel heart still held out. The pain came and went, but my heart was still beating. And I had not lost—I shall never lose, I think—my old gaiety. I could laugh at my own tragedy, and I could find a flash of sardonic mirth even in the world's tragedy. Yet I had always felt the vast impersonal anguish of life more deeply than

I had felt my own small—yet vast, too—personal misery.

A friend said to me this summer: "The people here think you so gay and attractive that they wonder why you write such sad books."

I laughed. "But my books are not sad! And there will always be, if God permits, a last laugh at the end." In the life of the mind, glad or sad, there will always be laughter, and the life of the mind alone, I have found, contains an antidote to experience. . . .

Yes, I have had my life. I have known ecstasy. I have known anguish. I have loved, and I have been loved. With one I loved, I have watched the light breaking over the Alps. If I have passed through "the dark night of the soul," I have had a far-off glimpse of the illumination beyond. For an infinitesimal point of time or eternity, I have caught a gleam, or imagined I caught a gleam, of the mystic vision. . . . It was enough, and it is now over. Not for everything that the world could give would I consent to live over my life unchanged, or to bring back, unchanged, my youth. . . .

Only on the surface of things have I ever trod the beaten path. So long as I could keep from hurting anyone else, I have lived, as completely as it was possible, the life of my choice. I have been free. Yet I have not ever stolen either the ponderable or the imponderable material of happiness. I have done the work I wished to do for the sake of that work alone. And I have come, at last, from the fleeting rebellion of youth into the steadfast—or is it merely the seasonable—accord without surrender of the unreconciled heart.

A Dull Note for Genealogists

During the Scottish wars in the seventeenth century (the exact date is not known), a branch of the Glasgow family fled from Ayrshire to the Counties Down and Antrim in northern Ireland.

In the year 1766, Arthur Glasgow, a ward and a boy of sixteen, came, with his mother and elder brothers, to America, and settled on a tract of land in Rockbridge County, Virginia. The place was named Green Forest because Glas Gow means green forest in Gaelic, and the green tree was a feature of the family arms. The modern towns of Buena Vista, Balcony Falls, and Glasgow are now contained in the original Green Forest plantation. The old brick house, built immediately after the Revolution, on the site probably of an earlier log house, is still standing in Buena Vista. About 1830, the original dwelling was partly burned; but it was rebuilt on the old foundations, with one or two rooms and the large columns of the square front porch still undestroyed. In more recent years a long porch and a railing have been added.

Until my own generation, every member of my father's family was born at Green Forest. The first American Arthur Glasgow (1750-1822) married Rebekah McNutt, the widow of Ensign John McCorkle, a youth who had fallen in the Revolution.

Their son Robert (1790-1839) married his cousin Catherine Anderson, the daughter of Col. William Anderson, of Walnut Hill, Botetourt County, Virginia, and his wife, Anne Thomas, daughter of Francis Thomas, of Montvue, near Frederick, Maryland.

The Andersons also were Scottish refugees in Ireland, in the seventeenth century. There, Robert Anderson married a Miss Graham (Margaret), the daughter of a Captain Graham, who was captured and executed in the Claverhouse wars. Family tradition relates that this young man was a near kinsman of the great Marquis of Montrose. But that is merely tradition, with an apocryphal flavour.

Colonel William Anderson, their descendant (1764-1839), of Walnut Hill, lived all his long life in the pioneer homestead of stone and round logs. Botetourt County was nearer the frontier than was Rockbridge, and in his youth Indians were still roaming the wilderness. As a boy of sixteen, he ran away from home in the night, and traveled two days and nights through the forest, with savages around him, in order to join the Revolution. He fought in the Battles of Cowpens and Guilford Courthouse, and in the War of 1812 he served as a colonel. In his later years, because he was called in to decide so many disputes among his neighbors, he was known as Squire Anderson. His three sons were all distinguished in the Virginia of their period. They were Colonel John T. Anderson, of Mount Joy, Botetourt County; Judge Francis Thomas Anderson, of Lexington, Judge of the Supreme Court of Appeals of Virginia, and rector of Washington and Lee University; General Joseph Reid Anderson, president of the Tredegar Iron Works, Richmond.

Catherine, the daughter of Colonel William Anderson, was born in 1797. She was married to Robert Glasgow and was the mother of my father.

My Mother (1831-93)

My mother, Anne Jane Gholson, was the daughter of Judge William Yates Gholson (1807-1870) and his first wife, Martha Anne Jane Taylor. Martha Anne, my grandmother, died before she was twenty, at the birth of her second child, and her husband, my grandfather, left Virginia, in his sorrow, and moved to Cincinnati, where he became a celebrated attorney, and one of the judges of the Supreme Court of Ohio. My mother was adopted by her great-uncle Chancellor Creed Taylor, of the famous Needham Law School.

While my father was of Valley stock, and Scottish in every nerve and sinew, my mother was a perfect flower of the Tidewater. She was descended from the Randolphs, through Colonel William Randolph, of Turkey Island; from the Yates through William Yates, Colonial President of the College of William and Mary, and rector of Bruton Parish Church; from the Bakers through Henry and Lawrence Baker, of the House of Burgesses; from the Woodsons, through Dr. John Woodson, who came from St. John's College,

Oxford, in the year 1619, as surgeon to Sir John Harvey's Expedition; from the De Graffenrieds through Christophe De Graffenried, Landgrave of the Carolinas under Queen Anne; from the Pendletons, the Blands, the Taylors, the Booths, the Gholsons, the Creeds. . . .

She was married to my father at Needham in the year 1853. After the War Between the States, they tried to restore the old place at Green Forest; but an invasion had passed over it, and the family fortunes were irretrievably ruined. In the end, the old homestead passed out of the family, and my parents spent the rest of their lives in Botetourt County, and in Richmond. For more than half a century my father was a managing director of the Tredegar Iron Works.

My parents had ten children, of which I was, unhappily, the eighth child. A little brother named Samuel Creed, who lived only a week, came between me and my sister Rebe, who is three years and nine months younger than I am.

When my grandmother died, she gave her baby, my mother, into the keeping of Mammy Rhoda, and said: "Mammy, bring her up for me." The baby was only two weeks old, and she and her little brother, Samuel Creed, were adopted by their elderly great-uncle, Creed Taylor, of "Needham," Cumberland County, Virginia. Both children were born at "Needham," where the oldest part of the house is still standing, though it has fallen upon degenerate days.

Creed Taylor

Born in 1766, trained in the law in the office of Colonel George Carrington, whom he later succeeded in practice, Creed Taylor,* at twenty-two, entered the General Assembly of Virginia, continuing in the house from 1788 until 1798, when he was elected to the senate, serving as a member of that body until he was appointed to the bench. He was one of the commissioners to locate the University of Virginia, and served with General Joseph Martin and Archibald Stuart, on the commission to settle the boundary lines between Virginia, Kentucky, and Ohio, when Virginia ceded her western lands to the United States. In 1805 he was appointed Judge of the

* The following account of Creed Taylor, Sally Woodson Taylor and Miss Glasgow's father, Francis Thomas Glasgow, is taken from the *History of the De Graffenried Family* by Thomas P. De Graffenried.

General Court and in 1806, upon the death of Chancellor George Wythe, became Chancellor of the Superior Court of Law and Chancery. Some of the most distinguished members of the Virginia bar, including John Minor Botts, Samuel Taylor, and William Yates Gholson, were trained in the famous law school and moot court which the Chancellor opened at "Needham" in 1821.

Sally Woodson Taylor

Sally Woodson Taylor, according to tradition, was of a somewhat high-strung and nervous temperament, but of the most generous and hospitable disposition. A woman of proud and stately bearing, she continued, long after the advent of modern fashions, to make her visits in her great swinging red morocco coach, high, with numerous steps to be let down, and a footman standing behind. The portraits of Chancellor Taylor and his wife, by St. Memin, now hang in the drawing-room of Miss Ellen Glasgow, the novelist, at Richmond. Miss Glasgow is the great-grandniece of Chancellor Taylor and the grandniece of Sally Woodson Taylor. It was Mrs. Taylor's fondness for reading *The Mysteries of Udolpho* in bed which Miss Glasgow has attributed to one of her characters, "Mrs. Lightfoot." Mrs. Taylor lived to an advanced age, dying in or about the year 1861.

Francis Thomas Glasgow (1829-1916)

Francis Thomas Glasgow, born September 13th, 1829, was the son of Robert Glasgow, and grandson of Arthur Glasgow, of "Green Forest," now Buena Vista, and Balcony Falls, now Glasgow, in Rockbridge Country, Virginia. He entered Washington College, now Washington and Lee University (at the age of fifteen) in 1844, and was graduated with the degree of A.B. in 1847. He read law in Richmond for two years, and then, at the request of his uncle, General Joseph R. Anderson, its president, became, at the age of twenty, associated with the Tredegar Iron Works, an association which endured for more than sixty-three years. He was among the first to volunteer for service in the Confederate Army at the outbreak of the Civil War, but General Anderson refused to permit his enlistment because he could be of greater service at the Tredegar plant.

A large part of the munitions and ordnance used by the Confederate Government was manufactured at the Tredegar Works, and the *Merrimac,* the Confederate ram, was over-hauled and outfitted there. The only available supply of ore was in the Valley of Virginia, where, in a territory frequently overrun by Federal troops, Mr. Glasgow successfully superintended the operation of blast furnaces employing several hundred men. After the war, the Tredegar having been taken by the Union troops, he went to his father's plantations, and rehabilitated the country house which had been devastated. He then returned to Richmond to become manager of the Tredegar Works, retaining his connection with the plant until 1912. Although of quiet and retiring disposition, and little inclined toward public life, Mr. Glasgow served as a member of the Board of the State Penitentiary, having early become interested in the subject of prison reform. He was a "Gold Democrat" in 1896, and chairman of the Richmond Committee Opposing Free Silver. He possessed an excellent library and was an omnivorous reader. Devoted to the Presbyterian faith, he was an elder of the church, as had been his father and grandfather before him. He died at his home in Richmond, January 29th, 1916.

INDEX